Understanding Children's Literature

Understanding Children's Literature

Edited by Peter Hunt

Key essays from the *International Companion Encyclopedia of Children's Literature*

London and New York

First published 1999
by Routledge
11 New Fetter Lane, London EC4P 4EE

Simultaneously published in the USA and Canada
by Routledge
29 West 35th Street, New York, NY 10001

Typeset in Ehrhardt and Frutiger by Routledge
Printed and bound in Great Britain by Page Brothers, Norwich

British Library Cataloguing in Publication Data
A catalogue record for this book is available from the British Library

Library of Congress Cataloging in Publication Data
Understanding children's literature / [edited by] Peter Hunt
     p.   cm.
Includes bibliographical references and index.
1. Children's literature–History and criticism. I. Hunt, Peter
PN1009.A1U44 1998
809' .89282–dc21   98–8226

     ISBN 0–415–19546–2

Contents

Contributors

Michael Benton is a Professor of Education in the Research and Graduate School of Education, University of Southampton. His main critical orientation is that of reader-response theory and practice; the main argument of his research is that a pedagogy grounded in reader-response offers English teachers the most coherent position in relation to their work because it focuses upon the live processes of literary experience. Two co-authored books written from this standpoint are: *Teaching Literature 9–14*, with Geoff Fox (1985) and *Young Readers Responding to Poems*, with three teachers (1988). In recent years, his research has widened its remit to encompass aspects of the visual arts, especially painting and picture books. This development is represented by *Secondary Worlds: Literature Teaching and the Visual Arts* (1992), by several articles in *The British Journal of Aesthetics* and in the *Journal of Aesthetic Education*, and by three classroom anthologies of paired paintings and poems, compiled and edited with his brother: *Double Vision* (1990), *Painting with Words* (1995) and *Picture Poems* (1997), all published by Hodder and Stoughton.

Hamida Bosmajian is Professor of English at Seattle University where she teaches children's literature, mythology, and literary theory as well as a seminar in literature and law. She has published widely in children's literature, but her main scholarly focus is literature for young readers about Nazism and the Holocaust. In her book *Metaphors of Evil: Contemporary German Literature and the Shadow of Nazism* (1979) she noticed that many adults remember the child in historical traumas. Children have far fewer defence mechanisms than adults; they confront trauma without analysis and interpretation. In later life such experiences haunt them differently than do traumatic events experienced by adults. Her current project is called 'Sparing the Child: Young Readers' Literature About Nazism and the Holocaust'. She always tells her students: 'Whenever and wherever the nightmare of history occurs – there are children there'.

Hugh Crago is currently co-editor with Maureen Crago of *The Australian and New Zealand Journal of Family Therapy*. He has worked as an individual and family therapist for the past sixteen years, and was Senior Lecturer in Counselling at the University of New England (Australia) until 1997. He has also studied and taught English. He is co-author, with Maureen, of *Prelude to Literacy* (1983), and of a number of other empirical and theoretical studies of children's and adults' interactions with stories, which combine the perspectives of reader-response and psychoanalytic criticism. His new book, *A Circle Unbroken: How Our Unique Lives Unfold in Predictable Patterns* will be published in 1999 in Australia).

Peter Hunt is Professor of English and Children's Literature in the School of English, Communications and Philosophy at the University of Wales, Cardiff. He has written or edited eleven books on children's literature, including *An Introduction to Children's Literature* (1994), the *International Companion Encyclopedia of Children's Literature* (1996), and six books for children and adolescents.

Karín Lesnik-Oberstein is a lecturer in English, American and Children's Literature at the University of Reading. She teaches extensively on the MA in Children's Literature and is an associate director of the Centre for International Research in Childhood: Literature, Culture, Media (CIRCL) at the University. Principal publications include her books *Children's Literature: Criticism and the Fictional Child* (1994) and (as editor) *Children in Culture: Approaches to Childhood* (1998), as well as articles and chapters on children's literature and theory. All her work on children explores childhood as a culturally and historically constructed category, rather than as a biological or psychological given, and uses anthropology, sociology, psychoanalysis, and literary and critical theory to support this argument. Ongoing research includes work on psychoanalysis, feminist theory, and theory in general but her overall interest continues to lie with working from interdisciplinary and multidisciplinary perspectives in the social sciences and humanities.

Robyn McCallum has a background in literature and visual arts and is involved in teaching and research in children's literature at Macquarie University. She has published articles on children's and adolescent literature, film and television and is author of *Ideologies of Identity in Adolescent Fictions* (1999) and co-author with John Stephens of *Retelling Stories, Framing Culture: Traditional Stories and Metanarratives in Children's Literature* (1998). Research interests include: critical theory relating to children's texts and culture; literature, film and television for children and adolescents; and picture books.

Perry Nodelman spent five years as editor of *The Children's Literature Association Quarterly*, and has published a hundred or so articles on various aspects of children's literature in scholarly journals, many of them focusing on literary theory as a context for understanding books for children. He has also written two books on the subject: *Words About Pictures: The Narrative Art of Children's Picture Books* (1988), and *The Pleasures of Children's Literature* (1992), currently in its second edition. In recent years, Nodelman has begun a new career as a writer of fiction for children, producing two children's fantasies, *The Same Place But Different* (1993) and its sequel *A Completely Different Place* (1996), and a picture book, *Alice Falls Apart* (1996). *Behaving Bradley* (1998), a comic novel about life in a high school, appeared in the spring of 1998. He has also collaborated on two young adult fantasies with Carol Matas: *Of Two Minds* (1994) and its sequels *More Minds*; (1996) and *Out of Their Minds*, (1998).

Lissa Paul is a Professor in the Faculty of Education at the University of New Brunswick where she teaches five courses on children's literature and literary theory. Her new book, *Reading Otherways* (1998), provides a practical demonstration of the ways in which contemporary literary theories, especially feminist theories, enable new readings of books for children – readings in touch with contemporary sensibilities. Lissa writes and reviews regularly for Canadian, American and British children's literature journals, most frequently as a contributor to *Signal*. She has also served as one of two non-British judges for the *Signal* poetry award. She holds workshops in schools, and lectures widely internationally; her current research interests include maternal literacies, chaos theory and new poetics, contemporary poetry and post-colonial studies.

Charles Sarland is a Senior Lecturer in Education at Liverpool John Moores University. He is interested in culture – the meanings that, in particular, the young make of the world – and is thus interested in the texts, written or visual that become canonical in that process. He is concerned about the potential for educational research to make a difference, to mount a critique rather than just to process data, and is interested in ways of both re-introducing, and in some way accounting for, commitment in the research process.

John Stephens is Associate Professor in English at Macquarie University, where his main teaching commitment is children's literature, but he also teaches and supervises postgraduate research in medieval studies, post-colonial literature, and discourse analysis. He is the author of *Language and Ideology in Children's Fiction* (1992), two books about discourse analysis, and around sixty articles about children's (and other) literature. More recently, he has co-authored, with Robyn McCallum, *Retelling Stories, Framing Culture: Traditional Story and Metanarratives in Children's Literature* (1998). His primary research focus is on the relationships between texts produced for children (especially literature and film) and cultural formations and practices.

Tony Watkins is lecturer in English, Director of the MA in Children's Literature and Director of the Centre for International Research in Childhood: Literature, Culture, Media (CIRCL) at the University of Reading. Under his direction, CIRCL is co-ordinating an international collaborative research project on 'National and Cultural Identity in Children's Literature and Media'. Tony Watkins has lectured on Children's Literature at universities and conferences in Europe, the USA and Australia and has been awarded a Fellowship at the International Centre for Research in Children's Literature in Osaka, Japan. He has just finished co-editing a collection of essays on *The Heroic Figure in Children's Popular Culture* and is currently editing another collection on *Children's Literature and Theory*. He has a particular interest in representations of space, place and history and their relationship to national and cultural identity in children's literature and media.

Christine Wilkie lectures in English and is the Director of the MA programme in Children's Literature Studies at the University of Warwick, teaching courses on Literary Theory, Twentieth Century Children's Literature and Women's Writing. She has published a book on the works of Russell Hoban,

Through the Narrow Gate (1989), and several articles in international journals on various aspects of children's literature. She is currently researching literary subjectivity in the contemporary children's novel.

Geoffrey Williams is interested in ways that children reflect on experience through reading, play, and conversation. He is a linguist, working in the Department of English at Sydney University, where he teaches courses in children's literature, functional linguistics and language variation. His recent research has explored children's uses of functional 'grammar' in learning about how written texts mean. In this project he worked closely with groups of young children, including a year in conversations with eleven-year-olds in an after-school literacy club. Dr Williams is also investigating children's play with language prior to formal schooling. He is the co-editor, with Ruqaiya Hasan, of *Literacy in Society*, a volume which presents debates about genre-based literacy education in English-speaking countries. He has also contributed to the volume *Literacy and Schooling*, (1998).

1 Introduction: The World of Children's Literature Studies

Peter Hunt

So what good is literary theory? Will it keep our children singing? Well perhaps not. But understanding something of literary theory will give us some understanding of how the literature we give to our children works. It might also keep us engaged with the texts that surround us, keep us singing even if it is a more mature song than we sang as youthful readers of texts. As long as we keep singing, we have a chance of passing along our singing spirit to those we teach.

McGillis 1996: 206

Children's Literature

'Children's Literature' sounds like an enticing study; because children's books have been largely beneath the notice of intellectual and cultural gurus, they are (apparently) blissfully free of the 'oughts' – what we ought to think and say about them. More than that, to many readers, children's books are a matter of private delight, which means, perhaps, that they are *real* literature – if 'literature' consists of texts which engage, change, and provoke intense responses in readers.

But if private delight seems a somewhat indefensible justification for a study, then we can reflect on the direct or indirect influence that children's books have, and have had, socially, culturally, and historically. They are overtly important educationally and commercially – with consequences across the culture, from language to politics: most adults, and almost certainly the vast majority in positions of power and influence, read children's books as children, and it is inconceivable that the ideologies permeating those books had no influence on their development.

The books have, nonetheless, been marginalised. Childhood is, after all, a state we grow away from; children's books – from writing to publication to interaction with children – are the province of that culturally marginalised species, the female. But this marginalisation has had certain advantages; because it has been culturally low-profile, 'children's literature' has not become the 'property' of any group or discipline: it does not 'belong' to the Department of Literature or the Library School, or the local parents' organisation. It is attractive and interesting to students (official or unofficial) of literature, education, library studies, history, psychology, art, popular culture, media, the caring professions, and so on, and it can be approached from any specialist viewpoint. Its nature, both as a group of texts and as a subject for study, has been to break down barriers between disciplines, and between types of readers. It is, at once, one of the liveliest and most original of the arts, and the site of the crudest commercial exploitation.

This means that just as children's books do not exist in a vacuum – they have real, argumentative readers and visible, practical, consequential *uses* – so the theory of children's literature constantly blends into the practice of bringing books and readers together.

The slightly uncomfortable (or very inspiring) corollary of this is that we have to accept that children's books are *complex*, and the study of them infinitely varied. Many students around the world who have been enticed onto children's literature at courses at all 'levels' rapidly find that things are more complicated than they had assumed. There cannot be many teachers of children's literature who have not been greeted with a querulous 'But it's only a children's book', 'Children won't see that in it', or 'You're making it more difficult than it should be'. But the complexities are not mere problematising by academics eager to ensure their meal tickets; the most apparently straightforward act of communication is amazingly intricate – and we are dealing here with fundamental questions of communication and understanding between adults and children, or, more exactly, between individuals and individuals.

If children's literature is more complex than it seems, even more complex, perhaps, is the position it finds itself in between adult writers, readers, critics and practitioners, and the child readers. Children's literature is an obvious point at which theory encounters real life, where we are forced to ask: what can we say about a book, why should we say it, how can we say it, and what effect will what we say have? We are also forced to confront our preconceptions. Many people will deny that they were influenced by their childhood reading ('I read *xyz* when *I* was a child, and it didn't do *me* any harm'), and yet these are the same people who accept that childhood is an important phase in our lives (as is almost universally acknowledged), and that children are vulnerable, susceptible, and must be protected from manipulation. Children's literature is important – and yet it is not.

Consequently, before setting off into the somewhat tangled jungle that is 'children's literature' we need to establish some basic concepts, ideas, and methods: to work through fundamental arguments, to look at which techniques of criticism, which discourses, and which strategies are appropriate to – or even unique to – our subject. It can be argued that we can (and should) harness the considerable theoretical and analytical apparatus of every discipline from philosophy to psychotherapy; or that we should evolve a critical theory and practice tailored to the precise needs of 'children's literature'.

This book, which selects the key essays from the *International Companion Encyclopedia of Children's Literature*, provides the essential theory for any adventure into 'children's literature', outlines practical approaches, suggests areas of research, and provides up-to-date bibliographies to help readers to find their own, individual, appropriate paths.

Literature and Children

All the writers in this book share an unspoken conviction that children's literature is worth reading, worth discussing, and worth thinking about *for adults*. Aidan Chambers has summed up the motivation of many 'liberal humanist' teachers and writers:

> I belong to the demotic tradition; I believe literature belongs to all the people all the time, that it ought to be cheaply and easily available, that it ought to be fun to read as well as challenging, subversive, refreshing, comforting, and all the other qualities we claim for it. Finally, I hold that in literature we find the best expression of the human imagination, and the most useful means by which we come to grips with our ideas about ourselves and what we are.
>
> Chambers 1985: 16

Such a faith in literature underlies a great deal of day-to-day teaching and thinking about children and books; it lies behind the connection between literature and literacy – whether or not children's books are seen as valuable in themselves, or as stepping-stones to higher things ('adult' or 'great' literature).

It is, however, clearly not a neutral statement: it embodies some very obvious (and some not-so-obvious) ideology (aspects of ideology are considered in Chapter 4), and it brings us up against the question of 'literature'. Oceans of ink have been spilt on this matter, but it is essential to recognise that there is no such thing as 'literary' quality or value inherent in any set of words on a page. As Jonathan Culler sums it up, 'Literature . . . is a speech act or textual event that elicits certain kinds of attention' (1997: 27) – or which is accorded a certain value by those members of the culture in a position to accord values.

This is fundamental to children's literature, where practitioners (those who work with books and children, and who generally have more pressing concerns than subtle theoretical nuances) want to know – as simply as possible – what is *good*? The shadow of what they 'ought' to value lies over them, and it is difficult to convince many people that 'good' doesn't belong to somebody else – to the great 'they'. Outside academia, arguments about what is 'good' very often collapse into a rather weary 'well, it's all a matter of taste' – but people are usually a little uneasy – or defiant – about that, as if somebody, somewhere, knows better than they do what is 'good' (and they don't necessarily like it).

This leads to the common situation that people will privately like, or value, one type of book, while publicly recommending something else. Books which would have a low status on some cosmic value-scale (and which are highly successful commercially) are excluded from serious consideration; others – 'classics', perhaps – are taught and prescribed and written about. In primary and secondary education, this can lead to a backlash against reading: if children read one kind of book in school, and another outside school, then certain books will be regarded as 'other'.

This division leads to inappropriate critical approaches being taken to the books. Children's books are different from adults' books: they are written for a different audience, with different skills, different needs, and different ways of reading; equally, children experience texts in ways which are often unknowable, but which many of us strongly suspect to be very rich and complex. If we judge children's books (even if we do it unconsciously) by the same value systems as we use for adult books – where they are *bound by definition* to emerge as *lesser* – then we give ourselves unnecessary problems. To say that, for example, Judy Blume is not as good as Jane Austen, is like saying that this apple is an inadequate orange because it is green, and that oranges are innately superior anyway. 'Literature', then, is only a useful concept if we want to educate children into a particular kind of culture: but it can be misleading or pernicious if we are 'using' the texts in other ways.

If the word 'literature' presents obvious problems, the word 'children' proves to be equally slippery. Childhood changes from place to place, from time to time (see, for example, Hoyles (1979), the meticulous research of Pollock (1983) and Cunningham (1995), and in a lighter but no less revealing vein, Hardyment (1995)); in non-western countries, the relationships between story and storyteller, adult and child, can be radically different from those in the west (see, for example, Pellowski 1990). Even the sciences which have underpinned adult behaviour towards (and thus the 'construction' of) children have shifted their emphases and theories (Sommerville 1982). Consequently, making judgements on behalf of present or past children – as those adults who work with children and books are inclined (or bound) to do – is fraught with difficulty. This in itself draws our attention to the gross simplifications made about readers in very many critical texts: in children's literature, the 'reader' is a much more obviously immanent character.

A central example of this confusion may be seen in the discussion of poetry for children. Can such a thing exist, if we assume that 'poetry' is a kind of literature which is structured so as to invite or require a special kind of reading – a kind of reading that 'children' (it is widely assumed) cannot provide. Neil Philip effectively demolishes this proposition in the 'Introduction' to *The New Oxford Book of Children's Verse*:

> Some would argue that the very notion of poetry for children is a nonsense. . . . Yet there is a recognisable tradition of children's verse. It is, most crucially, a tradition of immediate apprehension. There is in the best children's poetry a sense of the world being seen as for the first time, and of language being plucked from the air to describe it. . . . This does not necessarily mean that children's poems are 'simple' in any reductive sense. I would argue that no poem can be called a poem that does not have at its heart some unknowable mystery.
>
> Philip 1996: xxv.

But while the study of childhood and its relationship to children is a fascinating study, the actuality of childhood (in so far as it can be generally deduced) may be not entirely relevant to criticism: as Karín Lesnik-Oberstein points out in Chapter 2, it is the way in which critics (and, by implication, writers) 'construct' childhood which is important.

History, Ideology, Politics

It will be clear by now that both the range of children's books and the ways in which they can be studied are very extensive. Just as children's books are part of the ideological structures of the cultures of the world, so their history is constructed ideologically (some of these issues are dealt with in Chapters 4, 5 and 9). The two most obvious constructions of history are from an Anglocentric viewpoint, and from a male viewpoint (although, of course, those 'viewpoints' are far from stable). Other constructions of history – such as a feminist, a feminine, or a 'childist' approach – wait to be written. (Some progress is being made with books such as Lynne Vallone's *Disciplines of Virtue. Girls' Culture in the Eighteenth and Nineteenth Centuries*, Kimberley Reynolds's *Girls Only? Gender and Popular Children's Fiction in Britain, 1880–1910*, and, more theoretically (and evangelistically) Roberta Seelinger Trites's *Waking Sleeping Beauty: Feminist Voices in Children's Novels*).

Children's books have a long history around the world, and they have absorbed into themselves elements of folk and fairy tale, and the oral tradition. In many places, such as many parts of Africa, they have a postcolonial tinge, and an uneasy relationship with indigenous culture; elsewhere, they have seemed sufficiently important to totalitarian states as to suffer severe censorship. It is also possible to perceive similar patterns throughout the world. As Sheila Ray has observed:

> In the early stages of a printed literature, there are few or no books published specifically for children. There are perhaps a few books intended for broadly educational purposes, such as the courtesy or behaviour books printed in the fifteenth or sixteenth centuries in European countries, or the twentieth-century text books published to support the formal school curriculum in developing countries. In this situation children, as they learn to read, also take over adult books which appeal to them, a process helped by the fact that the early printed literature in any society is likely to draw on traditional stories which contain elements which appeal to every age group. Religion is also an important factor... Gradually stories written specially for children begin to appear... [and eventually] demands for books to meet a variety of interests and special needs emerge. One of the problems which face developing countries in the twentieth century is that they are expected to go through all the stages in a relatively short space of time – thirty or forty years at most – whereas European countries have taken five hundred years over the same process.
>
> Ray 1996: 654

If we argue that recognisable children's literature requires a recognisable childhood, and should not be totally shared with adults, then we might argue that only in the eighteenth century, with British publishers such as Mary Cooper and John Newbery, did English-language children's books emerge. They have since been immensely influential; the first book 'especially prepared for North American youth', John Cotton's *Spiritual Milk for Boston Babes*, was printed in London (in 1646) (Griswold, 1996: 871); in India, children's books began in Calcutta with the establishment of the School Book Society by missionaries in 1817 (Jafa 1996: 808). This dominance has continued: in 1988, half the children's books published in France were translations from the English (Bouvaist 1990: 30). (In contrast, France was the dominant influence on early German children's books.) Today, the traffic between English and other languages remains virtually one-way.

Earliest books for children were, as in Ray's formulation, based on traditional materials, or overtly didactic; children's literature in its modern form is largely a nineteenth-century phenomenon. For example, at the end of the eighteenth century in the Netherlands there was a rapid growth in fiction for children; whereas in Spain, despite translations of Grimm, Andersen, and Perrault, 'true' children's books did not emerge until the end of the nineteenth century.

Thereafter, histories of children's books worldwide demonstrate tensions between educational, religious and political exercises of power on the one hand, and various concepts associated with 'freedom' (notably fantasy and the imagination) on the other. The literatures that result demonstrate very clearly those societies' concepts of childhood and its power-relationship to adults. (Notable English-language histories include Avery 1994; Darton 1932/1982; Gilderdale 1982; Hunt 1995; Saxby 1969, 1971; Townsend 1965/1990.)

Both the construction of history, and what it generally shows is that (obviously enough) adults can and do control the production of children's literature – however subversive the child's reading might be (see Chapter 7). Censorship operates both before and after the texts are produced, often in bizarre circumstances. As Mark West has observed:

> Throughout the history of children's literature, the people who have tried to censor children's books, for all their ideological differences, share a rather romantic view about the power of books. They believe, or at least profess to believe, that books are such a major influence in the formation of children's values and attitudes that adults need to monitor nearly every word that children read.
>
> West, 1996: 506.

Censorship is relative: if books are withdrawn from classrooms, as they have often been, is that being protective or restrictive? Many of the most forceful actions taken against books, publishers, libraries and teachers have been in the USA by right-wing organisations, usually fundamentalist Christian in origin. Perhaps the most famous has been Educational Research Analysts, a Texas-based organisation run by Mel and Norma Gabler, which has provided 'evidence' for local campaigners and has sought to influence publishers (sometimes through state textbook-buying boards). Books which have been banned locally have included *The Diary of Anne Frank*, *The Wizard of Oz*, and adult books widely read by children and young adults such as *The Catcher in the Rye*.

The fact that children may well read 'against' the text (making simple cause-and-effect arguments very questionable) means that children's books have been potentially highly subversive. Ironically, their power can be demonstrated by the fact that although they were tightly controlled in Nazi Germany as part of the *Gleichschaltung*, Erich Kästner's classic *Emil and the Detectives* (1929) remained available – even though his other books had been burned by the Nazis.

Censorship tends to characterise children as impressionable and simple-minded, unable to take a balanced view of, for example, sexual or racial issues, unless the balance is explicitly stated. Judy Blume's books, which include the first example of explicitly described sexual intercourse in a children's book (in *Forever* (1975)) have been widely condemned, but have been bought in huge numbers by adolescents. Attempts have been made to censor or influence writers as diverse as Beatrix Potter (undressed kittens in *The Tale of Tom Kitten* (1907)) or Alan Garner (unsupervised sledging in *Tom Fobble's Day* (1977)). Difficulties have arisen over books which contain attitudes which were quite acceptable to the majority in their day. British examples are the racial caricatures in, for example, Hugh Lofting's *The Story of Dr Dolittle* (1922), or the gender bias in Enid Blyton's work; new editions of these books have been modified, as Britain has become increasingly multi-cultural – or at least, more aware of multicultural issues.

The question of how far children are likely to be influenced by what they may or may not perceive in the texts has been a shifting conundrum throughout children's book history: recent debates have involved Toshi Maruki's *Hiroshima No Pika* (1982) with its unstinting depiction of death and destruction, and Babette Cole's *Mummy Laid an Egg* (1993) with its witty and ironic explanations of conception and birth.

Different cultures exercise 'censorship' in different ways. In Britain, it operates through selection, notably by large booksellers and wholesalers; in the USA, direct and vocal action is more the norm; elsewhere, just as totalitarian states 'manufactured' politically acceptable texts, so post-totalitarian (and post-colonial) societies have reacted against their previous masters.

Children's literature, then, has its own histories, and immense influence – but this has not, until recently, been reflected in serious study of the form. Perhaps the most neglected area has been bibliography – the history of the books as books. As Brian Alderson has observed, 'there can be no doubt that scientific bibliography is able to play as important a role in supporting the very varied activity which is taking place among children's books as it does in the field of literary studies elsewhere' (1977: 203; see also Chapter 10). However, because the study of children's literature has been skewed towards the reader and affect, rather than towards the book as artefact, we are in the position of having a great deal of speculative and theoretical criticism, but relatively little 'solid' bibliographical backup. How far this is necessary will remain a matter of debate, but with vast collections of children's literature in libraries across the world, most of them very little used, there is immense potential for bibliographic and historical research.

Reading Children's Literature

As might be expected, it is unwise to assume that reading and interpreting children's books is a simple process, and one of the recurrent themes in this volume is the relationship between reader and text. How far can the writer, by implying a reader (that is, a type of reader or a reader with certain knowledge, skills, and attitudes) control what is understood in a text? How can we discover what has been understood? What are the mechanisms by which understanding is produced?

Chapter 5 of this book, 'Analysing Texts for Children: Linguistics and Stylistics', and Chapter 6, 'Decoding the Images: Illustration and Picture Books', take us to the basics of textual analysis. In the first case, it is important to have an understanding of text as language; this is particularly true of children's literature – given that the primary audience is still learning about language as it uses it. Such a detailed approach also militates against the temptation to see children's literature as an amorphous mass, and suggests that it can be profitably read in this 'literary' way. Jonathan Culler has pointed out that literary studies tend to encourage 'close reading', a type of reading that is 'alert to the details of narrative structure and attends to complexities of meaning'. In contrast, cultural studies (which usually deal with 'non-literary' texts, such as television – and often children's books) tend 'towards "symptomatic interpretation" – that is, identifying broad, portable themes' (Culler 1997: 52).

There is a simple philosophical problem at the root of understanding reading, to take the most conservative viewpoint:

> It is known that the reader's understanding of a text will be conditioned by what he [*sic*] already knows, and by the availability of that knowledge during the reading process. Given that different purposes and motivations for reading result in different levels of processing and outcome... it is likely that different readers will to some extent interpret different texts in varied ways. This, indeed, is notoriously the case for literary texts, where it is often said that there are as many interpretations as there are readers to interpret. Yet it is intuitively unsatisfying to claim that a text can mean anything to any reader. The text itself must to some extent condition the nature of the understanding that the reader constructs.
>
> Alderson and Short 1989: 72

Equally, this kind of analysis allows us access to possible meanings in the text, which a 'theme hunting' approach might miss. As Perry Nodelman has noted:

> Unfortunately, many readers approach texts with the idea that their themes or messages can be easily identified and stated in a few words... Reading in this way directs attention away from the more immediate pleasures of a text: away from language... away from other, deeper kinds of meaning the text might imply.
>
> Nodelman 1996: 54

But above all, a stylistic-linguistic approach points out (especially if taken in conjunction with reader-response criticism – see Chapter 7) the inevitable complexity of texts. This is no more obvious than in the case of the picture-book – where it is often assumed that pictures are in some way 'easier' to interpret than words. As Scott McCloud points out in his revolutionary *Understanding Comics: the Invisible Art*, it is 'nothing short of incredible' that the human mind can understand icons – symbolic representations or abstractions from reality, as readily as it does (1993: 31, and see 30–45). Picture-books cannot help but be polyphonic; even the 'simplest' require complex interpretative skills. What is missing is as complex an interpretative vocabulary as exists for words, although this is rapidly being supplied through the work of Nodelman (1988), Doonan (1993) and others.

Underestimating the power of the picture-book (or the comic book) is tantamount to underestimating the 'child' as reader – which, as I hope I have demonstrated, is a central error. Doonan, for example, is concerned less with the complex mechanics of reading pictures than with aesthetics:

> A less common view, and the one I believe honours the picture-book most fully, holds that pictures, through their expressive powers, enable the book to fuction as an art object.... The value lies... in the aesthetic experience and the contribution the picture book can make to our aesthetic development. In an aesthetic experience we are engaged in play of the most enjoyable and demanding kind.... And in that play we have... to deal with abstract concepts logically, intuitively and imaginatively.
>
> Doonan 1993: 7

Of course, the experience of a book starts before – and goes beyond – the words or the pictures on the page. The total book-as-object is an experience, one that has become increasingly the province of book designer: 'each book is different and none so elementary as not to benefit from considered design... The designer sometimes has to take the initiative for presenting the author's material visually and thereby transforming it into a marketable product' (Martin 1996: 463).

Although we have been considering texts, it is obvious that the study of children's literature involves the audience – the child, the reader and the circumstance of reading. Text is also a context; readers are made, or un-made, by the 'reading environment' as Aidan Chambers has called it. Nor do 'texts' need to be written. As Chambers observes: 'Storytelling is indispensable in enabling people to become literary readers' (Chambers 1991: 46), and the study of how stories are told orally contributes to our understanding of how story – and communication – work.

Storytelling also (to return to questions of ideology, which are never very far away) has a political axis. Jack Zipes, a distinguished American expert on children's literature, folklore, and storytelling, believes passionately in the subversive virtues of storytelling. Schools in the West (with the collusion of society in general), he notes:

> are geared towards making children into successful consumers and competitors in a 'free' world dictated by market conditions.... If storytellers are to be effective on behalf of children in schools... it is important to try to instil a sense of community, self-reflecting and self-critical community, in the children to demonstrate how the ordinary can become extraordinary.... Schools are an ideal setting for this 'subversive' type of storytelling... if schools want... to show that they can be other than the institutions of correction, discipline, and distraction that they tend to be.
>
> Zipes 1995: 6.

How a story is communicated, then, by spoken word or written word, by picture or symbol, the circumstances of that communication, and the possible effect – all these have become an integral part of the study of children's literature. This means that the concerns of what might be broadly called 'criticism' extend beyond the traditional bounds of literary criticism.

Criticising Children's Literature

There is a happy irony that people involved with the apparently simple subject of children's literature have (often unwittingly) been at the forefront of literary and critical theory.

It has been widely argued that children's literature studies should not ghettoise themselves, but make every use of critical techniques. There is no shortage, as a sceptic might remark, of schools of criticism, nor of books which will outline their principles. But the fact that the work of such schools can be productively applied to children's literature is demonstrated by Roderick McGillis's *The Nimble Reader* (1996), which shows the relevance of schools of thought from formalism to feminism. (General textbooks such as Raman Selden's *Practising Theory and Reading Literature* (1989) are also useful.)

In the present book, four chapters (5, 7, 8, and 9) cover the major general areas of literary theory and practice; other particularly fruitful approaches for children's literature are those concerned with the analysis of narrative, discourse in general, and the cultural structures reflected in texts. 'Structuralism', for example, although perhaps somewhat outmoded as a critical fashion, can be very fruitfully employed even if, as Rex Gibson observed in the context of education, 'it might appear to have little to offer.... Its insistence on systems, wholes, relationships, together with the apparent devaluation of the individual in its "decentring of the subject", all run counter to the child-centred, individualistic, humanistic assumptions that those working with children might be supposed to share' (Gibson 1984: 105). Yet it is precisely this level of abstraction which is valuable to those concerned with individual reactions of readers to texts.

Structural readings may well, therefore, provide a starting point for the study of myth, legend, folk- and fairy-tales – but only a starting point; the way in which approaches may be combined, and barriers crossed, can be demonstrated by looking at Jack Zipes's approach to these texts. It is a sociological and historical oddity that children's literature has come to include and absorb these (initially) crude, violent, and sexually-charged texts, but by understanding their structures, and then relating them to broader cultural movements, as well as historical moments, they may be seen as other than they are generally supposed to be. The idea that folk-tales and myths contain archetypal patterns, for example, may be valuable; the idea that these archetypes are appropriate, because of their 'simple' form, to a particular audience, will not stand up to much scrutiny. Jack Zipes's *The Trials and Tribulations of Little Red Riding Hood* (1993) is an excellent example of the way in which structural analyses can be combined with psychological, sociological, and historical studies. 'Little Red Riding Hood' may seem to the casual observer to be merely a simple, children's story. Zipes rejects such a view:

> It is impossible to exaggerate the impact and importance of the Little Red Riding Hood syndrome as a dominant cultural pattern in Western societies. [One reading is that] *Little Red Riding Hood* reflects men's fear of women's sexuality – and of their own as well. The curbing and regulation of sexual drives is fully portrayed in this bourgeois literary fairy tale of the basis of

deprived male needs. [Alternatively] given the conditions of Western society where women have been prey for men, there is a positive feature to the tale: its warning about the possibility of sexual molestation continues to serve a useful purpose.

Zipes, 1993: 80–1; see also Zipes, 1997

Zipes's critical practice – which reflects his multiple roles as translator, oral storyteller, and critical analyst – exemplifies the way in which children's literature rewards the application of a wide range of critical skills.

The Uses of Children's Literature

> When academics are born, a good fairy at the christening promises them that when they grow up they will be able to read and understand books. Hardly has she finished speaking, however, when a bad fairy interrupts to say, with a threatening gesture, 'but you must never, never look out of the window'.
>
> Joan Rockwell, quoted in Parker 1994: 194

As we have seen, the study of children's literature brings us back to some very fundamental concerns: why are we reading? What are books *for*? The answers may be, as in the case of Chambers, a general liberal-humanist faith in the book and in human civilisation; but very often, children's literature is seen as the last repository of the *ducis et utile* philosophy: the books may be pleasant, yes, but essentially they have to be *useful*. Children's books are of the world, and one of the features of critical theory which has made it unattractive to many children's book practitioners has been its solipsistic turn.

In the judgement of children's books, then, *for* is often the key word. What are books 'good' *for*? Children's books are used for different purposes at different times – for more things than most books are. Some are 'good' time-passers; others 'good' for acquiring literacy; others 'good' for expanding the imagination or 'good' for inculcating general (or specific) social attitudes, or 'good' for dealing with issues or coping with problems, or 'good' for reading in that 'literary' way which is a small part of adult culture, or 'good' for dealing with racism . . . and most books do several things. This is not a scale where some purposes stand higher than others – it is a matrix where hundreds of subtle meanings are generated: what you think is good depends on you, the children, and on what you're using the book for – and every reading is different.

The two chapters of this book which address practical outcomes of reading children's books, 'Children Becoming Readers: Reading and Literacy' (13) and 'Can stories Heal?' (14), demonstrate how theory and practice, psychological probability and practical outcome, and awareness of words, people, and their environments, are all inextricably linked. But the same could be said of other 'practical' applications of children's literature. For example, Eileen Colwell, one of the most distinguished of British storytellers, felt that 'There are particular people in a community who *need* stories . . . I would make a special plea for storytelling to the visually impaired' (1991: 82). Children's literature, then, is relevant to an even more marginalised section of the community, those with special needs. As Beverley

Mathias, of the British National Resource Centre for Children with Reading Difficulties wrote:

> What was not addressed until recently was the fact that for some children print is not the means by which they will be able to enjoy reading, and for others, reading is complicated by some intellectual, sensory or physical problem. Some children find it extremely difficult or even impossible to use print at all, and therefore... some of these children will never aspire to be 'readers' in the commonly accepted sense.

Mathias 1996: 644

It is the awareness that the study of children's literature encompasses not only subtle textual distinctions but practical, life-affecting actions which holds the 'subject' of children's literature together. The phenomenal range of prizes for 'the best' children's books awarded each year covers books which are not just abstractly 'the best', but which portray minorities, or promote peace – or which are chosen by children.

Thus while writers, publishers, librarians, teachers, parents, and children, and very many others discuss the applications of children's literature, they are talking about the same interactive area as those who look into the books themselves. This seems to me the source, potentially, of immense strength and of immense innovation. In 1997, an issue of the prestigious Yale journal, *Children's Literature*, was devoted to 'cross-writing', based on the idea that 'a dialogic mix of older and younger voices occurs in texts too often read as univocal. Authors who write for children inevitably create a colloquy between past and present selves'. This, the editors concluded, involves 'interplay and cross-fertilisation' (Knoepflmacher and Myers 1997: vii). That image could stand for much of children's literature studies, and it is an understanding of the meanings behind those many voices that this book addresses.

References

Alderson, B. (1977) *Bibliography and Children's Books: The Present Position*, London: The Bibliographical Society. Reprinted from *The Library* 32, 3: 203–213.

Alderson, J. C. and Short, M. (1989) 'Reading literature', in Short, M. (ed.) *Reading, Analysing and Teaching Literature*, London: Longman.

Avery, G. (1994) *Behold the Child. American Children and their Books, 1621–1922*, London: The Bodley Head.

Bouvaist, J. M. (1990) *Les Enjeux de l'édition-jeunesse à la veille de 1992*, Montreuil: Salon du Livre de jeuness.

Chambers, A. (1985) *Booktalk. Occasional Writing on Literature and Children*, London: The Bodley Head.

—— (1991) *The Reading Environment. How Adults Help Children Enjoy Books*, South Woodchester: Thimble Press

Colwell, E. (1991) *Storytelling*, South Woodchester: Thimble Press.

Culler, J. (1997) *Literary Theory: A Very Short Introduction*, Oxford: Oxford University Press.

Cunningham, H. (1995) *Children and Childhood in Western Society since 1500*, London: Longman.

Darton, F. J. H. (1932/1982) *Children's Books in England: Five Centuries of Social Life*, 3rd edn, rev. B. Alderson, Cambridge: Cambridge University Press.

Doonan, J. (1993), *Looking at Pictures in Picture-Books*, South Woodchester: Thimble Press.

Gibson, R. (1984) *Structuralism and Education*, London: Hodder and Stoughton.

Gilderdale, B. (1982) *A Sea Change: 145 Years of New Zealand Junior Fiction*, Auckland: Longman Paul.

Griswold, J. (1996) 'Children's literature in the U.S.A.: A historical overview' in Hunt, P. (ed.) *International Companion Encyclopedia of Children's Literature*, London: Routledge.

Hardyment, C. (1995) *Perfect Parents. Baby-Care Advice Past and Present*, Oxford: Oxford University Press.

Hoyles, M. (ed.) (1979) *Changing Childhood*, London: Writers and Readers Publishing Cooperative.

Hunt, P. (ed.) (1995) *Children's Literature: An Illustrated History*, Oxford: Oxford University Press.

Jafa, M. (1996) 'The Indian sub-continent' in Hunt, P. (ed.) *International Companion Encyclopedia of Children's Literature*, London: Routledge.

Knoepflmacher, U. C. and Myers, M. (1997) 'From the editors: "cross-writing" and the reconceptualizing of children's literary studies', *Children's Literature*, 25, New Haven, CT: Yale University Press, vii–xvii.

McCloud, S. (1993) *Understanding Comics: The Invisible Art*, Northampton, MA: Tundra.

McGillis, R. (1996) *The Nimble Reader*, New York: Twayne.

Martin, D. (1996) 'Children's book design' in Hunt, P. (ed.) *International Companion Encyclopedia of Children's Literature*, London: Routledge.

Mathias, B. (1996) 'Publishing for special needs', in Hunt, P. (ed.) *International Companion Encyclopedia of Children's Literature*, London: Routledge.

Nodelman, P. (1988) *Words About Pictures*, Athens, GA: University of Georgia Press.

—— (1996) *The Pleasures of Children's Literature*, 2nd edn, White Plains, NY: Longman.

Parker, J. (1994) 'Unravelling the romance: strategies for understanding textual ideology' in Corcoran, B., Hayhoe, M., and Pradl, G. M. (eds), *Knowledge in the Making. Challenging the Text in the Classroom*, Portsmouth, NH: Boynton/Cook, Heinemann.

Pellowski, A. (1980) *The World of Storytelling*, rev. edn, New York: H. W. Wilson.

Philip, N. (ed.) (1996) *The New Oxford Book of Children's Verse*, Oxford: Oxford University Press.

Pollock, L. A. (1983) *Forgotten Children: Parent–Child Relations from 1500 to 1900*, Cambridge: Cambridge University Press.

Ray, S. (1996) 'The world of children's literature: An introduction', in Hunt, P. (ed.) *International Companion Encyclopedia of Children's Literature*, London: Routledge.

Reynolds, K. (1990) *Girls Only? Gender and Popular Children's Fiction in Britain, 1880–1910*, Hemel Hempstead: Harvester Wheatsheaf.

Saxby, H. M. (1969) *A History of Australian Children's Literature 1841–1941*, Sydney: Wentworth Books.

—— (1971) *A History of Australian Children's Literature 1941–1970*, Sydney: Wentworth Books.

Selden, R. (1989) *Practising Theory and Reading Literature*, Hemel Hempstead: Harvester Wheatsheaf.

Sommerville, J. (1982) *The Rise and Fall of Childhood*, Beverly Hills, CA: Sage.

Townsend, J. R. (1965/1990) *Written for Children: An Outline of English-Language Children's Literature*, London: Penguin.

Trites, R. S. (1997) *Waking Sleeping Beauty: Feminist Voices in Children's Novels*, Iowa City, IA: University of Iowa Press.

Vallone, L. (1995) *Disciplines of Virtue. Girls' Culture in the Eighteenth and Nineteenth Centuries*, New Haven, CT: Yale University Press.

West, M. (1988) *Trust Your Children, Voices Against Censorship in Children's Literature*, New York: Neal-Schuman.

—— (1996) 'Censorship' in Hunt, P. (ed.) *International Companion Encyclopedia of Children's Literature*, London: Routledge.

Zipes, J. (ed.) (1993) *The Trials and Tribulations of Little Red Riding Hood*, 2nd edn, New York: Routledge.
—— (1995) *Storytelling. Building Community, Changing Lives*, New York: Routledge.
—— (1997) *Happily Ever After. Fairy Tales, Children, and the Culture Industry*, New York: Routledge.

2 Essentials: What is Children's Literature? What is Childhood?

Karín Lesnik-Oberstein

Editor's introduction

The study of children's literature involves three elements – the literature, the children, and the adult critics. The relationship between these is complex, partly because childhood and 'the child' are difficult to define, partly because adults need to 'construct' the child in order to talk about the books, and partly because the literature is assumed to be 'good for' children in some way. The tensions which are generated are fundamental to the ways in which we think and talk about the subject; in this chapter, Karín Lesnik-Oberstein sets out the fascinating range of positions that can be taken in the search for working definitions.

P. H.

The definition of 'children's literature' lies at the heart of its endeavour: it is a category of books the existence of which absolutely depends on supposed relationships with a particular reading audience: children. The definition of 'children's literature' therefore is underpinned by purpose: it wants to be something in particular, because this is supposed to connect it with that reading audience – 'children' – with which it declares itself to be overtly and purposefully concerned. But is a children's book a book written by children, or for children? And, crucially: what does it mean to write a book 'for' children? If it is a book written 'for' children, is it then still a children's book if it is (only) read by adults? What of 'adult' books read also by children – are they 'children's literature'? As the British critic John Rowe Townsend points out:

> Surely *Robinson Crusoe* was not written for children, and do not the *Alice* books appeal at least as much to grown ups?; if *Tom Sawyer* is children's literature, what about *Huckleberry Finn*?; if the *Jungle Books* are children's literature, what about *Kim* or *Stalky*? and if *The Wind in the Willows* is children's literature, what about *The Golden Age*?; and so on.
>
> Townsend 1980: 196

Attempts to dismiss categorisation and definition of texts as a side issue which should not be an end in itself are very problematic when it comes to children's literature: how do we know which books are best for children if we do not even know which books *are* 'children's books'? For this is what 'children's literature' means in its most fundamental sense to every critic who uses the term: books which are good for children, and most particularly good in terms of emotional and moral values. We can see this view reflected in Canadian critic Michele Landsberg's belief that

> good books can do so much for children. At their best, they expand horizons and instil in children a sense of the wonderful complexity of life ... No other pastime available to children is so conducive to empathy and the enlargement of human sympathies. No other pleasure can so richly furnish a child's mind with the symbols, patterns, depths, and possibilities of civilisation.
>
> Landsberg 1987: 34

The meaning of children's literature as 'books which are good for children' in turn crucially indicates that the two constituent terms – 'children' and 'literature' – within the label 'children's literature' cannot be separated and traced back to original independent meanings, and then reassembled to achieve a greater understanding of what 'children's literature' is. Within the label the two terms totally qualify each other and transform each other's meaning for the purposes of the field. In short: the 'children' of 'children's literature' are constituted as specialised ideas of 'children', not necessarily related in any way to other 'children' (for instance those within education, psychology, sociology, history, art, or literature), and the 'literature' of 'children's literature' is a special idea of 'literature', not necessarily related to any other 'literature' (most particularly 'adult literature').

Having said this, one of the primary characteristics of most children's literature criticism and theory is that it assumes that the terms 'children' and 'literature' within 'children's literature' *are* separable and more or less independent of one another, and that they are directly related to other 'children' and 'literatures'; critics often make use of, or refer to, theories from education, psychology, sociology, history, art or literature, in buttressing their opinions. But in every case they transform the material from other disciplines to fit their own particular argument.

This complexity arises partly because the reading 'child' of children's literature is primarily discussed in terms of emotional responses and consciousness. Children's literature criticism, for instance, actually devotes little systematic discussion (but many random comments) to cognitive issues such as the correspondence between vocabulary lists composed by educational psychologists and the vocabulary levels in books, or to levels of cognitive development thought to be necessary to understanding the content of a book. These areas are regarded as the province of child psychologists, or as appropriate to the devising of strictly functional reading schemes which are not held to fall within 'children's literature'. This is the case even with the teachers' guides to children's literature (such as those of Lonsdale and Mackintosh 1973; Huck 1976; Sadker and Sadker 1977; Smith and Park 1977; Glazer and Williams 1979; and Norton 1983) which purport to be able to draw connections between psychological and educative investigations and children's books. (This exercise, even when it is seriously attempted, is in any case fraught with difficulties, and even in the best cases produces very limited results – one need only think of the ongoing debates in education on how to teach children the basic mechanics of reading itself.) In fact, in the actual discussion of works of children's literature, the critics' attention is primarily focused on whether and how they think the book will attract the 'child' – whether the 'child' will 'love' or 'like' the book.

But it is even more relevant to the problems of children's literature criticism that, although the idea that 'children's literature' might pose problems of definition is often accepted and discussed by critics, the idea that the 'child' might pose equal – if not greater – problems of definition is strenuously resisted. This is despite the fact that historians such as Philippe Ariès and anthropologists such as Margaret Mead and Martha Wolfenstein (1955) have argued in classic studies that – at the very least – definitions of 'childhood' have differed throughout history, and from culture to culture. As Ariès writes:

> the point is that ideas entertained about these [family] relations may be dissimilar at moments separated by lengthy periods of time. It is the history of the idea of the family which concerns us here, not the description of manners or the nature of law ... The idea of childhood is not to be confused with affection for children: it corresponds to an awareness of the particular nature of childhood, that particular nature which distinguishes the child from the adult, even the young adult.
>
> Ariès 1973: 8, 125

Ariès makes clear that the 'family' and 'childhood' are ideas that function within cultural and social frameworks as carriers of changeable social, moral, and ethical values and motives.

British theorist Jacqueline Rose further elaborates views such as those of Ariès with respect specifically to children's literature by applying them to contemporary processes within Western culture, rather than by tracing historical or cultural shifts. Rose argues that

> children's fiction rests on the idea that there is a child who is simply there to be addressed and that speaking to it might be simple. It is an idea whose innocent generality covers up a multitude of sins ... *Peter Pan* stands in our culture as a monument to the impossibility of its own claims – that it represents the child, speaks to and for children, addresses them as a group which is knowable and exists for the book.
>
> Rose 1984: 1

Rose points out that, to begin with, 'children' are divided by class, race, ethnic origins, gender, and so on, but her argument is more radical than that: to Rose, the 'child' is a construction invented for the needs of the children's literature authors and critics, and not an 'observable', 'objective', 'scientific', entity. Within Rose's argument the adults' needs are discussed within a Freudian terminology involving the unconscious, and Rose is therefore emphatically not arguing that this process of constructing the 'child', or books for it, can – or should – simply be stopped: it serves important functions which she is attempting to understand better in her terms. Children's literature and children's literature criticism have not, in fact, made much use of Rose's argument, and, indeed, in many ways they cannot, for the very existence of these fields depends utterly on a posited existence of the 'child':

all their work is ostensibly on this 'child's' behalf. Yet, with or without Rose's argument, children's literature and its criticism continue to assume many different – and often contradictory – 'children', and this can only be accounted for by either accepting the notion of the 'child' as constructed (which, again, it should be noted, should not be taken to mean that it is superfluous or irrelevant: this use of 'construction' has to do with wider philosophical ideas about the way meaning works), or by maintaining that some critics are more correct about the child than others and adhering to their view.

The problems of children's literature criticism and theory, then, occur within the confines of the field of tension established by the contradictions and gaps between the assumption that 'children' and 'literature' have self-evident, consistent or logically derived meanings, and the actual use of 'children' and 'literature' within 'children's literature' in very specific, and often variable and inconsistent, ways. Attempts to define 'children's literature' and the reading 'child' thus also operate within this field of tensions. The British cultural theorist Fred Inglis argues that

> it is simply ignorant not to admit that children's novelists have developed a set of conventions for their work. Such development is a natural extension of the elaborate and implicit system of rules, orthodoxies, improvisations, customs, forms and adjustments which characterize the way any adult tells stories or simply talks at length to children.
>
> Inglis 1981: 101

Australian critic Barbara Wall agrees, and bases her whole analysis of children's books on 'the conviction that adults … speak differently in fiction when they are aware that they are addressing children … [This is] translated, sometimes subtly, sometimes obviously, into the narrator's voice … [which defines] a children's book' (Wall 1991: 2–3). But British critic Nicholas Tucker points out that Inglis and Wall's type of view does not avoid the difficulty that: 'although most people would agree that there are obvious differences between adult and children's literature, when pressed they may find it quite difficult to establish what exactly such differences amount to' (Tucker 1981: 8).

Because it has been precisely the self-imposed task of children's literature critics to judge which books are good for children and why, all children's literature criticism and reviews abound with both implicit and overt statements concerning the definitions of 'children's literature', 'children' and 'literature'. When critics state in some way or another that this is a book they judge to be good for children this actually involves saying that the book is good because of what they think a book does for children, and this in turn cannot avoid revealing what they think children are and do (especially when they read). Joan Aiken, for instance, says she does not purposefully incorporate moral messages into her books because she feels that 'children have a strong natural resistance to phoney morality. They can see through the adult with some moral axe to grind almost before he opens his mouth' (Aiken 1973: 149), but Rosemary Sutcliff writes that 'I *am* aware of the responsibility of my job; and I do try to put over to the child reading any book of mine some kind of ethic' (Sutcliff 1973: 306). Pamela Travers, creator of *Mary Poppins* feels that 'You do not chop off a section of your imaginative substance and make a book specifically for children for – if you are honest – you have, in fact, no idea where childhood ends and maturity begins. It is all endless and all one' (Cott 1984: xxii), and E. B. White states that 'you have to write up, not down. Children are demanding ... They accept, almost without question, anything you present them with, as long as it is presented honestly, fearlessly, and clearly ... They love words that give them a hard time' (White 1973: 140). Austrian critic Maria Lypp, in line with Travers and White, argues that the adaptations children's authors introduce to children's literature depend on an 'asymmetrical relationship' which forms the 'code of children's fiction', but that there is an 'ideal of *symmetrical* communication' which implies true understanding between author and reader, and this becomes Lypp's prescriptive criterion for children's literature (Heimeriks and Van Toorn 1989: 370–372). However, Barbara Wall argues in contrast to Travers, White, and Lypp, that

> All writers for children must, in a sense, be writing down. If they write with an educated adult audience in mind – their own peers – their stories will surely be, at best not always interesting and probably often intelligible, and at worst positively harmful, to children, even when a child appears as a central character, as in *The Go-Between* or *What Maisie Knew*. Whenever a writer shows consciousness of an immature audience, in the sense of adapting the material of the story or the techniques of the discourse for the benefit of child readers, that writer might be said to be writing down, that is, acknowledging that there is a difference in the skills, interests and frame of reference of children and adults.
>
> Wall 1991: 15

But where Wall worries about harm to the child, Gillian Avery in turn believes that '[the child] has his own defence against what he doesn't like or doesn't understand in the book ... He ignores it, subconsciously perhaps, or he makes something different from it ... [Children] extract what they want from a book and no more' (Avery 1976: 33). This adult critics' defining of the 'child' cannot be formed or disrupted by any child's own voiced opinions or ideas because these are interpreted – selected or edited ('heard') – by adults for their purposes and from their perspectives. One aspect of this is reflected by Nicholas Tucker when he explains that

> Trying to discover some of the nature and effects of the interaction between children and their favourite books is by no means easy ... One simple-minded approach to the problem has always been to ask children themselves through various questionnaires and surveys, what exactly their books mean to them. Turning a powerful searchlight of this sort onto complex, sometimes diffuse patterns of reaction is a clumsy way of going about things, however, and children can be particularly elusive when interrogated like this, with laconic comments like 'Not bad' or 'The story's good' adding little to any researchers' understanding.
>
> Tucker 1981: 2

It may be noted at this point that children's literature's constant underlying assumption of the 'child' as a generic universality connects children's literature criticism all over the world. Children's literature criticism in different cultures is united by speaking of the 'child' as an existing entity – even though this 'existing entity' may be described differently in different cultures as it is described differently within cultures. The 'child' and its attendant 'children's literature' are often, in this sense, described as Western imports by critics from other cultures: Indonesian critic Sunindyo points out that

> as with other countries, Indonesian literature had its origins in an oral tradition ... The history of children's books in Indonesia at this time is to be found entirely within the history of Balai Pustaka, a government publishing agency established in 1908 by the Government of the Netherlands East Indies [when Indonesia was a Dutch colony].
>
> Sunindyo 1987: 44–45

Japanese critic Tadashi Matsui notes that in 1920s Japan the growth of 'large cities with dense populations generated the birth of a middle class ... among [whom] the ideas of European liberalism, the urban mode of living, free mass education and a modern concept of the child were being fostered' (Matsui 1986–1987: 14). Birgit Dankert, when noting the background to the development of children's literature in Africa, draws attention to another aspect of response to Western influences:

> In addition to many other cultural 'achievements', the former colonial powers also introduced children's books to Africa. These cultural imports elicited then (and elicit still today) the same ambivalent mixture of respect and rejection which characterises African reactions to so many other borrowings from former colonial powers ... If arguments in favor of children's books are brought up, then they resemble those of the early years of European children's literature: that children's books should educate, that they should preserve folk culture, that they should help guarantee Africa's transition to a culture of the written word, that they should support African cultural identity.
>
> Hunt 1992: 112

The disparities between the various definitions of 'children's literature', 'children', and 'literature', are problematic to children's literature criticism because they undermine the goal it sets itself. In this situation, children's literature criticism's prescriptions or suggestions of reading for children become problematic, with critics attempting in different ways to assert the validity of their particular views. Important social issues, such as racism, have led critics with the same anti-racist orientation to differ utterly in their judgement of a book. For instance, British critic Bob Dixon praises Paula Fox's *The Slave Dancer* (1973) as being 'a novel of great horror and as great humanity ... [approaching] perfection as a work of art' (Dixon 1977: 125), while American views have included Sharon Bell Mathis's: 'an insult to black children' (Mathis 1977: 146), and Binnie Tate's claim that it 'perpetuates racism ... [with] constantly repeated racist implications and negative illusions [*sic*]' (Tate 1977: 152–153). The assumption that children's books somehow affect children makes the issues crucial: does, or can, *The Slave Dancer* perpetuate racism or does it counteract it (or does it do other things altogether)? In each case children's literature critics inevitably ultimately resort to one basic claim: that they know more about children or the child and how and why it reads than the critics they disagree with.

In examining various attempts to define 'children's literature' we find a constant assumption of the existence of the (reading) child (that is: the assumption that there is such a thing as a unified, consistent, 'objective' 'child reader') together with the capacity for knowing it that each critic claims for him- or herself. This holds true for all children's literature critics, even if they claim to be 'literary' critics of children's books, because the 'literary' is defined in terms of how the book is supposed to affect the 'child'. Examining the processes of defining 'children's literature' and the 'child' which is essential to its project also illustrates the extent to which differences of opinion exist and threaten the coherence of children's literature criticism: in other words, how and why the definitions of children's literature and childhood matter so much to children's literature critics.

The first and most basic step critics take in defining 'children's literature' – and one which still receives primary emphasis in discussions around children's books – is to differentiate books used for didactic or educational purposes from 'children's literature'. F. J. Harvey Darton classically outlined this split that critics make between didactic books for children and children's 'literature': 'by "children's books" I mean printed works produced ostensibly to give children spontaneous pleasure and not primarily to teach them, nor solely to make them good, nor to keep them profitably quiet' (Darton 1932/1982: 1). To the children's literature critic the outstanding characteristic of 'children's literature' is that it is supposed to speak to the reading child through amusement and inherent appeal, and not through primarily didactic messages, which are described as being merely instructive, coercive, intrusive, or dull to the reading child. This also often comes to be the main means of indicating the 'literary' qualities of children's books. As Margery Fisher writes:

> We should not *expect* children's stories to be sermons or judicial arguments or sociological pamphlets. As independent works of art they must be allowed to appeal to the imagination, the mind, the heart on their own terms ... If a writer cannot say what he really feels, if he cannot be serious in developing a theme ... [If he has in any way to minimise] that approach to books for the young must eventually dilute their quality as mainstream literature.
>
> Haviland 1973: 273

This is how 'children's literature' defines 'literature': as something that in itself is good for children – that affects children better or more than non-literature – and this of course implies a world of assumptions about what the reading 'child' is and how it reads. Charlotte Huck sums up this view when she writes that 'good writing, or effective use of language ... will help the reader to experience the delight of beauty, wonder, and humor ... He will be challenged to dream dreams, to ponder, and to ask questions to himself' (Huck 1976: 4). This concept of the 'literary' causes many children's literature critics considerable problems in its own right. In attempting to preserve both an essential, coherent, consistent, 'child', and a concept of 'literature', critics find themselves struggling with statements which in their self-contradiction inadvertently betray the ways in which the 'child' and 'literature' mutually qualify and construct each other within children's literature criticism. Joan Glazer and Gurney Williams, for instance, first state that good children's books are characterised by 'strong materials – good plots, rich settings, well-developed characters, important themes, and artistic styles ... bold and imaginative language' (Glazer and Williams 1979: 34, 19), and that this 'freshness ... comes from the author. And in the author it begins with an understanding of who the child is' (22). Then they continue, however, by arguing that even if children don't like these books which are good for them, they may still be 'good literature ... built of strong materials ... the likes and dislikes of children do not determine the quality of literature ... Books must be judged as literature on their own merits. And children should be given excellent literature' (34).

'Children' in relation to reading have something to do with particular ideas about freedom and about emotion and consciousness, as Darton's statement implies; the 'child' develops as a concept produced by ideas of liberation from restriction and force, and is assigned various particular niches within cultural and societal structures. These ideas of literature and liberation are in fact derived from the ideals of Western liberal humanism, originating in classical Greek culture. This is clear if we compare Michele Landsberg, Charlotte Huck and Glazer and Williams's statements of the value of children's literature with the statement of the sixteenth-century humanist educationist Juan Luis Vives:

> poems contain subjects of extraordinary effectiveness, and they display human passions in a wonderful and vivid manner. This is called *energia*. There breathes in them a certain great and lofty spirit so that the readers are themselves caught into it, and seem to rise above their own intellect, and even above their own nature.
>
> Vives 1913: 126

There are not many clearer articulations of the power ascribed to literature in the intellectual, moral or emotional education of children that dominates the concern of children's literature critics despite all their protestations of resistance to education or the dreaded 'didacticism'.

We may, incidentally – with respect to this relationship between the 'child' and specific formulations of liberty or freedom – refer back to Tadashi Matsui's linking of 'the ideas of European liberalism, the urban mode of living, [and] free mass education' with 'a modern concept of the child', as well as to Birgit Dankert's statement on African children's literature, which highlights the complex status of children's literature. It is written of as if it can be a value-free carrier of an oral home culture (an 'innocent text'), when it is inevitable that as a product of a written culture's liberal arts educational ideals it carries these values with it, whatever the actual content of the book.

The Swedish critic Boel Westin echoes Darton while specifying further how this ostensible move away from didacticism is seen by the critics as moving from adult coercion to a consideration of the 'child':

Well into the nineteenth century, [Swedish] children's books sought primarily to impress upon their young readers good morals, proper manners, and a sense of religion. In Sweden it was not until the turn of the twentieth century that children's literature began to respond to the needs of children rather than adults.

Westin 1991: 7

'Children's literature' becomes defined as containing, both in form and content, the 'needs of children', and, therefore, this is how 'children's books' – written, published, sold, and usually bought, by adults – come to be spoken of as if the 'child' were *in the book*. As the New Zealand critic Sydney Melbourne states while discussing the portrayal of the Maori in children's books: 'What are we after? Not just cultural trappings – that's for sure. The essence of children? Yes ...' (Melbourne 1987: 102).

The intimate interconnections between definitions of reading children and children's literature are fully evident here: in many ways, critics define them as one and the same thing, and children's literature is often spoken of as if it had been written by children expressing their needs, emotions and experiences. As Lissa Paul writes when she compares the situations of women's writing and children's literature:

as long as the signs and language of women's literature and children's literature are foreign, other, to male-order critics, it is almost impossible to play with meaning. So one of the primary problems feminist critics and children's literature critics have is how to recognize, define, and accord value to otherness.

Paul 1990: 150

Paul discusses children's literature as if it were written by children and as if the situation were therefore the same as with books written by women, as she writes: 'But women make up more than half of the population of the world – and all of us once were children. It is almost inconceivable that women and children have been invisible and voiceless for so long' (150). In this way Paul submerges the fact that children's literature (when it is not written by women) may well be written by the very 'male-order critics' she is seeking release from (unless she is assuming, as many critics do, that writing children's literature involves becoming a child again). Myles McDowell, too, for instance, describes his 'child in the book' when he claims that

Children's books are generally shorter; they tend to favour an active rather than a passive treatment, with dialogue and incident rather than description and introspection; child protagonists are the rule; conventions are much used; the story develops within a clear-cut moral schematism which much adult fiction ignores; children's books tend to be optimistic rather than depressive; language is child-oriented; plots are of a distinctive order, probability is often disregarded; and one could go on endlessly talking of magic, and fantasy, and simplicity, and adventure.

McDowell 1973: 51

American critic and author Natalie Babbitt, on the other hand, argues with respect to these type of criteria – and her 'child in the book' – that children's books are neither necessarily less serious than adults' books, nor necessarily concerned with 'simpler' or 'different' emotions: 'there is, in point of fact, no such thing as an exclusively adult emotion, and children's literature deals with them all' (Babbitt 1973: 157). Babbitt then claims that there is also no genuine disparity in range or scope, 'Everyman' being just as present, for instance, in *The Wind in the Willows* as in, say, James Joyce's *Ulysses*. Furthermore, to Babbitt, there are few differences in content between adult and children's literature: 'war, disability, poverty, cruelty, all the harshest aspects of life are present in children's literature' (157), as is fantasy. Language usage does not seem to Babbitt necessarily to distinguish children's literature from adult literature either:

A children's book uses simple vocabulary geared to the untrained mind? Compare a little Kipling to a little Hemingway and think again. Opening sentence of *A Farewell to Arms*: 'Now in the fall the trees were all bare and the roads were muddy'. Opening sentence of *How the Rhinoceros Got His Skin*: 'Once upon a time, on an uninhabited island on the shores of the Red Sea, there lived a Parsee from whose hat the rays of the sun were reflected in more-than-oriental splendour'. So much for that!

Babbit 1973: 157

One side-effect, incidentally, of the idea that 'children's literature' originated from a historical revelation of the 'child' and 'its needs' (John Locke and Jean-Jacques Rousseau are quoted as standard in this context as the 'discoverers' of childhood) is that many (although not all) critics tend to describe and define 'children's literature' in evolutionary terms: consciously or unconsciously 'children's literature' is described as progressing towards an ever better and more accurate inclusion of the 'child' in the book. As Boel Westin writes with respect to the history of Swedish children's literature:

After the Second World War, new trends in child psychology and a freer educational approach, prompted by such figures as Bertrand Russell and A. S. Neill, gained widespread acceptance in Sweden. The child's urge to play and seek pleasure was now to be gratified at the different stages of growth. In children's literature the world was now to be portrayed through the eyes and voice of the child itself.

Westin 1991: 22

Within this type of thinking the 'classics' of 'children's literature' are often described as being avant garde or exceptionally and anachronistically perspicacious with respect to the 'child'. Barbara Wall, for instance, explains the classic status of *Alice in Wonderland*, by arguing that

Alice's became the first child-mind, in the history of children's fiction, to occupy the centre ... No narrator of a story for children had stood so close to a child protagonist, observing nothing except that child, describing, never criticising, showing only what that child saw.

Wall 1991: 98

The children's literature critics' didactic–literary split continues and maintains its career as one of the ultimate judgements of the value – and therefore definition – of 'children's literature'. It is in these statements that the 'child' in the book – in all its various manifestations – is defined by each critic. Sheila Egoff, for instance, writes:

> May I suggest that the aim of children's writing be delight not edification; that its attributes be the eternal childlike qualities of wonder; simplicity, laughter and warmth; and that in the worldwide realm of children's books, the literature be kept inside, the sociology and pedagogy out.
>
> Egoff 1987: 355

Yoko Inokuma, similarly, in discussing writing about minority groups in Japanese children's literature, argues that

> the didactic motive of the authoress is quite clear ... There is no doubt about the legitimacy of her motive. But both Korean and Japanese readers will find it difficult to identify themselves with the characters who are only one dimensional ... Finally ... his [Imao Hirano's] desire to enlighten Japanese children ... betrayed him into producing an autobiography of a mediocre literary value ... Books of high literary value are, after all, short cuts to the real understanding of and sympathy with minority groups.
>
> Inokuma 1987: 75, 76, 82

Inokuma's statement introduces a word which is a mainstay of children's literature critics: 'identification'. The idea of 'identification' as an explanation of how and why the 'child' reads in turn supports the assumption that the 'child' is in the good 'children's book': the 'child' is supposed to be inherently and voluntarily attracted to books in which it recognises itself. As the Israeli critic Adir Cohen claims:

> Writers have become aware that, for the child, a book is a source of satisfaction that derives from identification and participation, and an expansion of his own experience. They provide him with an opportunity for catharsis, self-knowledge, and broadening his psychic experience. The process of reading, identification, participation and relating brings the reader into the reality of the book in dynamic fashion.
>
> Cohen 1988: 31

But 'identification' is caught up in the same debates concerning the definition of the 'child'. Since the supposed process of 'identification' depends on the definition of the 'child' the critic employs; different definitions lead to different evaluations of a book's ability to lead to the child reader achieving 'identification', and this also involves different concepts of what 'identification' actually is and does. The whole discussion, however, emphasises the persistence and depth of the assumption of the existence of an essential 'child': how otherwise could the notion of 'identification' be thought to function with respect to children's fiction, which by definition has a complex relationship to 'reality'? An essential 'child' in fiction is still supposed to be recognised by the 'reading child' as 'real'.

Implicit and overt assumptions about the 'child' and children's literature thus permeate explanations of 'identification', as we saw already in Adir Cohen's statement. Donna Norton describes 'identification' as a 'process [which] requires emotional ties with the model; children believe they are like these models and their thoughts, feelings, and characteristics become similar to them' (Norton 1983: 20). American critics Judith Thompson and Gloria Woodard draw the conclusion from this premise that

> one limitation to [many] books, however, is their emphasis on, identification with, and relevance only to middle class children. For too many black children, they depict an environment removed from their immediate experience ... Identification for the young black reader rests in the central character's intimate knowledge of the black subculture.
>
> Thompson and Woodard 1972: 23

But British critic Robert Leeson complicates this type of 'identification' as a description of the central mechanism of the emotional process of reading by pointing out that although he feels the 'child' needs 'to recognise himself or herself ... it is [also] argued that the working-class child does not want "only to read about itself" and likes to escape into a different world in its reading ... to escape and have vicarious pleasure and thrills' (Leeson 1977: 43). For Leeson, the good book for the 'child' offers not only the 'child' back to itself, but also needs to offer the 'child' that which is not itself. 'Identification' – despite its widespread and often unquestioned use – remains a problematic concept: it must assume a 'child in the book'; even if that 'child's' presence is assumed, 'identification' cannot account for reading which is not a perpetual reading of the self; and, finally, it cannot account therefore for other hypothetical processes in reading such as a possible learning of the new, or escapism, or what D. W. Harding has called 'imaginative insight into what another person may be feeling, and the contemplation of possible human experiences which we are not at that moment going through ourselves' (Harding 1967: 7).

The definitions of children's literature and childhood are thus enmeshed within the discourse of children's literature. They mutually qualify each other. Tension and problems arise within children's literature criticism because children's literature critics implicitly assume that there are independent, essential definitions of 'literature' and 'childhood' which only meet, to their mutual benefit, within children's literature and its criticism. Children's literature critics reveal this inherent assumption throughout their writings: besides the inherent contradictions and disagreements that I have touched on, this becomes most clear when critics attempt to divide themselves, for instance, into 'book people' and 'child people' (Townsend 1980: 199). Townsend argues that

> most disputes over standards are fruitless because the antagonists suppose their criteria to be mutually exclusive; if one is right the other must be wrong. This is not necessarily so. Different kinds of assessment are valid for different purposes ... I would only remark that the viewpoints of psychologists, sociologists, and educationists of various descriptions have

rather little in common with each other or with those whose approach is mainly literary.

Townsend 1980: 193–207

Townsend's suggestion, however, has not lessened the problem (for children's literature itself!) of differing 'children' – and thus conflicting interpretations of books – occurring within even the works of critics who regard themselves as belonging to the same 'camp'. Children's literature and children's literature criticism define themselves as existing because of, and for, 'children', and it is these 'children' who remain the passion of – and therefore the source of conflict for – children's authors and critics.

References

Aiken, J. (1973) 'Purely for love', in Haviland, V. (ed.) *Children and Literature: Views and Reviews*, London: Bodley Head.

Ariès, P. (1973) *Centuries of Childhood*, Harmondsworth: Penguin.

Avery, G. (1976) 'A sense of audience – 2', in Fox, G. *et al.* (eds) *Writers, Critics, and Children: Articles from 'Children's Literature in Education'*, London: Heinemann Educational Books.

Babbitt, N. (1973) 'Happy endings? Of course, and also joy', in Haviland, V. (ed.) *Children and Literature: Views and Reviews*, London: Bodley Head.

Cohen, A. (1988) 'The changing face of Israeli children's literature: forty years of creativity', *Modern Hebrew Literature* new series 1: 25–31.

Cott, J. (1984) *Pipers at the Gates of Dawn: The Wisdom of Children's Literature*, London: Viking.

Darton, F. J. H. (1932/1982) *Children's Books In England: Five Centuries of Social Life*, 3rd edn, rev. B. Alderson, Cambridge: Cambridge University Press.

Dixon, B. (1977) *Catching Them Young*. Vol. 1: *Sex, Race and Class in Children's Fiction*, London: Pluto Press.

Egoff, S. (1987) 'Inside and out: a Canadian's view of trends in contemporary children's literature', in Lees, S. (ed.) *A Track to Unknown Water: Proceedings of the Second Pacific Rim Conference on Children's Literature*, Metuchen, NJ: Scarecrow Press.

Glazer, J. I. and Williams G, III (1979) *Introduction to Children's Literature*, New York: McGraw-Hill.

Harding, D. W. (1967) 'Considered experience: the invitation of the novel', *English in Education* 2, 1: 3–14.

Haviland, V. (ed.) (1973) *Children and Literature: Views and Reviews*, London: Bodley Head.

Heimeriks, N. and Van Toorn, W. (eds) (1989) *De Hele Bibelebontse Berg. De Geschiedenis van het Kinderboek in Nederland en Vlaanderen van de Middeleeuwen tot Heden [The Whole 'Bibelebonts' Mountain: The History of Children's Books in The Netherlands and Flanders from the Middle Ages to the Present]*, Amsterdam: Em. Querido.

Huck, C. S. (1976) *Children's Literature in the Elementary School*, 3rd edn, New York: Holt, Rinehart and Winston.

Hunt, P. (ed.) (1992) *Literature for Children: Contemporary Criticism*, London: Routledge.

Inglis, F. (1981) *The Promise of Happiness: Value and Meaning in Children's Literature*, Cambridge: Cambridge University Press.

Inokuma, Y. (1987) 'The present situation of stories about minority groups in Japan', in Lees, S. (ed.) *A Track to Unknown Water: Proceedings of the Second Pacific Rim Conference on Children's Literature*, Metuchen, NJ: Scarecrow Press.

Landsberg, M. (1987) *Reading for the Love of It: Best Books for Young Readers*, New York: Prentice-Hall.

Leeson, R. (1977) *Children's Books and Class Society: Past and Present*, Children's Rights Workshop (ed.) Papers on Children's Literature no. 3, London: Writers and Readers Publishing Cooperative.

Lonsdale, B. J. and Mackintosh, H. K. (1973) *Children Experience Literature*, New York: Random House.

McDowell, M. (1973) 'Fiction for children and adults: some essential differences', *Children's Literature in Education* 10: 551-563.

Mathis, S. B. (1977) '*The Slave Dancer* is an insult to Black children', in MacCann, D. and Woodard, G. (eds) *Cultural Conformity in Books for Children: Further Readings in Racism*, Metuchen, NJ: Scarecrow Press.

Matsui, Tadashi (1986–1987) 'A personal encounter with Kodomo no kuni: a vanguard Tokyo periodical of the twenties and thirties', *Phaedrus: An International Annual of Children's Literature Research* 7, 2/3: 14–18.

Mead, M. and Wolfenstein, M. (1955) *Childhood in Contemporary Cultures*, Chicago: University of Chicago Press.

Melbourne, S. (1987) 'The portrayal of the Maori in New Zealand children's fiction', in Lees, S. (ed.) *A Track to Unknown Water: Proceedings of the Second Pacific Rim Conference on Children's Literature*, Metuchen, NJ: Scarecrow Press.

Norton, D. E. (1983) *Through the Eyes of a Child: An Introduction to Children's Literature*, Columbus, OH: Charles E. Merrill.

Paul, L. (1990) 'Enigma variations: what feminist theory knows about children's literature', in Hunt, P. (ed.) *Children's Literature: The Development of Criticism*, London: Routledge.

Rose, J. (1984) *The Case of Peter Pan or: The Impossibility of Children's Fiction*, London: Macmillan.

Sadker, M. P. and Sadker, D. M. (1977) *Now Upon A Time: A Contemporary View of Children's Literature*, New York: Harper and Row.

Smith, J. A. and Park, D. M. (1977) *Word Music and Word Magic: Children's Literature Methods*, Boston: Allyn and Bacon.

Sunindyo (1987) 'Publishing and translating in Indonesia', in Lees, S. (ed.) *A Track to Unknown Water: Proceedings of the Second Pacific Rim Conference on Children's Literature*, Metuchen, NJ: Scarecrow Press.

Sutcliff, R. (1973) 'History is people', in Haviland, V. (ed.) *Children and Literature: Views and Reviews*, London: Bodley Head.

Tate, B. (1977) 'Racism and distortions pervade *The Slave Dancer*', in MacCann, D. and Woodard, G. (eds) *Cultural Conformity in Books for Children: Further Readings in Racism*, Metuchen, NJ: Scarecrow Press.

Thompson, J. and Woodard, G. (1972) 'Black perspective in books for children', in MacCann, D. and Woodard, G. (eds) *The Black American in Books for Children: Readings in Racism*, Metuchen, NJ: Scarecrow Press.

Townsend, J. R. (1980) 'Standards of criticism for children's literature', in Chambers, N. (ed.) *The Signal Approach to Children's Books*, London: Kestrel Books.

Tucker, N. (1981) *The Child and the Book: A Psychological and Literary Exploration*, Cambridge: Cambridge University Press.

Vives, J. L. (1913) *On Education: A Translation of the 'De Tradendis Disciplinis' of Juan Luis Vives*, intro. and trans. F. Watson, Cambridge: Cambridge University Press.

Wall, B. (1991) *The Narrator's Voice: The Dilemma of Children's Fiction*, London: Macmillan.

Westin, B. (1991) *Children's Literature in Sweden*, trans. S. Croall, Stockholm: The Swedish Institute.

White, E. B. (1973) 'On writing for children', in Haviland, V. (ed.) *Children and Literature: Views and Reviews*, London: Bodley Head.

Further Reading

Barker, M. (1989) *Comics: Ideology, Power and the Critics*, Manchester: Manchester University Press.

Hunt, P. (ed.) (1990) *Children's Literature: The Development of Criticism*, London: Routledge.

——(ed.) (1991) *Criticism, Theory and Children's Literature*, Oxford: Basil Blackwell.

James, A., and Prout, A. (eds) (1997) *Constructing and Reconstructing Childhood: Contemporary Issues in the Sociological Study of Childhood*, London: Falmer Press.

Jenks, C. (1996) *Childhood*, London: Routledge.

Lesnik-Oberstein, K. (1994) *Children's Literature: Criticism and the Fictional Child*, Oxford: Clarendon Press.

Shavit, Z. (1986) *Poetics of Children's Literature*, Athens, GA: University of Georgia Press.

Stainton Rogers, R., and Stainton Rogers, W. (1992) *Stories of Childhood: Shifting Agendas of Child Concern*, London: Harvester Wheatsheaf.

3 The Setting of Children's Literature: History and Culture

Tony Watkins

Editor's introduction

In recent years there has been a move away from thinking of history as a fixed, neutral 'background' to literature towards complex ideas of history as forms of narrative, culturally constructed in the present. Tony Watkins explores these new concepts of history and culture and considers the implications of studying children's literature as part of the broad, ideologically-aware field of cultural studies.

P. H.

Until the late 1970s, there was (outside Marxist criticism) a generally accepted view of the nature of history and its place in literary studies. Perkins (1991) points out that during most of the nineteenth century, literary history was popular and enjoyed prestige because it produced a more complete appreciation of the literary work than was otherwise possible. It functioned, too, as a form of historiography, revealing the ' "spirit", mentality or *Weltanschauung* of a time and place with unrivaled precision and intimacy' (Perkins 1991: 2). For much of the twentieth century, especially in Renaissance studies, history was seen as outside literature and as guaranteeing the truth of a literary interpretation: 'History ... was the single, unified, unproblematic, extra-textual, extra-discursive real that guaranteed our readings of the texts which constituted its cultural *expression*' (Belsey 1991: 26). In the traditional literary view of history and culture, there was no difficulty in relating text to context: history was singular and operated as a 'background' to the reading of a work of literature ('the foreground'); and culture was something which the work reproduced or expressed, or could be set against. Literary history was 'a hybrid but recognizable genre that co-ordinated literary criticism, biography, and intellectual/social background within a narrative of development' (Buell 1993: 216).

Such notions have, until recently, remained the dominant ones behind the histories of children's literature. Thus, John Rowe Townsend, in the fifth edition (1990) of his standard one-volume history of children's literature, *Written for Children*, writes 'While I have tried to see children's literature in its historical and social contexts, my standards are essentially literary' (xi). However, in the 1970s, there was 'a Turn toward History' (Cox and Reynolds 1993: 3) in American adult literary theory as it began to move away from the dominance of deconstruction. The consequent reconceptualisation of history and its relationship to literature had its roots in the work of such theorists and critics as Michel Foucault, Raymond Williams, Edward Said and Frank Lentricchia. In the 1980s, new terms associated with literary history (including 'the new history', 'cultural poetics' and, especially, 'the New Historicism') entered the critical vocabulary through the work of such critics as Stephen Greenblatt, Louis Montrose and Jerome McGann.

The '*new* historicism' is distinguished from the old by a lack of faith in the objectivity of historical study and, instead, an emphasis on the way the past is constructed or invented in the present. Felperin quotes the opening paragraph of Catherine Belsey's *The Subject of Tragedy* (1985):

> History is always in practice a reading of the past. We make a narrative out of the available 'documents', the written texts (and maps and buildings and suits of armour) we interpret in order to produce a knowledge of a world which is no longer present. And yet it is always from the present that we produce this knowledge: from the present in the sense that it is only from what is still extant, still available that we make it; and from the present in the sense that we make it out of an understanding formed by the present. We bring what we know now to bear on what remains from the past to produce an intelligible history.

He comments: ' "history" is freely acknowledged to be a kind of story-telling towards the present, that is, a textual construct at once itself an interpretation and itself open to interpretation' (Felperin 1991: 89). The idea of a single 'History' is rejected in favour of the postmodern concept (Belsey 1991: 27) of 'histories', 'an ongoing series of human constructions, each representing the past at particular present moments for particular present purposes' (Cox and Reynolds 1993: 4).

The growth of radical alternative histories, such as women's history, oral history, and post-colonial rewriting of Eurocentric and other imperialist view-points, together with the more general blurring of disciplinary boundaries between historiography, sociology, anthropology and cultural studies, have all cast doubt on the validity, relevance or accessibility of historical 'facts' (Barker *et al.* 1991: 4). Cultural history draws closer to the concerns of the humanities and anthropology: 'The deciphering of meaning ... is taken to be the central task of cultural history, just as it was posed by Geertz to be the central task of cultural anthropology' (Hunt 1989: 12). With the emergence of the postmodern concept of 'histories' several questions have been put on the agenda of theory: for example, what valid distinctions can be made between the 'narrative' of history and the 'fiction' of texts? (Montrose (1989: 20) called for the recognition of 'the historicity of texts and the textuality of history'; see also White (1973).) What are the implications of our construction of the past from our present situation? What is the relationship between 'histories' and power?

The rise of newer forms of literary historicism is connected, in part, with social change and the effort to recover histories for blacks, women and minority groups within society. In turn, these social aims are linked with the recuperation of forgotten texts, including texts that have never been considered worthy of academic study. Such changes have, of course, benefited the academic study of children's literature.

The major influence in all this is that of Michel Foucault. As David Perkins puts it,

> [Foucault] encouraged his readers to reject the traditional Romantic model of literary change as continuous development, to resituate literary texts by relating them to discourses and representations that were not literary, and to explore the ideological aspects of texts in order to intervene in the social struggles of the present, and these remain characteristic practices of present-day historical contextualism – of New Historicism, feminist historiography, and cultural criticism.
>
> Perkins 1991: 4

Not everyone, however, would agree with the implied radical political stance of the new historicist movements. H. Aram Veeser, in his introduction to a 1994 collection of readings, asks of New Historicism, 'Is it liberal or Leftist? Literary or historical? Feminist or neuter? Reformist or radical? Canon-making or canon-smashing? Stabilizing or capsizing?' (Veeser 1994: 2) and points out that many believe that New Historicism is 'bent on neutralizing solidarity, subversion, disruption, and struggle' and that it 'entertained from the first the heresy of a good capitalism' (3). But he manages to give the following five-point definition of the assumptions held by New Historicists:

> 1) that every expressive act is embedded in a network of material practices;
> 2) that every act of unmasking, critique, and opposition uses the tools it condemns and risks falling prey to the practice it exposes;
> 3) that literary and non-literary 'texts' circulate inseparably;
> 4) that no discourse, imaginative or archival, gives access to unchanging truths or expresses unalterable human nature;
> 5) that a critical method and language adequate to describe culture under capitalism participate in the economy they describe.
>
> Veeser 1994: 2

Felperin argues that there are two broad schools of New Historicism, the American, sometimes called 'cultural poetics', and the British, often referred to as 'cultural materialism': 'Whereas cultural poetics inhabits a discursive field in which Marxism has never really been present, its British counterpart inhabits one from which Marxism has never really been absent' (Felperin 1991: 88). The radical nature of cultural materialism is made clear in books such as Dollimore and Sinfield's collection of essays, *Political Shakespeare*. In their foreword, the editors define cultural materialism as 'a combination of historical context, theoretical method, political commitment and textual analysis' (Dollimore and Sinfield 1985: vii). The historical context,

> undermines the transcendent significance traditionally accorded to the literary text and allows us to recover its histories; theoretical method detaches the text from immanent criticism which seeks only to reproduce it in its own terms; socialist and feminist commitment confronts the conservative categories in which most criticism has hitherto been conducted;

textual analysis locates the critique of traditional approaches where it cannot be ignored. We call this 'cultural materialism'.

Dollimore and Sinfield 1985: vii

Examples of how some of these new historicist ideas could be applied to children's literature are provided by the work of Mitzi Myers (Myers 1988; 1989; 1992). In a statement which blends something of the American and the British brands, Myers argues that a new historicism of children's literature would

> integrate text and socio-historic context, demonstrating on the one hand how extraliterary cultural formations shape literary discourse and on the other how literary practices are actions that make things happen – by shaping the psychic and moral consciousness of young readers but also by performing many more diverse kinds of cultural work, from satisfying authorial fantasies to legitimating or subverting dominant class and gender ideologies ... It would want to know how and why a tale or poem came to say what it does, what the environing circumstances were (including the uses a particular sort of children's literature served for its author, its child and adult readers, and its culture), and what kinds of cultural statements and questions the work was responding to. It would pay particular attention to the conceptual and symbolic fault lines denoting a text's time-, place-, gender-, and class-specific ideological mechanisms ... It would examine ... a book's material production, its publishing history, its audiences and their reading practices, its initial reception, and its critical history, including how its got inscribed in or deleted from the canon.

Myers 1988: 42

Myers has also argued that 'Notions of the "child", "childhood" and "children's literature" are contingent, not essentialist; embodying the social construction of a particular historical context; they are useful fictions intended to redress reality as much as to reflect it' (Myers 1989: 52), and that such notions today are bound up with the language and ideology of Romantic literature and criticism (Myers 1992; see also McGann 1983).

These ideas have been applied by Myers to eighteenth-century children's authors such as Maria Edgeworth. The child constructed by Romantic ideology recurs as Wordsworth's 'child of nature' in such figures as Kipling's Mowgli and Frances Hodgson Burnett's Dickon in *The Secret Garden* (Knoepflmacher 1977; Richardson 1992) and, as one critic points out, 'many children's books that feature children obviously wiser than the adults they must deal with – like F. Anstey's *Vice Versa* or E. Nesbit's *Story of the Amulet* – would have been unthinkable without the Romantic revaluation of childhood' (Richardson 1992: 128).

The same crises in the humanities which resulted in radical questioning of the nature of history and the emergence of new historiographies of culture, including literary New Historicism, also brought forth cultural studies. It is difficult to define the field of cultural studies very precisely because, as Brantlinger argues, it has 'emerged from the current crises and contradictions of the humanities and social science disciplines not as a tightly coherent, unified movement with a fixed agenda, but as a loosely coherent group of tendencies, issues and questions' (1990: ix). Nevertheless, there are several points of similarity between the new literary historicism and cultural studies and their relevance to the study of children's literature. For example, it is possible to see such works as Grahame's *The Wind in the Willows* and Baum's *The Wizard of Oz*, not only operating as versions of the English and American national myth with their landscapes representing the 'real' England and the 'real' America, but becoming sites for ideological struggle and appropriation by, for example, the 'culture industries' (Watkins 1992).

In *Keywords*, Raymond Williams describes culture as 'one of the two or three most complicated words in the English language' (Williams 1976: 76). Culture is an ambiguous term: a problem shared, perhaps, by all concepts which are concerned with totality, including history, ideology, society, and myth. 'Cultural studies' is an equally ambiguous term, but most commentators would agree that cultural studies is 'concerned with the generation and circulation of meanings in industrial societies' (Fiske 1987: 254). An anthology published in 1992 suggests the following major categories of current work in the field:

> the history of cultural studies, gender and sexuality, nationhood and national identity, colonialism and post-colonialism, race and ethnicity, popular culture and its audiences, science and ecology, identity politics, pedagogy, the politics of aesthetics, cultural institutions, the politics of disciplinarity, discourse and textuality, history, and global culture in a postmodern age.
>
> Grossberg *et al.* 1992: 1

But the editors of the volume stress the shapeless nature of the field and the variety of methodologies in use: '[cultural studies] remains a diverse and often contentious enterprise, encompassing different positions and trajectories in specific contexts, addressing many questions, drawing nourishment from multiple roots, and shaping itself within different institutions and locations' (2–3). There are, for example, distinctions to be made between the British and American traditions of cultural studies. The British tradition may be traced back to the pioneering work of F. R. Leavis and Denys Thompson in the 1930s (Leavis and Thompson 1933), but, more particularly, it arises from the work of Raymond Williams (Williams 1958). The British tradition, it is claimed, believes that the study of culture involves both 'symbolic and material domains ... not privileging one domain over the other but interrogating the relation between the two ... Continually engaging with the political, economic, erotic, social, and ideological, cultural studies entails the study of all the relations between all the elements in a whole way of life' (Grossberg *et al.* 1992: 4; 14). From the later work of Raymond Williams, from the work of Stuart Hall and others at the University of Birmingham's Centre for Contemporary Cultural Studies, and from major bodies of theory such as Marxism, feminism, psychoanalysis and poststructuralism, the British tradition derived the central theoretical concepts of articulation, conjuncture, hegemony, ideology, identity, and representation. (See, for example, Williams 1975; 1976; 1977; 1989; Hall *et al.* 1980; Hall 1990.) But even British cultural studies is not a coherent and homogeneous body of work: it is characterised by disagreements, 'divergencies in direction and concern, by conflict among theoretical commitments and political agendas' (Grossberg *et al.* 1992: 10).

In the USA, a somewhat different inflection has been given to cultural studies by the 'new ethnography', rooted primarily in anthropological theory and practice (a 'postdisciplinary anthropology') which is, in turn, linked to work by feminists and black and postcolonial theorists concerned with identity, history and social relations. (Grossberg *et al.* 1992: 14).

In some of the cultural studies theorists, one can detect the following characteristics: first, a belief that reality can only be made sense of through language or other cultural systems which are embedded within history. Second, a focus upon power and struggle. In cultural terms, the struggle is for meaning: dominant groups attempt to render as 'natural' meanings which serve their interests, whereas subordinate groups resist this process in various ways, trying to make meanings that serve *their* interests. (Fiske 1987: 255). An obvious example is the cultural struggle between patriarchy and feminism; but, of course, divisions into groups in society can be along lines of race, class, age and so on, as well as gender. Third, cultural studies has tried to theorise subjectivity as a socio-cultural construction. Some theorists, under the influence of poststructuralist psycho-analytical thinking and Althusserian notions of ideology, replace the idea of the individual by the concept of the 'subject'. The 'subject' and his or her 'subjectivity' is a social construction: 'Thus a biological female can have a masculine subjectivity (that is, she can make sense of the world and of her self and her place in that world through patriarchal ideology). Similarly, a black can have a white subjectivity' (Fiske 1987: 258).

But, because subjectivity is a social construction, it is always open to change. All cultural systems, including language, literature and the products of mass communication, play a part in the construction and reconstruction of the subject. It is in this way, according to the Althusserian wing of cultural studies, that ideology is constantly reproduced in people.

This notion can be seen perhaps more clearly in the fourth characteristic of cultural studies – the way it views acts of communication, including the 'reading process'. As one theorist puts it when talking about the 'reading' of a television programme as cultural text: 'Reading becomes a negotiation between the social sense inscribed in the program and the meanings of social experience made by its wide variety of viewers: this negotiation is a discursive one' (Fiske 1987: 268). The relevance of this notion to children's literature is not difficult to perceive.

The fifth characteristic is that cultural studies is not exclusively concerned with popular culture to the exclusion of 'high' culture, or vice versa: 'Cultural studies does not require us to repudiate elite cultural forms ... rather cultural studies requires us to identify the operation of specific practices, of how they continuously reinscribe the line between legitimate and popular culture, and of what they accomplish in specific contexts' (Grossberg *et al.* 1992: 13). As a result, cultural studies does interest itself in the formation, continuation and changes in literary canons, including those of children's literature. For example, books originally denied inclusion in the canon of children's literature, such as Baum's *Oz* books, have later received recognition and have been included. Other books traditionally included in the canon of children's literature, such as Lewis's Narnia series, Tolkien's *The Hobbit*, and Kipling's *Jungle Book* have been criticised on the grounds that the values they contain are too exclusively male and white.

The sixth characteristic is the use of ideology as a central concept, either as a 'critical' concept or as a neutral concept. Materialist, political approaches deriving from Marxism and feminism obviously stress *power* as the major component of cultural text, power which is often hidden or rendered apparently 'natural' through the process of ideology. These approaches use what has been called the 'critical' concept of ideology which is 'essentially linked to the process of sustaining asymmetrical relations of power – that is, to the process of maintaining domination' (Thompson 1984: 4). If ideology is embodied in cultural text, the major task of the cultural critic is not only understanding the meaning of the text but also unmasking what appears as natural as a social construction which favours a particular class or group in society. This process of 'ideology critique' or ideological deconstruction is often carried out in literary studies using an approach, derived from Williams, involving a combination of textual analysis, theoretical method, study of historical context, and a political commitment to socialism and feminism.

However, ideology can also be used in a neutral sense (Ricoeur 1986) and this is reflected in the work of Fred Inglis, who has written at length on children's literature (for example, Inglis 1975; 1981). Inglis favours, not cultural materialism, but cultural hermeneutics. In *Cultural Studies* (1993), he argues in favour of making cultural studies 'synonymous with the study of values (and valuing)' (Inglis 1993: 190). The book is dedicated to the cultural anthropologist, Clifford Geertz, with his influential view that 'man is an animal suspended in webs of significance he himself has spun' and that those webs are what we call culture'. For Geertz, the analysis of culture, therefore, will be 'an interpretive one in search of meaning', and culture itself is defined as 'an assemblage of texts' and 'a story they tell themselves about themselves' (Geertz 1975: 5; 448). So the model of cultural analysis Inglis favours is the interpretative one which aims not to *unmask* texts, using such critical concepts as ideology or hegemony which deconstruct and demystify ideologies, but to *understand* intersubjective meanings (Inglis 1993: 148). He argues against the tendency within cultural studies to collapse 'both aesthetics and morality into politics' so that 'the study of culture translates into politics without remainder' (175; 181). He quotes Dollimore and Sinfield's statement (see above) that cultural materialism 'registers its commitment to the transformation of a social order which exploits people on grounds of race, gender and class' (Dollimore and Sinfield 1985: viii) but asks, using the same phrase which formed the title of his book about children's literature (Inglis 1981), 'What about the promise of happiness held out by art? What about art itself?' (Inglis 1993: 181).

Following Geertz's concept, Inglis defines culture as, 'an ensemble of *stories* we tell ourselves about ourselves' (Inglis 1993: 206) and argues that our historically changing identity is formed from experience and the 'narrative tradition' of which we are part. It is from this identity that we interpret the world. In a passage strongly relevant to the study of children's literature, (see, for example, Watkins 1994), he goes on to argue that

> the stories we tell ourselves about ourselves are not just a help to moral education; they comprise the only moral education which can gain purchase on the modern world. They are not aids to sensitivity nor adjuncts to the

cultivated life. They are theories with which to think forwards ... and understand backwards.

Inglis 1993: 214

Because of the variety within the cultural studies paradigm and the dynamic nature of the field, it is difficult to generalise about features which underlie such work in the study of children's literature. But the work of Fred Inglis (1981), Karin Lesnik-Oberstein (1994), Jacqueline Rose (1984), Marina Warner (1994) and Jack Zipes (1979), although in many respects very different, may be thought of as arising within a cultural studies framework.

References

Barker, F., Hulme, P. and Iversen, M. (eds) (1991) *Uses of History: Marxism, Postmodernism and the Renaissance*, Manchester: Manchester University Press.

Belsey, C. (1991) 'Making histories then and now: Shakespeare from *Richard II* to *Henry V*', in Barker, F., Hulme, P. and Iversen, M. (eds) *Uses of History: Marxism, Postmodernism and the Renaissance*, Manchester: Manchester University Press.

Brantlinger, P. (1990) *Crusoe's Footprints: Cultural Studies in Britain and America*, New York: Routledge.

Buell, L. (1993) 'Literary History as a Hybrid Genre', in Cox, J. and Reynolds, L. J. (eds) *New Historical Literary Study: Essays on Reproducing Texts, Representing History*, Princeton, NJ: Princeton University Press.

Cox, J. N. and Reynolds, L. J. (eds) (1993) *New Historical Literary Study: Essays on Reproducing Texts, Representing History*, Princeton, NJ: Princeton University Press.

Dollimore, J. and Sinfield, A. (eds) (1985) *Political Shakespeare: New Essays in Cultural Materialism*, Manchester: Manchester University Press.

Felperin, H. (1991) ' "Cultural poetics" versus "cultural materialism": the two New Historicisms in Renaissance studies', in Barker, F., Hulme, P. and Iversen, M. (eds) *Uses of History: Marxism, Postmodernism and the Renaissance*, Manchester: Manchester University Press.

Fiske, J. (1987) 'British cultural studies and television', in Allen, R. C. (ed.) *Channels of Discourse: Television and Contemporary Criticism*, London: Routledge.

Geertz, C. (1975) *The Interpretation of Cultures*, London: Hutchinson.

Grossberg, L., Nelson, C. and Treichler, P. (eds) (1992) *Cultural Studies*, New York: Routledge.

Hall, S. (1990) 'The emergence of cultural studies and the crisis of the humanities', *October* 53: 11–90.

—— et al. (eds) (1980) *Culture, Media, Language*, London: Hutchinson.

Hunt, L. (ed.) (1989) *The New Cultural History*, Berkeley: University of California Press.

Inglis, F. (1975) *Ideology and the Imagination*, Cambridge: Cambridge University Press.

—— (1981) *The Promise of Happiness: Value and Meaning in Children's Fiction*, Cambridge: Cambridge University Press.

—— (1993) *Cultural Studies*, Oxford: Blackwell.

Knoepflmacher, U. C. (1977) 'Mutations of the Wordsworthian child of nature', in Knoepflmacher, U. C. and Tennyson, G. B. (eds) *Nature and the Victorian Imagination*, Berkeley: University of California Press.

Leavis, F. R. and Thompson, D. (1933) *Culture and Environment*, London: Chatto and Windus.

Lesnik-Oberstein, K. (1994) *Children's Literature: Criticism and the Fictional Child*, Oxford: Clarendon Press.

McGann, J. J. (1983) *The Romantic Ideology: A Critical Investigation*, Chicago and London: University of Chicago Press.

Montrose, L. A. (1989) 'Professing the Renaissance: the poetics and politics of culture', in Veeser, H. A. (ed.) *The New Historicism*, London: Routledge.

Myers, M. (1988) 'Missed opportunities and critical malpractice: New Historicism and children's literature', *Children's Literature Association Quarterly* 13, 1: 41–43.

—— (1989) 'Socializing Rosamond: educational ideology and fictional form', *Children's Literature Association Quarterly*, 14, 2: 52–58.

—— (1992) 'Sociologizing juvenile ephemera: periodical contradictions, popular literacy, transhistorical readers', *Children's Literature Association Quarterly* 17: 1: 41–45.

Perkins, D. (ed.) (1991) *Theoretical Issues in Literary History*, Cambridge and London: Harvard University Press.

Richardson, A. (1992) 'Childhood and romanticism', in Sadler, G. E. (ed.) *Teaching Children's Literature: Issues, Pedagogy, Resources*, New York: The Modern Language Association of America.

Ricoeur, P. (1986) *Lectures on Ideology and Utopia*, New York: Columbia University Press.

Rose, J. (1984) *The Case of Peter Pan, or, The Impossibility of Children's Fiction*, London: Macmillan.

Thompson, J. B. (1984) *Studies in the Theory of Ideology*, Cambridge: Polity Press.

Townsend, J. R. (1990) *Written for Children: An Outline of English Language Children's Literature*, 5th edn, London: Bodley Head.

Veeser, H. A. (1989) (ed.) *The New Historicism*, London: Routledge.

—— (1994) *The New Historicism Reader*, London: Routledge.

Warner, M. (1994) *From the Beast to the Blonde: On Fairy Tales and Their Tellers*, London: Chatto and Windus.

Watkins, T. (1992) 'Cultural studies, new historicism and children's literature', in Hunt, P. (ed.) *Literature for Children: Contemporary Criticism*, London: Routledge.

—— (1994) 'Homelands: landscape and identity in children's literature', in Parsons, W. and Goodwin R. (eds) *Landscape and Identity: Perspectives from Australia*, Adelaide: Auslib Press.

White, H. (1973) *Metahistory: The Historical Imagination in Nineteenth-Century Europe*, Baltimore: Johns Hopkins University Press.

Williams R. (1958) *Culture and Society 1780–1950*, London: Chatto and Windus.

—— (1975) *The Country and the City*, St Albans: Paladin.

—— (1976) *Keywords: A Vocabulary of Culture and Society*, London: Fontana.

—— (1977) *Marxism and Literature*, Oxford: Oxford University Press.

—— (1989) *The Politics of Modernism: Against the New Conformists*, London: Verso.

Zipes, J. (1979) *Breaking the Magic Spell: Radical Theories of Folk and Fairy Tales*, London: Heinemann.

Further Reading

Children's Literature Association Quarterly (1996) 21, 3: 102–132. (Special issue on New Historicism and Children's Literature.)

Flynn, R. (1997) 'The intersection of children's literature and childhood studies', *Children's Literature Association Quarterly* 22, 3: 143–145.

Hawthorn, J. (1996) *Cunning Passages: New Historicism, Cultural Materialism and Marxism in the Contemporary Literary Debate*, London: Arnold.

Hunt, P. (1996) 'Passing on the past: the problem of books that are for children and that were for children', *Children's Literature Association Quarterly* 21, 1: 200–202.

Petzold, D. (1997) 'Another "Querelles des ancients et des modernes"? Some commonplaces to remember', *Children's Literature Association Quarterly*, 22, 3: 145–146.

Ryan, K. (1996) *New Historicism and Cultural Materialism: A Reader*, London: Arnold.

4 The Impossibility of Innocence: Ideology, Politics, and Children's Literature

Charles Sarland

Editor's introduction

It is sometimes assumed that because children's books are designed for a relatively inexperienced audience they must be uninfluenced by ideology and politics, and in some way can be free of concerns of gender, race, class and so on. Not only is it impossible for any text, however 'simple', to be innocent in this way, but the 'imbalance of power' between adult writers and child readers complicates the matter. Charles Sarland explores the ways in which critics have approached the interaction of ideology and literature, and the ways in which this relates to children and children's fiction.

P. H.

Introduction

Discourse on children's fiction sits at the crossroads of a number of other discourses. In the late twentieth century the most important among these, for the purposes of this chapter, are the discourses that surround the subject of 'literature' itself, and the discourses that surround the rearing, socialisation, and education of the young. Thus discussion of ideology in children's literature requires the consideration of a number of issues. The very use of the expression 'children's literature', for instance, brings with it a whole set of value judgements which have been variously espoused, attacked, defended, and counterattacked over the years. In addition, discussion of children's fiction – my preferred term in this chapter – has always been characterised by arguments about its purposes. These purposes, or in some cases these denials of purpose, stem from the particular characteristics of its intended readership, and are invariably a product of the views held within the adult population about children and young people themselves and their place in society. Since there is an imbalance of power between the children and young people who read the books, and the adults who write, publish and review the books, or who are otherwise engaged in commentary upon, or dissemination of the books, either as parents, or teachers, or librarians, or booksellers, or academics, there is here immediately a question of politics, a politics first and foremost of age differential.

But wider than this, the books themselves and the social practices that surround them will raise ideological issues. These issues may be related to specific debates in adult society, to do for instance with class, gender or ethnicity, or they may be instances of more general debate about the role of liberal humanist values in a capitalist democracy. In addition to all of this, there is a continuing debate about reader response (see Chapter 6), a debate which also impacts upon considerations of ideology in children's fiction. And finally, no consideration of ideology in children's fiction would be complete without a glance at the current developments by which children's fiction is becoming a commodity in a global market, controlled by a relatively small number of international publishers.

Moral Purpose and Didacticism

It is useful, in the first instance, to recognise the historical nature of the debate, a debate that initially centred around questions of didacticism and moral purpose. In the 'Preface' to *The Governess or Little Female Academy* in 1749, Sarah Fielding wrote:

> Before you begin the following sheets, I beg you will stop a Moment at this Preface, to consider with me, what is the true Use of reading: and if you can once fix this Truth in your Minds, namely that the true Use of Books is to make you wiser and better, you will then have both Profit and Pleasure from what you read.
>
> Fielding 1749/1968: 91

Lest it should be thought that such overt moral purpose is a thing of the past, here is Fred Inglis: 'Only a monster would not want to give a child books she will delight in and which will teach her to be good. It is the ancient and proper justification of reading and teaching literature that it helps you to live well' (Inglis 1981: 4).

Contrary views have almost as long a history; for instance, Elizabeth Rigby writing in 1844 in *The Quarterly Review*, while admitting that no one would deliberately put what she calls 'offensive' books in the way of children, goes on:

> but, should they fall in their way, we firmly believe no risk to exist – if they will read them at one time or another, the earlier, perhaps, the better. Such works are like the viper – they have a wholesome flesh as well as a poisonous sting; and children are perhaps the only class of readers which can partake of one without suffering from the other.
>
> Hunt 1990: 21

The debate was lively in the eighteenth and nineteenth centuries, but for the bulk of this century it appeared largely to have been settled. Thus Harvey Darton, in 1932, could introduce his history with the words: 'By "children's books" I mean printed works produced ostensibly to give children spontaneous pleasure, and not primarily to teach them, not solely to make them good, nor to keep them *profitably* quiet' (Darton 1932/1982: 1, his emphasis).

For a considerable time, then, the question of values was left in abeyance. There was discussion about both how to write for children in ways that were not condescending, and about what the differences might be between fiction written for children and fiction written for adults, but considerations of moral purpose were

not an issue. In the 1970s, however, the debate was revived, albeit in another form, and it was at this point that ideological considerations came to be labelled as such.

Ideology

Ideology is a problematic notion. In the current general discourse of the electronic media, for instance, it is often considered that ideology and bias are one and the same thing, and that ideology and 'common sense' can be set against each other. This distinction continues into party political debate: 'ideology' is what the other side is motivated by while 'our' side is again merely applying common sense. In the history of Marxist thought there has been a convoluted development of usage of the term, not unrelated to the distinction just outlined. For the purposes of this chapter, however, ideology will be taken to refer to all espousal, assumption, consideration, and discussion of social and cultural values, whether overt or covert. In that sense it will include common sense itself, for common sense is always concerned with the values and underlying assumptions of our everyday lives.

Volosinov (1929/1986) encapsulates the position when he argues that all language is ideological. All sign systems, including language, he argues, have not only a simple denotative role, they are also and at one and the same time, evaluative, and thus ideological. 'The domain of ideology coincides with the domain of signs' (10). From this perspective it will thus be seen that all writing is ideological since all writing either assumes values even when not overtly espousing them, or is produced and also read within a social and cultural framework which is itself inevitably suffused with values, that is to say, suffused with ideology. In addition, in Marxist terms, considerations of ideology can neither be divorced from considerations of the economic base, nor from considerations of power (that is, of politics), and that too is the position taken here.

Representation: Gender, Minority Groups, and Bias in the 1970s

In eighteenth- and nineteenth-century didacticism the promotion of values had often taken the overt form of direct preaching, while in the 1970s the specific form of the debate was to do with questions of character representation and character role. The analysis consisted in showing how children's fiction represented some groups at the expense of others, or how some groups were negatively represented in stereotypical terms. The argument was that by representing certain groups in certain ways children's books were promoting certain values – essentially white, male and middle-class, and that the books were thus class biased, racist and sexist. The fact that the protagonists of most children's books tended to be white middle-class boys was adduced in evidence. Black characters rarely made an appearance in children's fiction, and working-class characters were portrayed either as respectful to their middle-class 'betters', or as stupid – or they had the villain's role in the story. Girls were only represented in traditional female roles.

Geoffrey Trease (1949/1964) had led the way in drawing attention to the politically conservative bias of historical fiction, and had attempted to offer alternative points of view in his own writing. Nat Hentoff drew attention to the under-representation of teenagers in children's books, and saw the need to make 'contact with the sizeable number of the young who never read anything for pleasure because they are not in it' (Hentoff 1969: 400). Bob Dixon's work (1974) was characteristic of many attacks on the most prolific of British authors, Enid Blyton, and commentators were becoming increasingly aware of the white middle-class nature of many children's books, and of the sex-role stereotyping to be found within them. Zimet (1976) drew attention to the exclusion or the stereotypical presentation of ethnic minorities and women in children's fiction, and incidentally also in school textbooks, and espoused the use of positive images of girls and of ethnic minorities. Bob Dixon (1977), in a comprehensive survey, demonstrated the almost universally reactionary views on race, gender and class, together with a political conservatism, that informed most British children's books of the time, and Robert Leeson (1977) came up with similar findings. The Writers and Readers Publishing Co-operative (1979) drew attention to the racism inherent in a number of children's classics and one or two highly rated more modern books, and examined sex roles and other stereotyping.

In order to respond to what was seen as the bias in children's fiction, it was argued that books should be written with working-class, or female or black protagonists. In this way working-class, anti-racist and anti-sexist values would be promoted. Thus, in 1982 Dixon drew up what was essentially an annotated book list of 'stories which show a positive, overall attitude with regard to sex roles, race and social class' (Dixon 1982: 3), though he also insisted that the books should meet 'literary' standards that were essentially Leavisite. Such initiatives have multiplied in recent years and the practical outcome has been a proliferation of series aimed particularly at the teenage market, and the emergence of writers like Petronella Breinburg, Robert Leeson and Jan Needle in Britain, and Rosa Guy, Julius Lester, Louise Fitzhugh and Virginia Hamilton in the USA, who have offered different perspectives and attempted to redress the balance.

As has been indicated, the debate was essentially about representation, and 'literary standards' *per se* were not generally challenged. Thus more complex considerations of the ways in which ideology is inscribed in texts did not enter into the equation, nor did considerations of the complexity of reader response. What such initiatives did do, however, was to point out that all texts incorporated value positions, and that after all, as John Stephens has observed, 'Writing for children is usually purposeful' (Stephens 1992: 3)

It was therefore not long before questions were raised about the grounds of the judgements made about the quality of children's books, and that in turn relates to a wider consideration of such questions with regard to literary criticism as a whole.

The Development of Criticism of Children's Fiction: the Leavisite Paradigm

The criticism of children's fiction has been something of a poor relation in critical studies. For the first two-thirds of twentieth century there was little written that addressed the subject, and in an interesting article Felicity Hughes (1978/1990) offers some analysis as to why this was the case. She argues that at the turn of the century Henry James and others encapsulated the view that for the novel to fully come of age as an art form it had to break free of its family audience. Since then the tendency has increased to view writing for children as a 'mere' craft, not worthy of serious critical attention. Reviewing and commentary focused on advising parents, librarians and other interested adults on what to buy for children, or on advising teachers on how to encourage and develop the reading habits of their pupils. And while critical judgements were offered about the quality of the books, the criteria for such critical judgements were assumed rather than debated. When surveys of the field were published they also tended to sacrifice discussion of critical criteria to the need for comprehensive coverage.

However, a developing body of work did start to emerge in the 1960s and 1970s which was directly concerned with confronting the problem and trying to establish criteria for judgement. Such work drew on two traditions, the Leavisite tradition in Britain, and the New Criticism in the USA. Foremost amongst such initiatives was a collection of papers edited by Egoff *et al.* (1969). Rosenheim (1969) and Travers (1969), both from that collection, look specifically to New Critic Northrop Frye's mythic archetypes, as do Ted Hughes (1976), and Peter Hunt (1980). Wallace Hildick (1970) and Myles McDowell (1973) both address the question of the difference in writing for children and writing for adults, but both resort to Leavisite criteria for evaluating the quality of children's books, as does John Rowe Townsend (1971/1990). The Leavisite tradition perhaps reaches its apogee with Fred Inglis's *The Promise of Happiness.* Inglis's opening sentence directly quotes the opening of Leavis's *The Great Tradition* (1948): 'The great children's novelists are Lewis Carroll, Rudyard Kipling, Francis Hodgson Burnett, Arthur Ransome, William Mayne, and Philippa Pearce – to stop for a moment at that comparatively safe point on an uncertain list' (Inglis 1981: 1).

The tradition is not dead. Margery Fisher (1986) for instance, assumes that the definition of a children's classic is still essentially unproblematic. William Moebius (1986/1990) brings similar assumptions to bear upon picture books, and Peter Hunt's book on Arthur Ransome is still largely rooted in Leavisite practice in its judgements of quality and value (Hunt 1992).

One of the features of the tradition is its refusal to address questions of value at a theoretical level. Here is Townsend exemplifying the point.

> We find in fact that the literary critics, both modern and not-so-modern, are reluctant to pin themselves down to theoretical statements. In the introduction to *Determinations* (1934), F. R. Leavis expresses the belief that 'the way to forward true appreciation of literature and art is to examine and discuss it'; and again, 'out of agreement or disagreement with particular judgements of value a sense of relative value in the concrete will define itself, and without this, no amount of talk in the abstract is worth anything'.
>
> Townsend 1971/1990: 66

The values in question can be culled from a variety of sources. F. R. Leavis (1955) talks of 'intelligence', 'vitality', 'sensibility', 'depth, range and subtlety in the presentment of human experience', 'achieved creation' 'representative significance'. Inglis (1981) talks of 'sincerity' 'dignity', 'integrity', 'honesty', 'authenticity', 'fulfilment', 'freedom', 'innocence', 'nation', 'intelligence', 'home', 'heroism', 'friendship', 'history'. And Peter Hunt tells us that the virtues of Arthur Ransome are 'family, honour, skill, good sense, responsibility and mutual respect', and 'the idea of place' (Hunt 1992: 86). All of these terms and formulations are offered by their various authors as if they are essentially unproblematic, and they are thus rendered as common sense, naturalised and hidden in the discourse, and not raised for examination. We may have little difficulty, however, in recognising a liberal humanist consensus which runs through them, even if one or two of Inglis's choices are somewhat idiosyncratic. Nowhere, however, are we able to raise the question of the role that this liberal humanist discourse plays ideologically in a late capitalist world, and it is such a challenge that an ideological critique inevitably raises.

However, before moving on to such considerations, it is necessary to add that Inglis's book also marks a peak in the *educational* debate which has filled the pages of such journals as *English in Education* throughout the 1980s and into the 1990s, and which is also a debate between the Leavisites and the exponents of newer developments in structuralism and semiotics. As I have indicated above, the discourses of children's literature and education continuously overlap. Felicity Hughes (1976/1990) highlights Henry James's concern that the universal literacy that would follow from universal schooling would endanger the future of the novel as an art form, leading to inevitable vulgarisation, as the novel itself catered to popular taste – and children's literature itself catered to an even lower common denominator. As a result, and in order to try to return some status to children's literature, it was, and often still is seen as the training ground of adult literary taste. From such a perspective the distinction conferred by the term 'literature' is crucial, since by that means the Jamesian distinctions between the novel as an art form and other fiction as *commercial* entertainment is promoted.

It is perhaps ironic that the criticism of children's fiction should come of age at precisely the point when the newer perspectives of structuralism, semiotics, and Marxism were beginning to make their mark in literary criticism in Britain, and to undermine those very certainties after which Inglis was searching.

The Ideological Debate in Literary Studies

Character and action: structuralist insights

As already noted, the work of New Critic Northrop Frye (1957) had been influential in establishing a structuralist tradition in the criticism of children's fiction in the USA in the early 1970s. From Europe a different tradition began to make its influence felt in Britain in the later 1970s and 1980s, particularly with regard to the treatment of character and action. The Russian formalist, Vladimir Propp (1928/1968), suggested in his study of the Russian folktale that character was not the source of action, rather it was the product of plot. The hero was the hero because of his or her role in the plot. One can go back to Aristotle for similar insistence that it was not character but action that was important in tragedy (Aristotle 1965: 39) and such views were echoed by the pre-war critic Walter Benjamin (1970) and in Tzvetan Todorov's work (1971/1977).

The Leavisite tradition had, by contrast, tended to emphasise the importance of psychological insight in characterisation, and had seen characters themselves as the source of the action of the story, and it is easy to see how the work of authors such as Philippa Pearce, Nina Bawden, William Mayne, Maurice Sendak, Anthony Browne or Aidan Chambers, to take a list not entirely at random, lends itself to such approaches. By contrast the work of popular authors, such as Enid Blyton or Roald Dahl, more easily lends itself to structuralist analysis: their protagonists are heroines and heroes primarily because that is their plot role, not because there is anything in their psychological make up that makes them inherently 'heroic'.

Such structuralist approaches need not be limited to popular texts, and can be applied with equal usefulness to the work of authors at what is often regarded as the 'quality' end of the market. To take an example, the character of Toad in *The Wind in the Willows* (Grahame 1908) could be seen on the one hand as a rounded psychological creation, in turns blustering and repentant, selfish, self-seeking and replete with hubris. His exploits can then be seen entirely in terms of his personality. Structuralist analysis, on the other hand, might see him as comic hero, archetypal overreacher, functioning as the disruptive element in the social order that is necessary for the book's main plot to develop, and thus acting as a pivotal point for the articulation of the conflict between the uncertainties of the newer machine age, and the more settled life of the rural idyll, a conflict which is one of the major themes of the book.

Robert Leeson (1975/1980) led the attack on the application to children's fiction of the then prevailing tradition of adult literary criticism. He writes: 'these days, turning to adult lit-crit is like asking to be rescued by the *Titanic*' (209). He locates the debate about characterisation in a specifically ideological context, suggesting that enthusiasm for psychological characterisation is a bourgeois trait. The old tales, he argues, echoing Propp, didn't need psychology, they had action and moral. The claims made by traditional 'lit-crit' for such characterisation are elitist, and have little application for the general reader. J. S. Bratton, too, rejected the Leavisite tradition in her study of Victorian children's books: 'the liberal humanist tradition of literary criticism offers no effective approach to the material' (Bratton 1981: 19) although she draws on Frye as well as Propp in her resort to structuralism (see also Sarland 1991: 142).

The critique of the position which sees character as the source of meaning and action comes from a wider and more ideological perspective than that of structuralism alone, and structuralism itself has more to offer than insights about character and action. More widely, structuralism draws on semiotics to explore the whole range of codes that operate in texts and by which they construct their meanings; it also takes a lead from Lévi-Strauss (1963), who related structural elements in myths to structural elements in the society that gave rise to them. This becomes a central tool of ideological critique, allowing parallels to be drawn between ideological structures in the works and those in society at large.

The underlying ground of ideological value

Marxist literary criticism analyses literature in the light of prevailing economic class conflict in capitalist society. This conflict is not slavishly reproduced in the ideological superstructure, of which literature is a part, but it is always possible to trace it in some form in individual work. The liberal humanist tradition, by contrast, sees not class conflict as the major determining structure in understanding history and society, but materialism itself. The ideological conflict then becomes materialism versus humanism and the paradigm distinction to be made about the work, *pace* Henry James, is that between art and commerce. Terry Eagleton (1976) and Catherine Belsey (1980) are among the major critics of the Leavisite tradition, identifying its liberal humanist roots, and analysing its escapist response to the materialism of bourgeois capitalism. Furthermore, they argue, by 'naturalising' its values as common sense, liberal humanism conceals its reactionary political role, though the idealist nature of its position is often clear enough in its claim of transcendent status for those same values and for a universal 'human nature' in which they inhere.

To take an example, a liberal humanist reading of *The Wind in the Willows* might see it as celebrating the values enshrined in notions of home and good fellowship, in opposition to the threatening materialism of the wide world with its dominant symbol of the motor car. A case might be made that the recurrent plots and sub-plots, all of which involve explorations away from, and successive returns to warm secure homes, culminating in the retaking of Toad Hall from the marauding weasels and stoats, have a universal appeal, since such explorations and returns are the very condition of childhood itself. An ideological perspective might note, by contrast, the resemblance of those secure warm homes to the Victorian middle-class nursery, and comment upon the escapism of the response to the materialism of the wide world. Such an approach might further recognise the underlying feudalist presuppositions that are hidden within the 'common sense' assumptions of the book, and might identify in the weasels and stoats the emergence of an organised working class challenging the privileges of property and upper-middle-class idleness. Jan Needle's re-working of the book, *Wild Wood* (1981), starts from just such a premise. In addition the celebration of fellowship is an entirely male affair, the only women in the book – the jailer's daughter and the bargee – have distinctly subservient roles, and claims for universality just in terms of gender alone begin to look decidedly suspect.

In her continuing ideological critique Belsey suggests that from the liberal humanist perspective people are seen as the sole authors of their own actions, and hence of their own history, and meaning is the product of their individual intentions. In fact, she argues, the reverse is true: people are not the authors of their own history, they are rather the products of history itself, or less deterministically, engaged in a dialectical relationship with their history – both product and producer. The grounds for Leeson's argument, above, are now clear, for a criticism that espouses psychological characterisation as a central tenet of 'quality', and that insists that the stories in which those characters find themselves should be rooted in the intentionality of those characters' psyches, is liberal humanist in assumption, and will fail to expose the ideological nature both of the fiction to which it is giving attention, and of the fiction that it is ignoring.

In liberal humanist criticism it is the author who takes centre stage, and Belsey identifies 'expressive realism' as literature's dominant form over the past 150 years: reality, as experienced by a single gifted individual is expressed in such a way that the rest of us spontaneously perceive it as being the case. Grahame's intention is assumed to be that readers should see childhood as a time and place of adventure within a secure framework, and readers are to take his word for it. The resort to the author's intention as the source of meaning in the work, known to its critics as the 'intentional fallacy', had already come under attack for circularity from the New Critics, since the primary evidence for the author's intention was usually the work itself. Belsey takes the argument one step further, suggesting that expressive realism operates to support liberal humanism, and thus, effectively, in support of capitalism itself. Ideological perspectives insist, in contrast, that texts are constructions in and of ideology, generally operating unconsciously, and it is the job of the critic to deconstruct the work in order to expose its underlying ideological nature and role. Thus, far from being the unique insight of an individual with a privileged understanding of the world, *The Wind in the Willows* can be seen as resting securely within a continuum of escapist response to developing bourgeois capitalism that stretches all the way from *Hard Times* to *Lady Chatterley's Lover.*

Peter Hollindale (1988) takes on a number of the perspectives outlined above, and applies them to his discussion of ideology in children's books. He distinguishes three levels of ideology. There is first of all an overt, often proselytising or didactic level, as instanced in books like *The Turbulent Term of Tyke Tyler* (Kemp 1977). Then there is a second more passive level, where views of the world are put into characters mouths or otherwise incorporated into the narrative with no overt ironic distancing. (There is a famous example of this from Enid Blyton's *Five Run Away Together* (1944), analysed by Ken Watson (1992: 31), in which the reader is implicitly invited to side with the obnoxious middle-class Julian putting down a member of the 'lower orders'.) Finally, there is what Hollindale calls an 'underlying climate of belief' which he identifies as being inscribed in the basic material from which fiction is built. It is possible to detect a hankering after the old transcendent certainties in Hollindale's work. None the less he does substantially shift the ground of the debate in regard to children's fiction, recognising the complexity of the issues.

Circumstances of production

Within the Marxist tradition it has long been recognised that literature is a product of the particular historical and social formations that prevail at the time of its production (see for example Lenin, originally 1908, 1910, 1911/1978; Plekhanov 1913/1957; Trotsky 1924/1974). Children's books have not received such attention until comparatively recently. Bratton (1981) traced the relationship between Victorian children's fiction and its various markets – stories for girls to teach them the domestic virtues, stories for boys to teach them the virtues of military Christianity, stories for the newly literate poor, to teach them religion and morality. Leeson, in his history of children's fiction (Leeson 1985), suggests that there has always been a conflict between middle-class literature and popular literature, a distinction which can be traced in the content of the material, and related to the market that it found. He draws attention to the roots of popular fiction in folktale, which had political content which survived (somewhat subdued) into the written forms. Leeson thus raises a question mark over the perhaps somewhat more determinist analysis offered by Belsey and Eagleton.

More thorough exploration of the issues in contemporary children's fiction has come from feminist perspectives, with a collection of studies of popular teen romance fiction edited by Linda K. Christian-Smith (1993a). Christian-Smith herself (1993b) provides a particularly powerful analysis of the economic, political and ideological circumstances of the growth in production of romances for 'teenagers' or 'young adults', which is now a global industry, with most of the publishing houses based in the USA. She traces the relationship between the imperatives of 'Reaganomics', the emphasis on family values in the rise of the New Right in the 1980s, and the need to enculturate young women into the gendered roles that serve such interests. The collection as a whole analyses how such material both constructs and meets the needs of its market in a rich and subtle exegesis which I shall return to below.

In the meantime it is necessary to explore a further area which has important ideological implication, and that is the way in which the child reader is constructed by the texts he or she is reading.

The Construction of the Reader

The initiatives of the 1970s to redress the balance in the bias of children's fiction took a straightforward view about the relationship between the text and the reader. At its simplest an almost directly didactic relationship was assumed. If you wrote books with positive characterisations of, and roles for, girls, ethnic minorities and the working class, then readers' attitudes would be changed and all would be well with the world. I do not suggest that anyone, even then, thought it would be quite that simple, and since the 1970s there has been something of a revolution in our understandings of how readers are constructed by texts. The insights of reader-response theoreticians like Wolfgang Iser (1978), applied to children's books most notably by Aidan Chambers (1980), had alerted us to some of the textual devices by which an implied reader is written into the text. Iser himself had drawn attention to the fact that texts brought with them a cultural repertoire which had to be matched by the reader. Macherey (1978) brought Freudian perspectives to bear on ways in which ideology operated in hidden ways in the text, and by extension, also in the reader, and Catherine Belsey drew insights from Althusser, Derrida and Lacan to further explore the ways in which the subjectivity of the reader is ideologically constructed.

It is Jacqueline Rose (1984) who offers the most thoroughgoing exposition of this view with respect to children's fiction. She argues that, by a combination of textual devices, characterisation and assumptions of value position, children's books construct children, both as characters and as readers, as without sexuality, innocent, and denied politics, either a politics between themselves or within wider society. As such they are seen as beings with a privileged perception, untainted by culture. More recently, John Stephens (1992), engages in a detailed analysis of a number of books to show how they produce ideological constructions of implied child readers. He concentrates particularly on narrative focalisation and the shifts, moves and gaps of narrative viewpoint and attitude, showing how such techniques imply certain ideological assumptions and formulations, and construct implied readers who must be expected to share them.

Implied Readers and Real Readers

When real readers are introduced into the equation, however, the picture becomes more complicated, and it is here that the educational discourse overlaps with the discourse about fiction *per se*, for it is almost always within school that evidence is gathered, and intervention is proposed. The introduction of real readers has another effect, for it throws into relief some of the more determinist assumptions of the analysis offered above. The evidence comes under three headings: identification, the polysemous text, and contradictory readings.

Identification

The notion of identification has been a contentious issue for some time. The assumption is that readers 'identify with' the protagonists, and thus take on their particular value positions. Readers are thus ideologically constructed by their identification with the character. D. W. Harding (1977) offered an alternative formulation of the reader as an observer in a more detached and evaluative spectator role, and both Geoff Fox (1979) and Robert Protherough (1983) suggest that such a straightforward notion as identification does not account for the evidence that they collected from children and young people. It is clear from their evidence that readers take up a range of positions of greater or lesser involvement, and of varied focalisation. The ideological initiatives of the 1970s presupposed an identification model of response, and subsequent commentators are still most fearful of what happens should a young person engage in unmediated identification with characters constructed within ideologically undesirable formulations. Such fears underlie Stephens's analysis (1992) and the work of Christian–Smith and her co-contributors (1993).

The polysemous text

Roland Barthes (1974) alerted us to the notion that texts operated a plurality of codes that left them open to a plurality of readings, and Umberto Eco (1981) offers the most extensive analysis of that plurality. Specifically, with regard to ideology, Eco agrees that all texts carry ideological assumptions, whether overt or covert. But readers, he argues, have three options: they can assume the ideology of the text and subsume it into their own reading; they can miss or ignore the ideology of the text and import their own, thus producing 'aberrant' readings – 'where "aberrant" means only different from the ones envisaged by the sender' (22); or they can question the text in order to reveal the underlying ideology. This third option is, of course, the project that ideological critique undertakes. When real readers, other than critics, are questioned about their readings, it is clear that the second option is often taken up, and that 'aberrant' readings abound (Sarland 1991; Christian–Smith 1993a), though consensual readings also clearly occur. Texts, it seems, are contradictory, and so evidently are readings.

Contradictory readings

Macherey (1977, 1978) and Eagleton (1976), both assume that the world is riven with ideological conflict. To expect texts to resolve that conflict is mistaken, and the ideological contradictions that inform the world will also be found to inform the fictional texts that are part of that world. Some texts, Eagleton argues, are particularly good at revealing ideological conflict, in that they sit athwart the dominant ideology of the times in which they were written. Eagleton looks to examples from the traditional adult canon to make his point.

Jack Zipes (1979) takes the argument one stage further and suggests that popular work too will be found to be contradictory. He links popular literature and film with its precursors in folktale and romance, and suggests that it offers the hope of autonomy and self-determination, in admittedly utopian forms, while at the same time affirming dominant capitalist ideology. In other words, while the closure of popular texts almost always reinforces dominant ideology, in the unfolding narratives there are always countering moves in which it is challenged. Zipes, then, denies the implications of Eagleton's work that only texts that sit athwart the prevailing ideology can be open to countervailing readings, and he denies too the implications of Belsey's work that popular forms sit within the classic expressive realist tradition, and as such demand readings that are congruent with the dominant ideology.

For example in Enid Blyton's *Famous Five* books, many of the plots are predicated on the refusal of the central female character, George, to accept her role as subservient, domesticated and non-adventurous, despite repeated exhortations to 'behave like a girl'. She even refuses to accept her 'real' name, which is Georgina. Countering this is the fact that Blyton only offers her the alternative of 'tomboy', an alternative that is itself determined by a predominantly male discourse; and the closures of the books re-establish traditional domestic order with the sexes acting according to conventional gender stereotype. (Zipes himself later turned his attention to children's fiction (Zipes 1983), and see also Sarland 1983.)

While this analysis is still essentially theoretical, supporting evidence is beginning to emerge from studies that have been done of readers themselves. The focus has been on popular fiction, and on teenagers. Popular fiction causes educationalists particular concern since it appears to reinforce the more reactionary values in society, particularly so far as girls and young women are concerned. The research evidence uncovers a complex picture of the young seeking ways to take control over their own lives, and using the fiction that they enjoy as one element in that negotiation of cultural meaning and value. Gemma Moss showed how teenage girls and boys were able to turn the popular forms of, respectively, the romance and the thriller to their own ends. She found unhelpful some of the more determinist ideological analysis that suggested that, by their reading of romance, girls were constructed as passive victims of a patriarchal society. The girls who liked the romances were tough, worldly wise working-class girls who were not subservient to their male counterparts. 'Girls didn't need to be told about male power, they were dealing with it every day of their lives' (Moss 1989: 7). The traditional assessment of 'teen romance' by most teachers as stereotyped drivel was applied to the girls' writing, too, when they chose to write in that form. However, Moss shows how the teenage girls she was working with were able to take the form into their own writing and use it to negotiate and dramatise their concerns with and experience of femininity and oppression. Romance offered them a form for this activity that was not necessarily limiting at all.

In *Young People Reading: Culture and Response* (Sarland 1991) I have argued that young people engaged in 'aberrant' readings of pulp violence and horror, readings which ran against the reactionary closure of such material, and they thus were able to explore aspirations of being in control of their own lives, and I further argued that the official school literature as often as not offered them negative perspectives on those same aspirations. Christian-Smith and her colleagues (1993) explore similar dualities and demonstrate the complexity of the problem. For instance, in her analysis of the Baby-Sitters Club books, Meredith Rogers Cherland shows how the characters are placed securely within feminine roles and functions, being prepared for domestic life and work in lowly paid 'caring' jobs. The 11-year-old girls who are reading them, however, 'saw the baby-sitters making money that they then used to achieve their own ends. They saw the baby-sitters shaping the action around them so that things worked out the way they wanted them to. They saw girls their age acting as agents in their own right' (Cherland with Edelsky 1993: 32). By contrast, horror, Cherland argues, which these girls were also beginning to read, casts women in increasingly helpless roles. In its association of sexuality with violence it seemed to offer the girls in Cherland's study a position of increasing powerlessness, living in fear and thus denied agency.

Research into the meanings that young people actually make of the books they are reading demonstrates the plural nature of the texts we are dealing with. While it was often claimed that texts within the canon had complexity and ambiguity, it was always thought that popular texts pandered to the lowest common denominator, and offered no purchase on complex ideological formulations. The evidence does not bear that out. Popular texts too are discovered to be open to more than one reading, and the deconstruction of those texts, and the readings young people bring to them, proves be a productive tool of analysis for exploring the ideological formulations which constitute them. There is yet to be a large mainstream study of what readers make of the more traditional central canon of children's fiction, though John Stephens and Susan Taylor's exploration of readings of two retellings of the Seal Wife legend (Stephens and Taylor 1992) is a useful start.

Ideology and Children's Fiction

We have learned from the debate in literary studies that ideology is inscribed in texts much more deeply and in much more subtle ways than we at first thought in the 1970s. The initial emphasis in the criticism of children's books was on the characters, and addressed questions of representation. The relationship between reader and text was assumed to be one of simple identification. Literary merit was an unproblematic notion built upon Leavisite assumptions. This was set in question by reconsideration of characterisation itself, and then by the revolution in literary studies. Hollindale (1988) made an initial attempt to explore the complexity of the problem, and Stephens (1992) has taken it further. Stephens brings powerful ideological perspectives to bear upon the themes of children's fiction, the ways in which the stories are shaped, as well as the ways in which implied readers are constructed by the texts. He looks at a range of texts, including picture books written for the youngest readers, and examines specific titles by a number of writers in the central canon – Judy Blume, Anthony Browne, Leon Garfield, Jan Mark, William Mayne, Jan Needle, Rosemary Sutcliffe, Maurice Sendak and others. The debate has been informed by a rerecognition of the moral/didactic role of children's fiction, now recoded as its ideological role. Unresolved conflicts remain between those who want to retain or renegotiate some literary criteria for judging the quality of children's fiction and those who are more sceptical of such judgements.

The overlap with the discourse of child rearing, and in particular, education, reveals another conflict, that between determinism and agency. One view of fiction is that it constructs readers in specific ideological formations, and thus enculturates them into the dominant discourses of capitalism – class division, paternalism, racism. Such views are not totally fatalistic, but do require of readers a very conscious effort to read against texts, to deconstruct them in order to reveal their underlying ideology. This then becomes the educational project. The opposing view is that readers are not nearly such victims of fiction as has been assumed, and that the fictions that are responsible for the transmission of such values are more complex than was at first thought. Evidence from the children and young people themselves is beginning to be collected in order to explore this complexity. The argument is that readers are not simply determined by what they read; rather there is a dialectical relationship between determinism and agency. With reference to her discussions of girls' reading, Cherland quotes J. M. Anyon:

> The dialectic of accommodation and resistance is a part of all human beings'
> response to contradiction and oppression. Most females engage in daily
> conscious and unconscious attempts to resist the psychological degradation
> and low self-esteem that would result from the total application of the
> cultural ideology of femininity: submissiveness, dependency, domesticity
> and passivity.
>
> Cherland with Edelsky 1993: 30

Applied to language itself, this analysis of a dialectic between individual identity and the ideological formulations of the culture within which it finds itself can be traced back to Volosinov. Within children's literature the dialectic will be found within the texts, and between the texts and the reader.

The collection of papers edited by Christian-Smith explores this dialectic in the greatest detail. There is initially the dialectic within the texts between feminine agency and patriarchy, traced by Pam Gilbert (1993) and Sandra Taylor (1993), who show how the female characters are agents of their own lives, finding spaces for decision making and autonomy within the gendered discourse of the culture, and in the case of younger characters, within the adult child power relationships of the family. They generally insist that boys treat them with respect, in an equal and caring relationship, yet they are trapped within stories that in their closure, suggest futures in domesticity, in poorly paid service and 'caring' jobs, and in monogamous heterosexual relationships.

There is, further, the dialectic between the mode of production, distribution and dissemination of the texts, and the fact that the girls themselves choose to read them despite whatever 'better' alternatives may be available (Christian-Smith 1993b; Willinsky and Hunniford 1993).

There is finally the dialectic in school itself as readers appropriate such texts as oppositional reading, and use them both to renegotiate their own gender roles in their writing (Moss 1993) and in their discussions (Willinsky and Hunniford 1993). Yet the schools' own rating of such reading as being beneath attention, and the tendency to regard the readers as therefore – and already – constructed by their reading in such a way that those readings do not merit serious attention, means that the young women and girls are themselves excluded from full educational opportunity (Taylor 1993, Davies 1993).

In Christian-Smith's collection *Texts of Desire: Essays on Fiction, Femininity and Schooling* (1993) ideological criticism of children's fiction has come of age. The collection as a whole addresses the complexity of the debate, analysing the ideologies of the texts themselves, the economic and political circumstances of their production, dissemination and distribution, the ideological features of the meanings their young readers make of them, and the political and economic circumstances of those young readers themselves. The focus of attention is the mass-produced material aimed at the female teen and just pre-teen market, but their study offers a paradigm for future exploration of children's fiction generally, if we are to fully understand its ideological construction within society.

References

Aristotle (1965) 'On the art of poetry', in Aristotle, Horace and Longinus, *Classical Literary Criticism*, trans. Dorsch, T., Harmondsworth: Penguin.

Barthes, R. (1974) *S/Z*, New York: Hill and Wang.

Belsey, C. (1980) *Critical Practice*, London: Methuen.

Benjamin, W. (1970) *Illuminations*, Glasgow: Collins Fontana.

Blyton, E. (1944) *Five Run Away Together*, London: Hodder and Stoughton.

Bratton, J. S. (1981) *The Impact of Victorian Children's Fiction*, London: Croom Helm.

Chambers, A. (1980) 'The reader in the book', in Chambers, N. (ed.) *The Signal Approach to Children's Books*, Harmondsworth: Kestrel.

Cherland, M. R., with Edelsky, C. (1993) 'Girls reading: the desire for agency and the horror of helplessness in fictional encounters', in Christian-Smith, L. K. (ed.) *Texts of Desire: Essays on Fiction, Femininity and Schooling*, London: Falmer Press.

Christian-Smith, L. K. (ed.) (1993a) *Texts of Desire: Essays on Fiction, Femininity and Schooling*, London: Falmer Press.

—— (1993b) 'Sweet dreams: gender and desire in teen romance novels', in Christian-Smith, L. K. (ed.) *Texts of Desire: Essays on Fiction, Femininity and Schooling*, London: Falmer Press.

Dahl, R. (1980) *The Twits*, Harmondsworth: Penguin.

Darton, F. J. H. (1932/1982) *Children's Books in England: Five Centuries of Social Life*, 3rd edn, rev. B. Alderson, Cambridge: Cambridge University Press.

Davies, B. (1993) 'Beyond dualism and towards multiple subjectivities', in Christian-Smith, L. K. (ed.) *Texts of Desire: Essays on Fiction, Femininity and Schooling*, London: Falmer Press.

Dixon, B. (1974) 'The nice, the naughty and the nasty: the tiny world of Enid Blyton', *Children's Literature in Education* 15: 43–62.

——— (1977) *Catching them Young* 2 vols, London: Pluto Press.

——— (1982) *Now Read On*, London: Pluto Press.

Eagleton, T. (1976) *Criticism and Ideology*, London: Verso.

Eco, U. (1981) *The Role of the Reader*, London: Hutchinson.

Egoff, S., Stubbs, G. T. and Ashley, L. F. (eds) (1969) *Only Connect*, Toronto: Oxford University Press.

Fielding, S. (1749/1968) *The Governess or, Little Female Academy*, London: Oxford University Press.

Fisher, M. (1986) *Classics for Children and Young People*, South Woodchester: Thimble Press.

Fox, G. (1979) 'Dark watchers: young readers and their fiction', in *English in Education* 13, 1: 32–35.

Frye, N. (1957) *Anatomy of Criticism*, Princeton, NJ: Princeton University Press.

Gilbert, P. (1993) 'Dolly fictions: teen romance down under', in Christian-Smith, L. K. (ed.) *Texts of Desire: Essays on Fiction, Femininity and Schooling*, London: Falmer Press.

Grahame, K. (1908) *The Wind in the Willows*, London: Methuen.

Harding, D. W. (1977) 'Psychological processes in the reading of fiction', in Meek, M., Warlow, A. and Barton, G. (eds) *The Cool Web*, London: Bodley Head.

Hentoff, N. (1969) 'Fiction for teenagers', in Egoff, S., Stubbs, G. T. and Ashley, L. F. (eds) *Only Connect*, Toronto: Oxford University Press.

Hildick, W. (1970) *Children and Fiction*, London: Evans.

Hollindale, P. (1988) 'Ideology and the children's book', *Signal* 55, 3–22.

Hughes, F. (1976/1990) 'Children's literature: theory and practice', in Hunt, P. (ed.) *Children's Literature: The Development of Criticism*, London: Routledge.

Hughes, T. (1976) 'Myth and education', in Fox, G., Hammond, G., Jones, T. and Sterk, K. (eds) *Writers, Critics and Children*, London: Heinemann.

Hunt, P. (1980) 'Children's books, children's literature, criticism and research', in Benton, M. (ed.) *Approaches to Research in Children's Literature*, Southampton: University of Southampton Department of Education.

——— (ed.) (1990) *Children's Literature: The Development of Criticism*, London: Routledge.

——— (1992) *Approaching Arthur Ransome*, London: Cape.

Inglis, F. (1981) *The Promise of Happiness*, Cambridge: Cambridge University Press.

Iser, W. (1978) *The Act of Reading*, London: Routledge and Kegan Paul.

Kemp, G. (1977) *The Turbulent Term of Tyke Tyler*, London: Faber and Faber.

Leavis, F. R. (1948) *The Great Tradition*, Harmondsworth: Penguin.

——— (1955) *D. H. Lawrence: Novelist*, Harmondsworth: Penguin.

Leeson, R. (1975/1980) 'To the toyland frontier', in Chambers, N. (ed.) *The Signal Approach to Children's Books*, Harmondsworth: Kestrel.

——— (1977) *Children's Books and Class Society*, London: Writers and Readers Publishing Co-operative.

——— (1985) *Reading and Righting*, London: Collins.

Lenin, V. (1908, 1910, 1911/1978) 'Lenin's articles on Tolstoy', in Macherey, P. (ed.) *A Theory of Literary Production*, London: Routledge and Kegan Paul.

Lévi-Strauss, C. (1963) *The Structural Study of Myth*, Harmondsworth: Penguin.

McDowell, M. (1973) 'Fiction for children and adults: some essential differences', *Children's Literature in Education* 10: 50–63.

Macherey, P. (1977) 'Problems of reflection', in Barker, F., Coombes, J., Hulme, P., Musselwhite, D. and Osborne, R. (eds) *Literature, Society, and the Sociology of Literature*, Colchester: University of Essex.

——— (1978) *A Theory of Literary Production*, London: Routledge and Kegan Paul.

Marx, K. and Engels, F. (1859/1892/1971) *Historical Materialism*, London: Pluto Press.

Moebius, W. (1985/1990) 'Introduction to picturebook codes', in Hunt, P. (ed.) *Children's Literature: The Development of Criticism*, London: Routledge.

Moss, G. (1989) *Un/Popular Fictions*, London: Virago.

—— (1993) 'The place for romance in young people's writing', in Christian-Smith, L. K. (ed.) *Texts of Desire: Essays on Fiction, Femininity and Schooling*, London: Falmer Press.

Needle, J. (1981) *Wild Wood*, London: André Deutsch.

Plekhanov, G. V. (1913/1957) *Art and Social Life*, Moscow: Progress Publishers.

Propp, V. (1928/1968) *Morphology of the Folktale*, Austin: Texas University Press.

Protherough, R. (1983) *Developing Response to Fiction*, Milton Keynes: Open University Press.

Rose, J. (1984) *The Case of Peter Pan or the Impossibility of Children's Fiction*, London: Macmillan.

Rosenheim, E. W. Jr (1969) 'Children's reading and adults' values', in Egoff, S., Stubbs, G. T. and Ashley, L. F. (eds) (1969) *Only Connect*, Toronto: Oxford University Press.

Sarland, C. (1983) 'The Secret Seven Versus The Twits', *Signal* 42: 155–171.

—— (1991) *Young People Reading: Culture and Response*, Milton Keynes: Open University Press.

Stephens, J. (1992) *Language and Ideology in Children's Fiction*, Harlow: Longman.

Stephens, J. and Taylor, S. (1992) 'No innocent texts', in Evans, E. (ed.) *Young Readers, New Readings*, Hull: Hull University Press.

Taylor, S. (1993) 'Transforming the texts: towards a feminist classroom practice', in Christian-Smith, L. K. (ed.) *Texts of Desire: Essays on Fiction, Femininity and Schooling*, London: Falmer Press.

Todorov, T. (1977) *The Poetics of Prose*, New York: Cornell University Press.

Townsend, J. R. (1971/1990) 'Standards of criticism for children's literature', in Hunt, P. (ed.) *Children's Literature: The Development of Criticism*, London: Routledge.

Travers, P. (1969) 'Only connect', in Egoff, S., Stubbs, G. T. and Ashley, L. F. (eds) *Only Connect*, Toronto: Oxford University Press.

Trease, G. (1949/1964) *Tales out of School*, London: Heinemann.

Trotsky, L. (1924/1974) *Class and Art*, London: New Park Publications.

Volosinov, V. N. (1929/1986) *Marxism and the Philosophy of Language*, Cambridge, MA: Harvard University Press.

Watson, K. (1992) 'Ideology in novels for young people', in Evans, E. (ed.) *Young Readers, New Readings*, Hull: Hull University Press.

Willinsky, J. and Hunniford, R. M. (1993) 'Reading the romance younger: the mirrors and fears of a preparatory literature', in Christian-Smith, L. K. (ed.) *Texts of Desire: Essays on Fiction, Femininity and Schooling*, London: Falmer Press.

Writers and Readers Publishing Co-operative (1979) *Racism and Sexism in Children's Books*, London: Writers and Readers.

Zimet, S. G. (1976) *Print and Prejudice*, Sevenoaks: Hodder and Stoughton.

Zipes, J. (1979) *Breaking the Magic Spell: Radical Theories of Folk and Fairy Tales*, London: Heinemann.

—— (1983) *Fairy Tales and the Art of Subversion*, London: Heinemann.

5   Analysing Texts for Children: Linguistics and Stylistics

John Stephens

Editor's introduction

Many assumptions are made about the language of children's books, not least by authors, who may feel obliged to use a specific type and range of vocabulary, styles, and structures. John Stephens argues that even when this happens, the form has 'access to textual strategies with the potential to offset the limitations', and demonstrates the value and fascination of recognising how words work on the page.

P. H.

Because the contexts in which children's literature is produced and disseminated are usually dominated by a focus on content and theme, the language of children's literature receives little explicit attention. Yet style – which is the *way* things are represented, based on complex codes and conventions of language and presuppositions about language – is an important component of texts, and the study of it allows us access to some of the key processes which shape text production (Scholes 1985: 2–3). The assumption that what is said can be extricated from how it is said, and that language is therefore only a transparent medium, is apt to result in readings with at best a limited grasp of written genres or of the social processes and movements with which genres and styles interrelate.

The language of fiction written for children readily appears to offer conventionalised discourses by means of which to 'encode' content (both story and message). The ubiquitous 'Once upon a time' of traditional story-telling, for example, not only serves as a formal story onset but also tends to imply that particular narrative forms, with a particular stock of lexical and syntactic forms, will ensue. But the contents and themes of that fiction are representations of social situations and values, and such social processes are inextricable from the linguistic processes which give them expression. In other words, the transactions between writers and readers take place within complex networks of social relations by means of language. Further, within the large language system of English, for example, it is possible for young readers to encounter in their reading an extensive range and variety of language uses. Some textual varieties will seem familiar and immediately accessible, consisting of a lexicon and syntax which will seem identifiably everyday, but others will seem much less familiar, either because the lexicon contains forms or uses specific to a different speech community (British 'Standard' English versus USA 'Standard' English, for example), or because writers may choose to employ linguistic forms whose occurrence is largely or wholly restricted to narrative fiction, or because particular kinds of fiction evolve specific discourses. Books which may be said to have a common theme or topic will differ not just because that theme can be expressed in a different content but because it is expressed through differing linguistic resources. For example, a large number of children's books express the theme of 'growing up', but since that theme can be discerned in texts as diverse as Tolkien's *The Hobbit* and Danziger's *Can You Sue Your Parents for Malpractice?*, it cannot in itself discriminate effectively between texts of different kinds.

Writers have many options to select from. Thus fiction offers a large range of generic options, such as the choice between fantasy and realism, with more specific differences within them, such as that between time-slip fantasy grounded in the knowable world, or fantasy set in an imaginary universe. To make such a choice involves entering into a *discourse*, a complex of story types and structures, social forms and linguistic practices. That discourse can be said to take on a distinctive style in so far as it is distinguished from other actualisations by recurrent patterns or codes. These might include choices in lexis and grammar; use, types and frequency of figurative language; characteristic modes of cohesion; orientation of narrative voice towards the text's existents (that is, events, characters, settings). Aspects of such a style may be shared by several writers working in the same period and with a common genre, as, for example, contemporary realistic adolescent fiction, but it is usually more personal, as when we speak of the style of Kenneth Grahame, or William Mayne or Zibby Oneal, and at times we may refer to the distinctive style of a particular text, such as Virginia Hamilton's *Arilla Sun Down*. Because the patterns of a particular style are a selection from a larger linguistic code, however, and exist in a relationship of sameness and difference with a more generalised discourse, a writer remains to some degree subject to the discourse, and the discourse can be said to determine at least part of the meaning of the text. Moreover, a narrative discourse also encodes a reading position which readers will adopt to varying extents, depending on their previous experience of the particular discourse, their similarities to or differences from the writer's language community, their level of linguistic sophistication, and other individual differences. At a more obviously linguistic level, a writer's choices among such options as first/third person narration, single/multiple focalisation, and direct/ indirect speech representation further define the encoded reading position. Between them, the broader elements of genre and the more precise linguistic processes appear to restrict the possibility of wildly deviant readings, though what might be considered more probable readings depends on an acquired recognition of the particular discourse. If that recognition is not available to readers, the readings they produce may well seem aberrant.

The communication which informs the transactions between writers and readers is a specialised aspect of socio–linguistic communication in general. The forms and meanings of reality are constructed in language: by analysing how language works, we come nearer to knowing how our culture constructs itself, and where we fit into that construction. Language enables individuals to compare their experiences with the experiences of others, a process which has always been a fundamental purpose of children's fiction. The representation of experiences such as growing up, evolving a sense of self, falling in love or into conflict and so on, occurs in language, and guarantees that the experiences represented are shared with human beings in general. Language can make present the felt experiences of people living in other places and at other times, thus enabling a reader to define his or her own subjectivity in terms of perceived potentialities and differences. Finally, the capacity of language to express things beyond everyday reality, such as abstract thought or possible transcendent experiences, is imparted to written texts with all its potentiality for extending the boundaries of intellectual and emotional experience. Readers (and writers) often like to think of this as a kind of 'word magic' (for example, Sullivan 1985) – and numerous fantastic fictions so represent it – though it is in fact an explicable linguistic function.

The socio-linguistic contexts of text production and reception are important considerations for any account of reading processes. But beyond satisfying a basic human need for contact, reading can also give many kinds of pleasure, though the pleasures of reading are not discovered in a social or linguistic vacuum: as we first learn how to read we also start learning what is pleasurable and what not, and even what is good writing and what not. Our socio-linguistic group, and especially its formal educational structures, tends to precondition what constitutes a good story, a good argument, a good joke, and the better our command of socio-linguistic codes the greater is our appreciation. In other words, we learn to enjoy the process as well as the product. Writing and reading are also very individual acts, however, and the pleasure of reading includes some sense of the distinctive style of a writer or a text. One primary function of stylistic description is to contribute to the pleasure in the text by defining the individual qualities of what is vaguely referred to as the 'style' of a writer or text.

Stylistic description can be attempted by means of several methodologies. These range from an impressionistic 'literary stylistics', which is characteristic of most discussions of the language of children's literature, to complex systemic analyses. The latter can offer very precise and delicate descriptions, but have the limitation that non-specialists may find them impenetrable. This article works within the semiotic analysis developed in contemporary critical linguistics (Fairclough 1989; Stephens 1992a).

To discuss the textuality of children's fiction one has to begin by considering some assumptions about the nature of language on which it is grounded. Linguists recognise that language is a social semiotic, a culturally patterned system of signs used to communicate about things, ideas or concepts. As a system constructed within culture, it is not founded on any essential bond between a verbal sign and its referent (Stephens 1992a: 246–247). This is an important point to grasp, because much children's fiction is written and mediated under the contrary, essentialist assumption, and this has major implications both for writing objectives and for the relationships between writers and readers. As mentioned above, fantasy writing in particular is apt to assert the inextricability of word and thing, but the assumption also underlies realistic writing which purports to minimise the distance between life and fiction, or which pivots on the evolution of a character's essential selfhood, and it often informs critical suspicion of texts which foreground the gap between signs and things. The essentialist position has been conveniently (over-)stated by Molly Hunter:

the belief underlying the practice of magic has a direct bearing on the whole concept of language ... The meaning of every word, it is argued, is innate to its sound and structure. Thus the word itself is the essence of what it names; and to capture that essence in speech is to be able to direct its power to a desired end.

Hunter 1976: 107–108

Later in the same paper Hunter balances this position against a writer's more sober awareness 'that words may be defined only to the extent of ensuring their correct use in context' (109), describing the difference as a contradiction which 'all creative writing is an attempt to solve'. But a creative writer cannot resolve those incompatible assumptions about the nature of language and linguistic function. The following passages throw some light on this difference:

> The glade in the ring of trees was evidently a meeting-place of the wolves ... in the middle of the circle was a great grey wolf. He spoke to them in the dreadful language of the Wargs. Gandalf understood it. Bilbo did not, but it sounded terrible to him, and as if all their talk was about cruel and wicked things, as it was.
>
> *The Hobbit*, Tolkien 1937/1987: 91

> Charlie did not know much about ice ... The only piece he had known came from a refrigerated boat, and was left on the wharf, cloudy white, not clear, not even very clean. Charlie had waited until the boat went with its load of lamb carcasses, and then gone for it. By then it had melted. There was a puddle, a wisp of lambswool, and nothing more.
>
> He did not even think this was the same stuff. He did not think this place was part of the world. He thought it was the mouth of some other existence coming up from the ground, being drilled through the rock. The pieces coming away were like the fragments from the bit of the carpentry brace Papa used for setting up shelves. An iron thing would come from the ground, Charlie thought, and another Papa would blow through the hole to make it clear. Last time all the dust had gone into Charlie's eye, because he was still looking through. Papa had thought him such a fool.
>
> *Low Tide*, Mayne 1992: 163–164

The Tolkien and Mayne passages represent a principal character at a moment of incomprehension: Bilbo hears a foreign language, and has no actual referents for the verbal signs; Charlie perceives a physical phenomenon (the point at which pieces of ice break from a glacier into a river, though *glacier* is not introduced for two more paragraphs) and struggles with the socio-linguistic resources at his disposal to find meaning in it. A significant difference between the two is the implication that the Wargs' language communicates meanings beyond sense. On a simple level, this is to say no more than that it is obvious what the sounds made by a nasty horde of wolves signify. But Tolkien directly raises the question of comprehension – 'Gandalf understood it' – and uses his overt, controlling narrative voice to confirm that Bilbo comprehends something which is a linguistic essential: the language is inherently 'dreadful' (presumably in the fuller sense of 'inspiring dread'); and the 'as it was' confirms the principle that 'the meaning is innate to its sound' suggested by the lexical set 'terrible, wicked and cruel'. Mayne focuses on the other side of the sign/thing relationship, in effect posing a question often posed in his novels: can a phenomenon be understood if it cannot be signified in language? Tolkien's shifts between narration and Bilbo's focalisation are clearly marked; Mayne slips much more ambiguously between these modes, a strategy which serves to emphasise the gap between phenomena and language. The first paragraph is a retrospective narration of Charlie's single relevant empirical experience, but because that ice then differed in colour and form ('cloudy white', 'a puddle') the past experience does not enable him to make sense of the present. Instead, in the second paragraph Charlie produces a fantastic (mis-)interpretation on the premise that what he sees is visually isomorphic with another previous experience. The upshot is that, once again, he seems 'such a fool', though that is only a temporary state induced by linguistic inadequacy, and is set aside by the novel's congruence of story and theme. As a story, *Low Tide* is a treasure hunt gone wrong and then marvellously recuperated; a major thematic concern, articulated through the child characters' struggles to make sense of phenomena, language, and the relationships between phenomena and language, is a child's struggle towards competence in his or her socio-linguistic context.

The texts thus demonstrate two very different approaches to the semiotic instability of language. A third, and very common, approach is to exploit that instability as a source of humour, and this partly explains why nonsense verse is considered to be almost entirely the province of childhood. A rich vein of narrative humour also runs from the same source. In Sendak's *Higglety Pigglety Pop!*, for example, humour is created by exploiting the arbitrary relationship between signs and things or actions, specifically the instabilities which can result when significations slip, multiply, or change. In the following extract, Jenny, the Sealyham terrier, has undertaken the task of feeding a mysterious and uncooperative baby:

Jennie wiped her beard on the rug. 'If you do not eat, you will not grow.'

'NO EAT! NO GROW! SHOUT!'

Jennie sighed and neatly tapped the top off the soft-boiled egg. 'Baby want a bite?'

'NO BITE!'

'GOOD!' snapped Jennie, and she gulped the egg, shell and all.

Breakfast was disappearing into Nurse, and suddenly Baby wanted some too. 'EAT!' she cried, pointing to the cereal.

Jennie thanked Baby and gobbled up the oatmeal.

'NO EAT!' Baby screamed.

Sendak 1967/1987: 24

Signification in this extract pivots on the Baby's shouted 'EAT!', which in its immediate context is an expression of the Baby's desire, but becomes an instruction when Jennie chooses to interpret it as such. Subsequently, 'NO EAT!', which initially signifies the Baby's act of refusal, shifts to become another instruction. The first line of the extract is itself a succinct example of how context determines meaning. As a discrete utterance, 'Jennie wiped her beard on the rug' would seem to violate two normal social assumptions: female names do not normally collocate with beards, and 'rug' does not belong to the lexical set comprising objects on which beards might be wiped (towel; handkerchief; sleeve; etc.). In such an example, 'correct use in context' extends beyond other nearby words and the grammar which combines them into intelligible form to include the situation of utterance and cultural context. The situation of utterance – the knowledge that Jennie is a dog – clarifies the focus of reference, but at the same time foregrounds how the 'same' utterance can have a very different meaning in different contexts. The instability of reference emerges even when we know Jennie is a dog, because the primary association of *beard* is with human (male) facial hair, and hence is always to some degree figurative when transferred to animals or plants. In such ways, *Higglety Pigglety Pop!* is a richly subversive text, playing on meanings to such an extent as to suggest that if allowed free play, language will tend to be uncontainable by situation, hovering always on the boundary of excess. Such a view of language, however, tends to be uncommon in the domain of children's literature.

The issue of sign/referent relationship is of central interest here because it bears directly on linguistic function in children's fiction and the notion of desirable significances. The assumption that the relationship is direct and unproblematic has the initial effect of producing what might be termed closed meanings. The Tolkien example is especially instructive because it explicitly shows how language which is potentially open, enabling a variety of potential reader responses, is narrowed by paradigmatic recursiveness and essentialism. Writers will, of course, often aim for such specification, but what are the implications if virtually all meaning in a text is implicitly closed? The outcome points to an invisible linguistic control by writer over reader. As Hunt has argued, attempts to exercise such control are much less obvious when conveyed by stylistic features than by lexis or story existents (Hunt 1991: 109).

A related linguistic concept of major importance for the issue of language choice and writerly control is register, the principle which governs the choice among various possible linguistic realisations of the same thing. Register refers to types of language variation which collocate with particular social situations and written genres. Socially, for example, people choose different appropriate language variations for formal and informal occasions, for friendly disputes and angry arguments, and for specialised discourses: science, sport, computing, skipping rope games, role-play, and so on, all have particular registers made up of configurations of lexical and syntactical choices. Narrative fictions will seek to replicate such registers, but also, as with a wide range of writing genres, develop distinctive registers of their own. Genres familiar in children's fiction such as folk and fairy stories, ghost and terror stories, school stories, teen romance, and a host of others – use some readily identifiable registers. Consider the use of register in the following passage from Anna Fienberg's *Ariel, Zed and the Secret of Life*. It describes three girls watching a horror movie, but one of them (Ariel) is giggling:

When the girls looked back at the screen, the scene had changed. It was dusk, and shadows bled over the ground. A moaning wind had sprung up, and somewhere, amongst the trees, an owl hooted.

'Ooh, *look*,' hissed Lynn, her nails digging into her friend Mandy's arm. 'Is that him there, crouching behind that bush? Tell me what happens. I'm not looking any more.'

'The nurse is saying goodnight,' Mandy whispered, 'she's leaving. She'll have to go right past him.'

The Monster From Out of Town was, indeed, breathing heavily behind a camellia bush. His clawed hands crushed flowers to a perfumed pulp, which made you think of what he would do to necks ...

Ariel grinned. The monster's mask was badly made and his costume looked much too tight ...

Fienberg 1992: 9–10

The scene from the movie is presented in the conventional register of the Gothic (dusk, shadows, bled, moaning wind, an owl hooted), though the unusual metaphor 'shadows bled' reconfigures the conventional elements with the effect of foregrounding the Gothic trait of overwording (or semantic overload). By then switching the retelling to the audience's perceptions and responses, Fienberg builds in a common Gothic narrative strategy, that of determining emotional response to scene or incident by building it in as a character's response. The switch also enables a version of the suspense so necessary to horror ('him ... behind that bush'; 'the nurse ... leaving'; 'his clawed hands'). These narrative strategies set up the deflation occurring with Ariel's response and the register shift which expresses it: detached and analytic, she epitomises the resistant reader who refuses the positioning implied by the genre. The deflation has the effect of retrospectively defining how far a genre can depend on its audience's unthinking acceptance of the emotional codes implied by its register.

Fienberg is making an important point about how fiction works (her novel is pervasively metafictive), and it is a point which is well applied to modes of fiction in which register is much less obtrusive. It is easy to assume that realistic fiction is based on a neutral register, though this is not really so, and a stylistic account can help disclose how its registers position readers even more thoroughly than do obvious registers such as that of Gothic. This is readily seen in the tradition of realism in adolescent fiction in the USA, which developed in the 1960s out of a psychology of adolescence based in the work of Erik Erikson re-routed through the textual influence of Salinger's *The Catcher in the Rye*. Thus a first-person, adolescent narrator represents significant issues of adolescent development, such as 'experience of physical sexual maturity, experience of withdrawal from adult benevolent protection, consciousness of self in interaction, re-evaluation of values, [and] experimentation' (Russell 1988: 61). Cultural institutions, genre and style interact with a material effect, not just to code human behaviour but to shape it. A stylistic analysis offers one position from which we can begin to unravel that shaping process. Danziger's *Can You Sue Your Parents for Malpractice?* is thematically focused on the five concepts of adolescent development listed above; most are evident in the following passage:

[Linda] says, 'How can you stop a buffalo from charging?'

'Take away his credit cards,' my mother answers.

My father turns to her. 'You should know that one. Now that you're going back to work, I bet you're going to be spending like mad, living outside my salary.'

'Why don't you just accept it and not feel so threatened?' My mother raises her voice. She hardly ever does that.

I can feel the knot in my stomach and I feel like I'm going to jump out of my skin.

'Who feels threatened?' he yells. 'That's ridiculous. Just because you won't have to depend on me, need me any more, why should I worry?'

So that's why he's acting this way. He thinks it's the money that makes him important. Sometimes I just don't understand his brain.

'Why can't you ever celebrate anything?' she yells again.

I throw my spoon on the table. That's it. I'm leaving.

Linda follows me out. It's like a revolution. Nothing like this has ever happened before.

Danziger 1979/1987: 64

An important part of the register here is the first person and – as often – present tense narration, particularly in so far as it constructs a precise orientation of narrative voice towards a conventional situation. The function of present tense narration is to convey an illusion of immediacy and instanteity, suppressing any suggestion that the outcome is knowable in advance. Thus Lauren, the narrator, proceeds through specific moments of recognition and decision – 'I can feel ...'; 'So that's why ...'; 'That's it. I'm leaving'; 'It's like a revolution' – but each of these moments, as with the depiction of the quarrel itself, is expressed by means of a register which consists of the clichés which pertain to it. Linguistically, this has a double function. It is, now at the other end of the creative spectrum, another use of language which assumes an essential link between sign and referent; and in doing that through cliché it constitutes the text as a surface without depth, an effect reinforced by the way present tense narration severely restricts the possibility of any temporal movement outside the present moment. The outcome, both linguistically and thematically, is a complete closing of meaning: there is no interpretative task for a reader to perform, no inference undrawn. This closure even extends to the joke with which the passage begins.

Another way to describe this is to say that the metonymic mode of writing which characterises realistic fiction, and which enables particular textual moments to relate to a larger signifying structure (Stephens 1992a: 248–249), has been directed towards a closing of meaning. Another aspect of the metonymic process is that a narrative may draw upon recognisable scenes repeatable from one text to another and which constitute a 'register' of metonyms of family life. This example could be categorised as: situation, the parental quarrel; pretext, money; actual focus, power and authority. With perhaps unintentional irony produced by the present tense verb, the repeatability of the scene is foregrounded by Lauren's remark that 'Nothing like this has ever happened before.' It happens all the time, especially in post-1960s realist adolescent fiction, and its function, paradoxically, is to confirm a model whereby the rational individual progresses to maturity under the ideal of liberal individuality, doing so through the assurance that the experience is metonymic of the experience of everybody in that age group.

The presence of a narrative voice which interprets the scene for the benefit of readers is a characteristic of another linguistic aspect of texts, the presentation of scene and incident through the representation of speech and thought and the strategy of focalisation. These are important aspects of point of view in narrative, the facet of narration through which a writer implicitly, but powerfully, controls how readers understand the text. Because readers are willing to surrender themselves to the flow of the discourse, especially by focusing attention on story or content, they are susceptible to the implicit power of point of view. Linguistically, point of view is established by focalisation strategies and by conversational pragmatics. The first is illustrated in the following passage from Paula Fox's *How Many Miles to Babylon?*, which exemplifies a common textual strategy in children's fiction, the narration of incidents as they impact on the mind of a single focalising character. Most novels which are third-person narrations include at least one focalising character, and this has important implications for the kind of language used, because in the vast majority of books written for children there is only one such focaliser, who is a child (or ersatz child, such as Bilbo in *The Hobbit*). Further, as with first person narrators, readers will tend to align themselves with that focalising character's point of view.

> [James] *knew* he shouldn't go into the house – it wasn't his house. But that wasn't the reason why he wanted the street to be empty when he walked up the little path. What he knew and what he felt were two different things. He felt that going into that house had to be something he did secretly, as though it were night and he moved among shadows.
>
> The door was open enough to let him slip in without pushing it. Sunlight didn't penetrate the dirty windows, so he stood still until his eyes grew accustomed to the darkness. Then, as he smelled the dusty old rooms and the dampness of the wallpaper that was peeling off the walls, other things he felt came swimming towards him through the gloom like fish.
>
> Fox 1967/1972: 28

The text is shaped by the presence of represented thought and by direct or implied acts of perception. The narrative representation of thought – marked here by the verbs 'knew' and 'felt' – situates events within the character's mind but also enables a separate narrating voice. This narration is always evident here in such aspects of register as the quite complex left-branching syntax of the final sentence and lexical items such as 'penetrate' and 'accustomed', and by the use of analogies and figurative language. James is a 10-year-old, whose own linguistic level is shown to be a scant competence with a *Dick and Jane* reader (20), and there is no evident attempt at this moment to match linguistic level of narrative discourse to that of the character, though that does often happen. There is, nevertheless, an obvious contrast with the Danziger passage, which, despite having a much older main character (14), has access to a more limited range of registers. Figurative language is likewise less complex. Lauren's 'I can feel the knot in my stomach and I feel like I'm going to jump out of my skin' are cliché analogies, whereas in 'other things he felt came swimming towards him through the gloom like fish' the ground of the concrete/abstract comparison foregrounds the double meanings of 'swimming' and 'gloom', opening out the space between sign and referent and giving readers an opportunity to draw inferences which are not fully determined by the text but have room to include more personal associations.

The last sentence of the Fox extract is unusual in its complexity, however, because complex sentences, especially in conjunction with complex focalisation, tend rather to be the province of more difficult Young Adult fiction. In general, most fiction for children up to early adolescence is characterised by a lexis and grammar simplified relative to the notional audience: sentences are right-branching, and within them clauses are mainly linked by coordination, temporality or causality; and the use of qualifiers and figurative language is restricted. Even the passage cited from *Low Tide*, which has a very subtle effect (and Mayne is often thought of as a writer of 'difficult' texts), is entirely right-branching and contains very few qualifiers. There, as elsewhere, subtlety depends on textual strategies which open, rather than close off, signification.

The second linguistic construction of point of view is by means of represented conversation. Various modes are available to a writer (see Leech and Short 1981), and all appear in children's fiction. These modes range from reported speech acts, which are mainly an aspect of narrative, to direct speech dialogues, which readers must interpret in the light of their knowledge of the principles and conventions of conversation. Because the intermediate forms of indirect and free indirect speech representation allow both for subtle interplay between narratorial and character points of view and for narratorial control, they have tended to receive most attention in discussions of general fiction. With children's fiction, however, more attention needs to be paid to direct speech dialogue, both because it exists in a higher proportion and because of the general principle that the narrator in the text appears to have less control over point of view in dialogue. Leech and Short envisage a cline running between 'bound' and 'free' forms, where 'free' corresponds with closeness to direct speech (324). But point of view in such conversations is affected by two factors: the presence of narratorial framing, especially speech-reporting tags, that is, the devices for identifying speakers which may in themselves suggest attitudes; and the pragmatic principles which shape conversation. The following passage illustrates these factors.

When they reached [the others] they slipped in behind Rebecca and Sue Stephens, and Juniper saw Ellie standing on the pavement buttoned up in her old red coat, Jake beside her. They waved and smiled.

'Your mum looks like … a pop star,' said Sue.

'No, someone in a TV series,' said Rebecca.

'It must be strange to have a mother looking like that,' went on Sue, still staring behind her.

'How would I know? I've only had her, haven't I? I don't know any different mother, so I don't know if it's strange or not.'

Sue kept on:

'Is that your dad? That one with the beard?'

'Shut up,' hissed Rebecca, then said very loudly and clearly, 'I liked your reading, Juniper. You were the best.'

'You sounded dead miserable but your arm didn't show. Nobody could tell. I expect Sir picked you because of being sorry for you. He's like that. What did you say?' asked Sue.

'I said Abbledy, Gabbledy Flook,' answered Juniper and then under her breath, Ere the sun begins to sink, May your nasty face all shrink, which came into her head out of nowhere, and wished herself away to a wide, pale beach with the sun shining down and a white horse galloping at the edge of the incoming tide, far, far away from the wind slicing down the pavement blowing up grit and rubbish as they made their way back to school.

Kemp 1982: 78–79

This exchange shows very clearly how meaning in conversations arises not from the simple sense of individual utterances but from the tenor of utterances in combination and as shaped by narratorial tagging. It also illustrates how a children's book makes use of the main principles which inform actual or represented conversations: the principle of cooperation, the principle of politeness and the principle of irony. In order to communicate in an orderly and productive way speakers accept five conventions which organise what we say to one another: an utterance should be of an appropriate size; it should be correct or truthful; it should relate back to the previous speaker's utterance (a change of subject and a change of register may both be breaches of relation); it should be clear, organised and unambiguous; and each speaker should have a fair share of the conversation, that is, be able to take his or her turn in an orderly way and be able to complete what s/he wants to say (Leech 1983; Stephens 1992b: 76–96). These conventions are very readily broken, and much of everyday conversation depends on simultaneously recognising and breaking one or more of them. In particular, many breaches are prompted by the operation of politeness in social exchange. Whenever conversational principles are breached, the product is apt to be humour, irony or conflict.

After a sequence of four utterances which more or less adhere to the principles of coherence and turn taking, but skirt the boundaries of politeness by drawing attention to Ellie's unusual appearance (shabby but beautiful, she doesn't conform to the girls' image of 'mother'), Kemp introduces a sequence built on crucial breaches of relation and politeness, beginning with Sue's 'Is that your dad?'. This is flagged contextually because readers know that Juniper's father is missing, and textually because of the cline in the speech reporting tags from the neutral 'said Sue' to the intrusively persistent 'Sue kept on', and the heavy tagging of Rebecca's interruption and shift of relation ('hissed Rebecca, then said very loudly and clearly'). Finally, of course, Juniper's escapist daydream cliché also serves as a narratorial comment on how painful she has found the exchange: indeed, the blowing 'grit and rubbish' becomes a metonym for the anguish at the heart of her being. Second, Sue's response to Rebecca's intervention is to apparently pursue relation but to breach politeness by turning attention to Juniper's missing arm. The upshot is Juniper's final spoken utterance – interrupting, impolite and nonsensical, it terminates the exchange and the discourse shifts into represented thought. Such an astute use of conversational principles is one of the most expressive linguistic tools available to a children's writer.

A stylistic examination of children's fiction can show us something very important, namely that a fiction with a high proportion of conversation and a moderately sophisticated use of focalisation has access to textual strategies with the potential to offset the limitations which may be implicit in a disinclination to employ the full range of lexical, syntactic and figurative possibilities of written discourse. But stylistic analysis is also never an end in itself, and is best carried out within a frame which considers the relationship of text to genre and to culture. Obviously enough, stylistics alone cannot determine the relative merits of Sue and Rebecca's preferences for 'a pop star' or 'someone in a TV series', and cannot determine whether a reader treats either category as prestigious or feels that both consign Ellie to a subject position without selfhood. The example illustrates two general principles in language analysis: that significance is influenced by the larger contexts of text and culture within which particular utterances are meaningful; and that particular language features or effects can have more than one function, simultaneously expressing both purposiveness and implicit, often unexamined, social assumptions.

Finally, attention to the language of children's fiction has an important implication for evaluation, adding another dimension to the practices of judging books according to their entertainment value as stories or to their socio-political correctness. It can be an important tool in distinguishing between 'restrictive texts' which allow little scope for active reader judgements (Hunt 1991: 117) and texts which enable critical and thoughtful responses.

References

Danziger, P. (1979/1987) *Can You Sue Your Parents for Malpractice?*, London: Pan.
Fairclough, N. (1989) *Language and Power*, London and New York: Longman.
Fienberg, A. (1992) *Ariel, Zed and the Secret of Life*, Sydney: Allen and Unwin.
Fox, P. (1967/1972) *How Many Miles to Babylon?*, Harmondsworth: Puffin.
Hamilton, V. (1976) *Arilla Sun Down*, London: Hamish Hamilton.
Hunt, P. (1991) *Criticism, Theory, and Children's Literature*, Oxford: Basil Blackwell.
Hunter, M. (1976) *Talent Is Not Enough*, New York: Harper and Row.
Kemp, G. (1986/1988) *Juniper*, Harmondsworth: Puffin.
Leech, G. N. (1983) *Principles of Pragmatics*, London and New York: Longman.
—— and Short, M. H. (1981) *Style in Fiction*, London and New York: Longman.
Mayne, W. (1992) *Low Tide*, London: Cape.

Russell, D. A. (1988) 'The common experience of adolescence: a requisite for the development of young adult literature, *Journal of Youth Services in Libraries* 2: 58–63.

Scholes, R. (1985) *Textual Power: Literary Theory and the Teaching of English*, New Haven and London: Yale University Press.

Sendak, M. (1967/1984) *Higglety Pigglety Pop! or There Must be More to Life*, Harmondsworth: Puffin.

Stephens, J. (1992a) *Language and Ideology in Children's Fiction*, London and New York: Longman.

—— (1992b) *Reading the Signs: Sense and Significance in Written Texts*, Sydney: Kangaroo Press.

Sullivan, C. W. III (1985) 'J. R. R. Tolkien's *The Hobbit*: the magic of words', in Nodelman, P. (ed.) *Touchstones: Reflections on the Best in Children's Literature*, vol. 1, West Lafayette, IN: Children's Literature Association.

Tolkien, J. R. R. (1937/1987) *The Hobbit*, London: Unwin Hyman.

Further Reading

Billman, C. (1979) 'Verbal creativity in children's literature', *English Quarterly* 12: 25–32.

Hunt, P. (1978) 'The cliché count: a practical aid for the selection of books for children', *Children's Literature in Education* 9, 3: 143–150.

—— (1988) 'Degrees of control: stylistics and the discourse of children's literature', in Coupland, N. (ed.) *Styles of Discourse*, London: Croom Helm.

Knowles, M., and Malmjoer, K. (1996) *Language and Control in Children's Literature*, London: Routledge.

Kuskin, K. (1980) 'The language of children's literature', in Michaels, L. and Ricks, C. (eds) *The State of the Language*, Berkeley: University of California Press.

Stephens, J. (1989) 'Language, discourse, picture books', *Children's Literature Association Quarterly* 14: 106–110.

6 Decoding the Images: Illustration and Picture Books

Perry Nodelman

This is Mr Gumpy.

From *Mr Gumpy's Outing* by John Burningham. Copyright ©1971 John Burningham. Reprinted by permission of Jonathan Cape and Henry Holt and Co. Inc.

Editor's introduction

The picture-book genre is a paradox. On the one hand it is seen as children's literature's one truly original contribution to literature in general, a 'polyphonic' form which absorbs and uses many codes, styles, and textual devices, and which frequently pushes at the borders of convention. On the other, it is seen as the province of the young child, and is therefore beneath serious critical notice. Taking this second view, it may seem unlikely that someone can write a 6,000-word chapter on a single picture from a picture-book. But Perry Nodelman's fascinating analysis of the first picture in John Burningham's *Mr Gumpy's Outing* demonstrates not only how much there is to say about a picture, but also how much there is to learn about reading pictures.

P. H.

I open a book. I see a picture of a man, standing on a path in front of a house. Under the picture, printed words appear: 'This', they tell me, 'is Mr Gumpy.'

What could be more straightforward, more easily understood? And for good reason: the book, John Burningham's *Mr Gumpy's Outing* (1970), is intended for the least experienced of audiences – young children; and therefore, it is a 'picture book', a combination of verbal texts and visual images. We provide children with books like this on the assumption that pictures communicate more naturally and more directly than words, and thus help young readers make sense of the texts they accompany.

But are pictures so readily understood? And are picture books really so straightforward? If I try for a moment to look at the picture of Mr Gumpy without engaging my usual assumptions, I realise that I'm taking much about it for granted.

Burningham's image does in some way actually resemble a man, as the words 'man' or 'Mr Gumpy' do not; it is what linguists identify as an 'iconic' representation, whereas the words are 'symbolic', arbitrary sounds or written marks which stand for something they do not resemble. Nevertheless, if I didn't know that what I'm actually looking at – marks on a page – represented something else, I would see nothing in the picture but meaningless patches of colour. I need some general understanding of what pictures are before I can read these patches as a person, apparently named Mr Gumpy, living in a real or fictional world which exists somewhere else, outside the picture.

Even so, my previous knowledge of pictures leads me to assume that this man is different from his image. He is not four inches tall. He is not flat and two-dimensional. His eyes are not small black dots, his mouth not a thin black crescent. His skin is not paper-white, nor scored with thin orange lines. I translate these qualities of the image into the objects they represent, and assume that the four-inch figure 'is' a man of normal height, the orange lines on white merely normal skin.

But before I can translate the lines into skin, I must know what skin is, and what it looks like. I must have a pre-existing knowledge of actual objects to understand which qualities of representations, like the orange colour here, do resemble those of the represented objects, and which, like the lines here, are merely features of the medium or style of representation, and therefore to be ignored.

For the same reason, I must assume that the sky I see above the man does not end a few inches above his head – that this is a border, an edge to the depiction, but not a representation of an edge in the world depicted. And I must realise that the house is not smaller than the man and attached to his arm, but merely at some distance behind him in the imaginary space the picture implies.

But now, perhaps, I'm exaggerating the degree to which the picture requires my previous knowledge of pictorial conventions? After all, more distant real objects do appear to us to be smaller than closer ones. But while that's true, it's also true that artists have been interested in trying to record that fact – what we call perspective – only since the Renaissance, and then mostly in Europe and European-influenced cultures. Not all pictures try to represent perspective, and it takes a culture-bound prejudice to look at visual images expecting to find perspective and therefore, knowing how to interpret it.

Children must learn these prejudices before they can make sense of this picture. Those who can accurately interpret the relative size of Mr Gumpy and the house do so on the expectation that the picture represents the way things do actually appear to a viewer. Applying that expectation might lead a viewer to be confused by Burningham's depiction of Mr Gumpy's eyes. These small black dots evoke a different style of representation, caricature, which conveys visual information by means of simplified exaggeration rather than resemblance. In order to make sense of this apparently straightforward picture, then, I must have knowledge of differing styles and their differing purposes, and perform the complex operation of interpreting different parts of the pictures in different ways.

So far I've dealt with my understanding of this image, and ignored the fact that I enjoy looking at it. I do; and my pleasure seems to be emotional rather than intellectual – a sensuous engagement with the colours, shapes, and textures that leads me to agree with Brian Alderson (1990: 114), when he names *Mr Gumpy's Outing* as one of 'those picture books which have no ambitions beyond conveying simple delight'. But Alderson forgets the extent to which experiencing that simple delight depends on still further complex and highly sophisticated assumptions about what pictures do and how viewers should respond to them.

These particular assumptions are especially relevant in considering art intended for children. Ruskin famously suggested in 1857 that taking sensuous pleasure in pictures requires adults to regain an 'innocence of the eye' he described as 'childish' (quoted in Herbert 1964: 2). The implication is that children themselves, not having yet learned the supposedly counterproductive sophistication that leads adults to view pictures only in terms of their potential to convey information, are automatically in possession of innocent eyes, automatically capable of taking spontaneous delight in the colours and textures of pictures.

But according to W. J. T. Mitchell (1986: 118), 'This sort of "pure" visual perception, freed from concerns with function, use, and labels, is perhaps the most highly sophisticated sort of seeing that we do; it is not the "natural" thing that the eye does (whatever that would be). The "innocent eye" is a metaphor for a highly experienced and cultivated sort of vision.' Indeed, I suspect my own pleasure in the way Burningham captures effects of light falling on grass and bricks relates strongly to the impressionist tradition the picture evokes for me – a tradition that built a whole morality upon the pleasure viewers could and should take in just such effects.

Could I have the pleasure innocently, without the knowledge of impressionism? I suspect not; as Arthur Danto asserts (1992: 431), 'To see something as art requires something the eye cannot descry – an atmosphere of artistic theory, a knowledge of the history of art: an artworld'. The 'simple delight' sophisticated adults like Brian Alderson and me take in this picture is not likely to be shared by children unaware of the ethical value of an 'innocent eye', untutored in the 'artworld'.

Nor is the picture the only thing I've read in the context of previous assumptions. There are also the words. 'This is Mr Gumpy', they say. But *what* is, exactly? The paper page I'm looking at? The entire image I see on it? Of course not – but I must know conventions of picture captioning to realise that these words are pointing me towards a perusal of the contents of the image, in order to find somewhere within it a depiction of the specific object named.

And besides, just *who* is telling me that this is Mr Gumpy? It's possible, even logical, that the speaker is the person in the picture – as it is, for instance, when we watch TV news broadcasts; and then, perhaps, he's telling us that Mr Gumpy is the name of the watering can he's holding? It's my prior knowledge of the narrative conventions of picture books that leads me to assume that the speaker is not the figure depicted but someone else, a narrator rather than a character in the story, and that the human being depicted is the important object in the picture, and therefore the most likely candidate to be 'Mr Gumpy'.

As does in fact turn out to be the case – but only for those who know the most elementary conventions of reading books: that the front of the book is the cover with the bound edge on the left, and that the pages must be looked at in a certain order, across each double-page spread from left to right and then a turn to the page on the other side of the right-hand sheet. And of course, these conventions do not operate for books printed in Israel or Japan, even if those books contain only pictures, and no Hebrew or Japanese words.

In other words: picture books like *Mr Gumpy's Outing* convey 'simple delight' by surprisingly complex means, and communicate only within a network of conventions and assumptions, about visual and verbal representations and about the real objects they represent. Picture books in general, and all their various components, are what semioticians call 'signs' – in Umberto Eco's words (1985: 176), 'something [which] stands to somebody for something else in some respect or capacity'.

The most significant fact about such representations is the degree to which we take them for granted. Both adults and children do see books like *Mr Gumpy* as simple, even obvious, and as I discovered myself in the exercise I report above, it takes effort to become aware of the arbitrary conventions and distinctions we unconsciously take for granted, to see the degree to which that which seems simply natural is complex and artificial.

It's for that reason that such exercises are so important, and that thinking of picture books in semiotic terms is our most valuable tool in coming to understand them. According to Marshall Blonsky, 'The semiotic "head", or eye, sees the world as an immense message, replete with signs that can and do deceive us and lie about the world's condition' (1985: vii). Because we assume that pictures, as iconic signs, do in some significant way actually resemble what they depict, they invite us to see objects *as* the pictures depict them – to see the actual in terms of the fictional visualisation of it.

Indeed, this dynamic is the essence of picture books. The pictures 'illustrate' the texts – that is, they purport to show us what is meant by the words, so that we come to understand the objects and actions the words refer to in terms of the qualities of the images that accompany them – the world outside the book in terms of the visual images within it. In persuading us that they do represent the actual world in a simple and obvious fashion, picture books are particularly powerful deceivers.

Furthermore, the intended audience of picture books is by definition inexperienced – in need of learning how to think about their world, how to see and understand themselves and others. Consequently, picture books are a significant means by which we integrate young children into the ideology of our culture.

As John Stephens suggests, 'Ideologies ... are not necessarily undesirable, and in the sense of a system of beliefs by which we make sense of the world, social life would be impossible without them' (1992: 8). But that does not mean that all aspects of social life are equally desirable, nor that all the ideology conveyed by picture books is equally acceptable. Picture books can and do often encourage children to take for granted views of reality that many adults find objectionable. It is for this reason above all that we need to make ourselves aware of the complex significations of the apparently simple and obvious words and pictures of a book like *Mr Gumpy's Outing*. As Blonsky says, 'Seeing the world as signs able to deceive, semiotics should teach the necessity to fix onto *every* fact, even the most mundane, and ask, "What do you mean?" ' (1985: xxvii).

What, then, do John Burningham's picture and text mean? What have I been lead to assume is 'natural' in agreeing that this *is*, in fact, Mr Gumpy?

Most obviously, I've accepted that what matters most about the picture is the human being in it: it encourages a not particularly surprising species–centricity. But it does so by establishing a hierarchic relationship among the objects depicted: only one of them is important enough to be named by the text, and so require more attention from the viewer. Intriguingly, young children tend to scan a picture with equal attention to all parts; the ability to pick out and focus on the human at the centre is therefore a learned activity, and one that reinforces important cultural assumptions, not just about the relative value of particular objects, but also about the general assumption that objects do indeed have different values and do therefore require different degrees of attention.

Not surprisingly, both the text and the picture place the human depicted within a social context. He is *Mr* Gumpy, male and adult, his authority signalled by the fact that he is known only by his title and last name and that he wears the sort of jacket which represents business-like adult behaviour. The jacket disappears in the central portions of the book, as visual evidence that Mr Gumpy's boat trip is a vacation from business as usual, during which the normal conventions are relaxed. Then, at the end, Mr Gumpy wears an even fancier jacket as host at a tea party which, like the meals provided to children by adults at the end of children's stories from 'Little Red Riding Hood' through Potter's *Peter Rabbit* (1902) and Sendak's *Where the Wild Things Are* (1963), confirms the benefits for children of an adult's authority.

But despite the absence of this visual sign of his authority in many of the pictures, Mr Gumpy always remains *Mr* Gumpy in the text – and he is always undeniably in charge of the children and animals who ask to accompany him on his ride, always entitled to make the rules for them. Apparently, then, his authority transcends the symbolism of the jacket, which might be donned by anybody and therefore represents the status resident in a position rather than the power attached to an individual person. Mr Gumpy's authority must then emerge from the only other things we know about him: that he is male and adult, and that as the text makes a point of telling us, he 'owned' the boat.

Apparently it is more important for us to know this than anything about Mr Gumpy's marital status or past history or occupation – about all of which the text is silent. Both by making ownership significant and by taking it for granted that adult male owners have the right to make rules for children and animals, who don't and presumably can't own boats, the book clearly implies a social hierarchy.

Nor is this the only way in which it supports conventional values. A later picture shows us that one of the children, the one with long hair, wears a pink dress, while the other has short hair and wears shorts and a top. In terms of the behaviour of actual children, both might be girls; but a repertoire of conventional visual codes would lead most viewers to assume that the child in shorts is male – just as we assume that trouser-wearing figures on signs signal men's washrooms, skirt-wearing figures women's washrooms. But whether male or not, the wearer of shorts behaves differently from the wearer of the dress. A later picture of the aftermath of a boating accident shows the one wet child in shorts sensibly topless, the other equally wet child still modestly sodden in her dress. This picture takes for granted and so confirms that traditionally female attire requires traditionally constraining feminine behaviour.

The story revolves around Mr Gumpy eliciting promises that the children not squabble, the cat not chase the rabbit, and so on, before he allows them on to his boat; the creatures break their promises, and the boat tips. My knowledge of the didactic impulse behind most picture book stories leads me to expect that an ethical judgement is about to be made: either Mr Gumpy was wrong to demand these promises, or the children and animals were wrong to make them.

Curiously, however, the book implies no such judgement. The pictures, which show Mr Gumpy as a soft, round man with a pleasant, bland face, suggest that he is anything but the sort of unreasonable disciplinarian we ought to despise; and even though the breaking of promises leads to a spill, nothing is said or shown to insist that we should make a negative judgement of the children and animals. After all, exactly such outbreaks of anarchy are the main source of pleasure in most stories for young children, and therefore to be enjoyed at least as much as condemned. Mr Gumpy himself is so little bothered that he rewards the miscreants with a meal, and even an invitation to come for another ride.

Not accidentally, furthermore, the promises all relate to behaviour so stereotypical as to seem inevitable: in the world as we most often represent it to children in books, on TV, and elsewhere, cats always chase rabbits – and children always squabble. In centring on their inability to act differently, and the fun of the confusion that ensues when they don't, this story reinforces both the validity of the stereotypes and the more general (and again, conservative) conviction that variation from type is unlikely.

But why, then, would Mr Gumpy elicit promises which, it seems, could not be kept? This too the text is silent on; but the silence allows us to become aware that his asking the children and animals to do what they are not sensible enough to do reinforces the story's unspoken but firm insistence on his right to have authority over them. If they ever did mature enough to keep their word, then we couldn't so blindly assume they were unwise enough to need his leadership. Someone else might be wearing that jacket at the final tea party.

Mr Gumpy's Outing thus reinforces for its implied young readers a not uncommon set of ideas about the similarity of children to animals, the inevitability of child-like irresponsibility in both, and the resultant need for adult authority. In accepting all this as natural, readers of *Mr Gumpy's Outing* and many other apparently 'simple' picture books gain complex knowledge, not just of the world they live in, but also of the place they occupy as individual beings within it – their sense of who they are.

This latter is important enough to deserve further exploration. Like most narrative, picture book stories most forcefully guide readers into culturally acceptable ideas about who they are through the privileging of the point of view from which they report on the events they describe. Knowing only what can be known from that perspective, we readers tend to assume it ourselves – to see and understand events and people as the narrative invites us to see them. Ideological theorists call such narrative perspectives 'subject positions': in occupying them, readers are provided with ways of understanding their own subjectivity – their selfhood or individuality. But, as John Stephens suggests, 'in taking up a position from which the text is most readily intelligible, [readers] are apt to be situated within the frame of the text's ideology; that is, they are subjected to and by that ideology' (1992: 67).

All stories imply subject positions for readers to occupy. Because picture books do so with pictures as well as words, their subject positions have much in common with what Christian Metz (1982) outlines as the one films offer their viewers. The pictures in both offer viewers a position of power. They exist only so that we can look at them: they invite us to observe – and to observe what, in its very nature as a representation, cannot observe us back.

In *Mr Gumpy's Outing*, Burningham makes the authority of our viewing position clear in the same way most picture book artists do: by almost always depicting all the characters with their faces turned towards us, even when that makes little sense in terms of the activities depicted. Indeed, the picture in which Mr Gumpy stands with his back to his house while smiling out at us makes sense only in terms of the conventions of photography or portrait painting; as in family snapshots, he is arranged so as to be most meaningfully observable by a (to him) unseen viewer who will be looking at the picture some time after it was made. In confirmation of the relationship between this image and such snapshots, the caption tells us, 'This *is* Mr Gumpy', in the same present tense we use to describe photographic images of events past (for example, 'This *is* me when I *was* a child'). The story that follows switches to the more conventional past tense of narratives.

In making their faces available to an unseen observer, the characters in *Mr Gumpy's Outing* imply, not just the observer's right to gaze, but also their somewhat veiled consciousness of an observer – and therefore, their own passive willingness, even desire, to be gazed at. Like the actors in a play or movie, and like characters in most picture books, they share in a somewhat less aggressive form the invitation to voyeurism that John Berger (1972) discovers in both pin-up photographs and traditional European paintings of nudes. Their implied viewer is a peeping Tom with the right to peep, to linger over details, to enjoy and interpret and make judgements.

But meanwhile, of course, the power such pictures offer is illusory. In allowing us to observe and to interpret, they encourage us to absorb all the codes and conventions, the signs that make them meaningful; they give us the freedom of uninvolved, egocentric observation only in order to enmesh us in a net of cultural constraints that work to control egocentricity. For that reason, they encourage a form of subjectivity that is inherently paradoxical. They demand that their implied viewers see themselves as both free and with their freedom constrained, and both enjoy their illusory egocentric separation from others and yet, in the process, learn to feel guilty about it.

Interestingly, *Mr Gumpy* confirms the central importance of such paradoxes by expressing them, not just in the position of its implied viewer, but also in the ambivalence of its story's resolution. Are we asked to admire or to condemn the children and animals for being triumphantly themselves and not giving in to Mr Gumpy's attempts to constrain them? In either case, does their triumphantly being themselves represent a celebration of individuality, or an anti-individualist conviction that all cats always act alike? And if all cats must always act in a cat-like way, what are we to make of the final scene, in which the animals all sit on chairs like humans and eat and drink out of the kinds of containers humans eat and drink from? Does this last image of animals and children successfully behaving according to adult human standards contradict the apparent message about their inability to do so earlier, or merely reinforce the unquestionable authority of the adult society Mr Gumpy represents throughout?

These unanswerable questions arise from the fact that the story deals with animals who both talk like humans and yet cannot resist bleating like sheep – who act sometimes like humans, sometimes like animals. While such creatures do not exist in reality, they appear frequently in picture books, and the stories about them almost always raise questions like the ones *Mr Gumpy* does. In the conventional world of children's picture books, the state of animals who talk like humans is a metaphor for the state of human childhood, in which children must learn to negotiate between the animal-like urges of their bodily desires and the demands of adults that they repress desire and behave in social acceptable ways – that is, as adult humans do. The strange world in which those who bleat as sheep naturally do, or squabble as children naturally do, must also sit on chairs and drink from teacups, is merely a version of the confusing world children actually live in. *Mr Gumpy* makes that obvious by treating the children as exactly equivalent to the other animals who go on the outing.

The attitude a picture book implies about whether children should act like the animals they naturally are or the civilised social beings adults want them to be is a key marker in identifying it either as a didactic book intended to teach children or as a pleasurable one intended to please them. Stories we identify as didactic encourage children towards acceptable adult behaviour, whereas pleasurable ones encourage their indulgence in what we see as natural behaviour. But of course, both types are didactic.

The first is more obviously so because it invites children to stop being 'child-like'. In the same way as much traditional adult literature assumes that normal behaviour is that typical of white middle-class males like those who authored it, this sort of children's story defines essentially human values and acceptably human behaviour as that of adults like those who produce it.

But books in the second category teach children *how* to be child-like, through what commentators like Jacqueline Rose (1984) and myself (1992) have identified as a process of colonisation: adults write books for children to persuade them of conceptions of themselves as children that suit adult needs and purposes. One such image is the intractable, anti-social self-indulgence that Mr Gumpy so assertively forbids and so passively accepts from his passengers. It affirms the inevitability and desirability of a sort of animal-likeness – and child-likeness – that both allows adults to indulge in nostalgia for the not-yet-civilised and keeps children other than, less sensible than, and therefore deserving of less power than, adults.

That picture books like *Mr Gumpy* play a part in the educative processes I've outlined here is merely inevitable. Like all human productions, they are enmeshed in the ideology of the culture that produced them, and the childlikeness they teach is merely what our culture views as natural in children. But as a form of representation which conveys information by means of both words and pictures, picture books evoke (and teach) a complex set of intersecting sign systems. For that reason, understanding of them can by enriched by knowledge from a variety of intellectual disciplines.

Psychological research into picture perception can help us understand the ways in which human beings – and particularly children – see and make sense of pictures; Evelyn Goldsmith (1984) provides a fine summary of much of the relevant research in this area. The *gestalt* psychologist Rudolph Arnheim (1974: 11) provides a particularly useful outline of ways in which the composition of pictures influences our understanding of what they depict, especially in terms of what he calls 'the interplay of directed tensions' among the objects depicted. Arnheim argues (11) that 'these tensions are as inherent in any precept as size, shape, location, or colour', but it can be argued that they might just as logically be viewed as signs – culturally engendered codes rather than forces inherent in nature.

In either case, the relationships among the objects in a picture create variations in 'visual weight': weightier objects attract our attention more than others. In the picture of Mr Gumpy in front of his house, for instance, the figure of Mr Gumpy has great weight because of its position in the middle of the picture, its relatively large size, and its mostly white colour, which makes it stand out from the darker surfaces surrounding it. If we think of the picture in terms of the three-dimensional space it implies, the figure of Mr Gumpy gains more weight through its frontal position, which causes it to overlap less important objects like the house, and because it stands over the focal point of the perspective. Meanwhile, however, the bright red colour of the house, and the arrow shape created by the path leading toward it, focus some attention on the house; and there is an interplay of tensions amongst the similarly blue sky, blue flowers and blue trousers, the similarly arched doorway and round-shouldered Mr Gumpy. Analysis of such compositional features can reveal much about how pictures cause us to interpret the relationships among the objects they represent.

Visual objects can have other kinds of meanings also: for a knowledgeable viewer, for instance, an object shaped like a cross can evoke Christian sentiments. Because picture books have the purpose of conveying complex information by visual means, they tend to refer to a wide range of visual symbolisms, and can sometimes be illuminated by knowledge of everything from the iconography of classical art to the semiotics of contemporary advertising. Consider, for instance, how the specific house Burningham provides Mr Gumpy conveys, to those familiar with the implications of architectural style, both an atmosphere of rural peacefulness and a sense of middle-class respectability.

Furthermore, anyone familiar with Freudian or Jungian psychoanalytical theory and their focus on the unconscious meanings of visual images will find ample material for analysis in picture books. There may be Freudian implications of phallic power in Mr Gumpy's punt pole, carefully placed in the first picture of him on his boat so that it almost appears to emerge from his crotch; in the later picture of the aftermath of the disastrous accident, there is nothing in front of Mr Gumpy's crotch but a length of limp rope. Meanwhile, Jungians might focus on the archetypal resonances of the watering can Mr Gumpy holds in the first few pictures, its spout positioned at the same angle as the punt pole in the picture that follows and the teapot he holds in the last picture, its spout also at the same angle. The fact that this story of a voyage over and into water begins and ends with Mr Gumpy holding objects that carry liquid, and thus takes him from providing sustenance for plants to providing sustenance for other humans and animals, might well suggest a complex tale of psychic and/or social integration.

Nor is it only the individual objects in pictures that have meaning: pictures as a whole can also express moods and meanings, through their use of already existing visual styles which convey information to viewers who know art history. Styles identified with specific individuals, or with whole periods or cultures, can evoke not just what they might have meant for their original viewers, but also, what those individuals or periods or cultures have come to mean to us. Thus, Burningham's pictures of Mr Gumpy suggest both the style of impressionism and the bucolic peacefulness that it now tends to signify.

In addition to disciplines which focus on pictures, there has been an extensive theoretical discussion of the relationships between pictures and words which is especially important in the study of picture books. Most studies in this area still focus on the differences Lessing (1776/1969) pointed out centuries ago in *Laocoön*: visual representations are better suited to depicting the appearance of objects in spaces, words to depicting the action of objects in time. In a picture book like *Mr Gumpy*, therefore, the text sensibly says nothing about the appearance of Mr Gumpy or his boat, and the pictures are incapable of actually moving as a boat or an animal does.

But pictures can and do provide information about sequential activity. In carefully choosing the best moment of stopped time to depict, and the most communicative compositional tensions among the objects depicted, Burningham can clearly convey the action of a boat tipping, what actions led the characters to take the fixed positions they are shown to occupy, and what further actions will result. Furthermore, the sequential pictures of a picture book imply all the actions that would take the character from the fixed position depicted in one picture to the fixed position in the next – from not quite having fallen into the water in one picture to already drying on the bank in the next. Indeed, it is this ability to imply unseen actions and the passage of time that allow the pictures in picture books to play the important part they do in the telling of stories.

Nevertheless, the actions implied by pictures are never the same as those named in words. The bland statement of Burningham's text, 'and into the water they fell', hardly begins to cover the rich array of actions and responses the picture of the boat tipping lays out for us. W. J. T. Mitchell (1986: 44) concludes that the relationship between pictures and accompanying texts is 'a complex one of mutual translation, interpretation, illustration, and enlightenment'. Once more, *Mr Gumpy's Outing* reveals just how complex.

Burningham's text on its own without these pictures would describe actions by characters with no character: it takes the pictures and a knowledge of visual codes to read meaning into these simple actions. Without a text, meanwhile, the pictures of animals that make up most of the book would seem only a set of portraits, perhaps illustrations for an informational guide to animals. Only the text reveals that the animals can talk, and that it is their desire to get on the boat. Indeed, the exact same pictures could easily support a different text, one about Mr Gumpy choosing to bring speechless animals on board until the boat sinks from their weight and he learns a lesson about greed. So the pictures provide information about the actions described in the words; and at the same time, the words provide information about the appearances shown in the pictures.

If we look carefully, in fact, the words in picture books always tell us that things are not merely as they appear in the pictures, and the pictures always show us that events are not exactly as the words describe them. Picture books are inherently ironic, therefore: a key pleasure they offer is a perception of the differences in the information offered by pictures and texts.

Such differences both make the information richer and cast doubt on the truthfulness of both of the means which convey it. The latter is particular significant: in their very nature, picture books work to make their audiences aware of the limitations and distortions in their representations of the world. Close attention to picture books automatically turns readers into semioticians. For young children as well as for adult theorists, realising that, and learning to become more aware of the distortions in picture book representations, can have two important results.

The first is that it encourages consciousness and appreciation of the cleverness and subtlety of both visual and verbal artists. The more readers and viewers of any age know about the codes of representation, the more they can enjoy the ways in which writers and illustrators use those codes in interesting and involving ways. They might, for instance, notice a variety of visual puns in *Mr Gumpy's Outing*: how the flowers in Burningham's picture of the rabbit are made up of repetitions of the same shapes as the rabbit's eyes, eyelashes and ears, or how his pig's snout is echoed by the snout-shaped tree branch behind it.

The second result of an awareness of signs is even more important: the more both adults and children realise the degree to which all representations misrepresent the world, the less likely they will be to confuse any particular representation with reality, or to be unconsciously influenced by ideologies they have not considered. Making ourselves and our children more conscious of the semiotics of the pictures books through which we show them their world and themselves will allow us to give them the power to negotiate their own subjectivities – surely a more desirable goal than repressing them into conformity to our own views.

References

Alderson, B. (1990) 'Picture book anatomy', *Lion and the Unicorn* 14, 2: 108–114.
Arnheim, R. (1974) *Art and Visual Perception: A Psychology of the Creative Eye*, Berkeley: University of California Press.
Berger, J. (1972) *Ways of Seeing*, London: BBC and Penguin.
Blonsky, M. (1985) *On Signs*, Baltimore: Johns Hopkins University Press.
Burningham, J. (1970) *Mr Gumpy's Outing*, London: Cape.
Danto, A. (1992) 'The artworld', in Alperson, P. (ed.) *The Philosophy of the Visual Arts*, New York and Oxford: Oxford University Press, 426–433.
Eco, U. (1985) 'Producing signs', in Blonsky, M. (ed.) *On Signs*, Baltimore: Johns Hopkins University Press.
Goldsmith, E. (1984) *Research into Illustration: An Approach and a Review*, Cambridge: Cambridge University Press.
Herbert, R. L. (ed.) (1964) *The Art Criticism of John Ruskin*, Garden City, NY: Doubleday Anchor.
Lessing, G. E. (1766/1969) *Laocoön: An Essay upon the Limits of Poetry and Painting*, trans. E. Frothingham, New York: Farrar Straus and Giroux.
Metz, C. (1982) *The Imaginary Signifier: Psychoanalysis and the Cinema*, Bloomington, IN: Indiana University Press.
Mitchell, W. J. T. (1986) *Iconology: Image, Text, Ideology*, Chicago: University of Chicago Press.
Nodelman, P. (1992) 'The other: orientalism, colonialism, and children's literature', *Children's Literature Association Quarterly* 17, 1: 29–35.
Potter, B. (1902) *The Tale of Peter Rabbit*, London: Frederick Warne.
Rose, J. (1984) *The Case of Peter Pan, or The Impossibility of Children's Fiction*, London: Macmillan.
Sendak, M. (1963) *Where the Wild Things Are*, New York: Harper and Row.
Stephens, J. (1992) *Language and Ideology in Children's Fiction*, London and New York: Longman.

Further Reading

Children's Literature 19 (1991). New Haven: Yale University Press. (An issue of this journal devoted to discussions of picture books.)
Gombrich, E. H. (1972) 'Visual image', *Scientific American* 227: 82–94.
Kiefer, B. Z. (1995) *The Potential of Picture Books: From Visual Literacy to Aesthetic Understanding*, Englewood Cliffs, NJ and Columbus, OH: Merrill.
Moebius, W. (1986) 'Introduction to picturebook codes', *Word and Image* 2, 2: 63–66.
Nodelman, P. (1988) *Words About Pictures: The Narrative Art of Children's Picture Books*, Athens, GA: University of Georgia Press.
—— (1992) *The Pleasures of Children's Literature*, New York: Longman.
Schwarcz, J. H. (1982) *Ways of the Illustrator: Visual Communication in Children's Literature*, Chicago: American Library Association.
Schwarcz, J. H. and C. (1991) *The Picture Book Comes of Age*, Chicago and London: American Library Association.

7   Readers, Texts, Contexts: Reader-Response Criticism

Michael Benton

Editor's introduction

Much critical theory stands at one remove from actual books and actual readers. Reader-response criticism, however, engages directly with the knotty problems of how readers understand texts and how we can elicit and interpret individual responses; it is thus particularly relevant to those who see the interaction of child and book as central to children's literature studies. Michael Benton's survey of this complex field includes theories of how children see the process of reading fiction, how children develop as readers of literature, and how texts may be better understood from the point of view of the readers' responses to them.

P. H.

The importance of reader–response criticism in the area of children's literature lies in what it tells us about two fundamental questions, one about the literature and the other about its young readers:

- who is the implied child reader inscribed in the text?
- how do actual child readers respond during the process of reading?

The main advocates of reader–response criticism acknowledge the complementary importance of text and reader. They attend both to the form and language of poem or story, and to the putative reader constructed there, acknowledging, as Henry James put it, that the author makes 'his reader very much as he makes his characters ... When he makes him well, that is makes him interested, then the reader does quite half the labour' (quoted in Booth 1961: 302). Equally, they attend to the covert activity of the reading process, deducing the elements of response from what readers say or write, and/or developing theoretical models of aesthetic experience.

Whatever the particular orientation of the reader–response critic, one central issue recurs: the mystery of what readers actually do and experience. The subject of the reader's response is the Loch Ness Monster of literary studies: when we set out to capture it, we cannot even be sure that it is there at all; and, if we assume that it is, we have to admit that the most sensitive probing with the most sophisticated instruments has so far succeeded only in producing pictures of dubious authenticity. That the nature and dimensions of this phenomenon are so uncertain is perhaps the reason why the hunters are so many and their approaches so various. Accordingly, it is necessary to map the main historical development of reader-response criticism and, second, to outline the theoretical bases which its advocates share, before going on to consider how this perspective – whose concepts have been formulated largely in the area of adult literary experience – has been taken up by researchers interested in young readers and their books.

A Shift of Critical Perspective

In the 1950s the criticism of literature was in a relatively stable state. In *The Mirror and the Lamp* (1953), M. H. Abrams was confidently able to describe 'the total situation' of the work of art as one with the text at the centre with the three elements of the author, the reader, and the signified world ranged like satellites around it. What has happened since has destabilised this model. In particular, reader-response critics have argued that it is readers who make meaning by the activities they perform on texts; they see the reader in the centre and thus the privileged position of the work of art is undermined and individual 'readings' become the focus of attention. This is not to say that the emphasis upon reading and response which emerged in the 1960s was entirely new. It had been initiated famously by I. A. Richards forty years earlier; but Richards's (1924, 1929) seminal work, with its twin concerns of pedagogy and criticism, influenced subsequent developments in criticism in two contrary ways. For, in one sense, Richards privileged the text, and the American New Critics, particularly, seized upon the evidence of *Practical Criticism* to insist that close analysis of the words on the page was the principal job of critic and teacher. Yet, in another sense, Richards privileged the reader; and subsequently, modern reader-response criticism has developed to give the reader freedoms that infuriate text-oriented critics. Hence, Stanley Fish writes: 'Interpretation is not the art of construing but the art of constructing. Interpreters do not decode poems: they make them' (Fish 1980: 327). Or, even more provocatively: 'It is the structure of the reader's experience rather than any structures available on the page that should be the object of description' (152). As Laurence Lerner (1983: 6) has pointed out, perhaps the most important division in contemporary literary studies is between those who see literature as a more or less self-contained system, and those who see it as interacting with real, extra-literary experience (that of the author, or of the reader or the social reality of the author's or the reader's world). Reader-response critics clearly fall within this second category.

Reader-response criticism is difficult to map because of its diversity, especially in two respects: first, there are several important figures whose work stands outside the normal boundaries of the term; and second, there is overlap but not identity in the relationship between German 'reception theory' and Anglo-American reader-response criticism. On the first issue, two highly influential writers, D. W. Harding and Louise Rosenblatt, began publishing work in the 1930s which was ahead of its time (for example, Harding 1937; Rosenblatt 1938/1970) and their explorations of the psychological and affective aspects of literary experience only really began to have an impact upon educational thinking (and hence upon children's experiences of poems and stories in school) when the educational and literary theorists began to rehabilitate the reader in the 1960s and

1970s. Subsequently, Harding's paper on 'Psychological approaches in the reading of fiction' (1962) and Rosenblatt's re-issued *Literature as Exploration* (1938/1970) have been widely regarded as two of the basic texts in this area.

It is an indication of the diversity and loose relationships which characterise response-oriented approaches to literature that Harding and Rosenblatt are reduced to complimentary footnotes in the standard introductions to reader-response criticism (Tompkins, 1980: xxvi; Suleiman and Crosman, 1980: 45; Freund, 1987: 158), and that writers in the German and Anglo-American traditions have, with the notable exception of Iser, little contact with or apparent influence upon one another. In a thorough account of German reception theory, Holub (1984) comments upon this divide and provides an excellent analysis of Iser's work to complement that of Freund (1987), whose book summarises the Anglo-American tradition.

The development of reader-response writings since the 1960s has steadily forged a new relationship between the act of reading and the act of teaching literature which, as is illustrated later, has significant consequences for the way the relationship between young readers and their books is conceptualised. Prior to this time, during the 1940s and 1950s, the reader was hidden from view as the critical landscape was dominated by the American New Criticism, whose adherents took a determinedly anti-reader stance to the extent that, despite a concern for 'close reading', the major statement of New Criticism views – Wellek and Warren's *Theory of Literature* (1949) – makes no mention of the reader and includes only two brief references to 'reading'. Subsequently, the development of reader-response studies has seen the momentum shift periodically from literary theory to educational enquiry and practice almost decade by decade.

The 1960s were dominated by education, with the most influential work published by The National Council of Teachers of English (Squire 1964; Purves and Rippere 1968), culminating in two surveys, one English and the other American (D'Arcy 1973; Purves and Beach 1972). The 1970s saw the full bloom of reader-response theorising by literary critics of whom Holland (1975), Culler (1975), Iser (1978) and Fish (1980) were perhaps the most notable figures, all of whom were well represented in the two compilations of papers that stand as a summary of work in this area at the end of the decade (Suleiman and Crosman 1980; Tompkins 1980). During the 1980s the emphasis moved back to education, where the main concern was to translate what had become known about response – both from literary theory and from classroom enquiry – into principles of good practice. Protherough (1983), Cooper (1985a), Benton and Fox (1985), Scholes (1985), Corcoran and Evans (1987), Benton *et al.* (1988), Dias and Hayhoe (1988), Hayhoe and Parker (1990), Benton (1992a), Many and Cox (1992) have all, in their different ways, considered the implications for practice of a philosophy of literature and learning based upon reader-response principles. In Britain, one of the more heartening results of this development was that the importance of the reader's response to literature was fully acknowledged in the new National Curriculum as embodied in the Cox Report (1989) and in the official documents that ensued. Such has been what one standard book on modern literary theory calls 'the vertiginous rise of reader-response criticism' (Jefferson and Robey, 1986: 142), that its authors see it as threatening to engulf all other approaches.

What are the theoretical bases that such writers share? Reader-response criticism is a broad church as a reading of the various overview books demonstrates (Tompkins, 1980; Suleiman and Crosman, 1980; Freund, 1987). None the less, a number of principles can be said to characterise this critical stance. First is the rejection of the notorious 'affective fallacy'. In describing the 'fallacy' as 'a confusion of the poem and its results', and in dismissing as mere 'impressionism and relativism' any critical judgements based on the psychological effects of literature, Wimsatt and Beardsley (1954/1970) had left no space for the reader to inhabit. They ignored the act of reading. New Criticism, it could be said, invented 'the assumed reader'; by contrast, reader-response criticism deals with real and implied readers. Iser, Holland, Bleich and Fish operate from a philosophical basis that displaces the notion of an autonomous text to be examined in and on its own terms from the centre of critical discussion and substitutes the reader's recreation of that text. Reading is not the discovering of meaning (like some sort of archaeological 'dig') but the creation of it. The purpose of rehearsing this familiar history is its importance for children's reading. The central concerns of response-oriented approaches focus upon

1   what constitutes the source of literary meaning; and
2   what is the nature of the interpretative process that creates it.

Both issues are fundamental to how young readers read, both in and out of school.

The works of Iser on fiction and Rosenblatt on poetry, despite some criticism that Iser has attracted on theoretical grounds, have none the less had greater influence upon the actual teaching of literature and our understanding of children as readers than those of any other theoretical writers. No doubt this is because they avoid what Frank Kermode calls 'free-floating theory' and concentrate, in Iser's words, on 'an analysis of what actually happens when one is reading' (Iser 1978: 19). Iser's theory of aesthetic response (1978) and Rosenblatt's transactional theory of the literary work (1978, 1985) have helped change the culture of the classroom to one which operates on the principle that the text cannot be said to have a meaningful existence outside the relationship between itself and its reader(s). This transfer of power represents a sea-change in critical emphasis and in pedagogical practice from the assumptions most critics and teachers held even a generation ago. Yet it is evolutionary change, not sudden revolution – a progressive rethinking of the way readers create literary experiences for themselves with poems and stories. In fact, reader-response is the evolutionary successor to Leavisite liberal humanism. It is perceived – within the area of literature teaching – as providing a framework of now familiar ideas which are widely accepted and to which other lines of critical activity often make reference: the plurality of meanings within a literary work; the creative participation of the reader; the acknowledgement that the reader is not a *tabula rasa* but brings idiosyncratic knowledge and personal style to the act of reading; and the awareness that interpretation is socially, historically and culturally formed. All these ideas are ones that have had a sharp impact upon the study of texts and upon research into young readers' reading in the field of children's literature.

Young Readers and Their Books

Reader-response approaches to children's literature which set out to answer the questions raised at the beginning of this chapter all have a direct relationship with pedagogy. Some are concerned with children's responses, mainly to fiction and poetry but latterly also to picture books, with the broad aim of improving our understanding of what constitutes good practice in literature teaching. Others employ reader-response methods in order to explore children's concepts and social attitudes. Others again, are text-focused and use concepts and ideas from reader-response criticism of adult literature in order to examine children's books, with the aim of uncovering their implied audience and, thence, something of the singularity of a specifically *children's* literature.

This diversity creates two problems: first, there is bound to be overlap. Many studies cover both textual qualities and children's responses as complementary aspects of a unitary experience which, as the foregoing discussion has argued, follows from the mainstream thinking of reader-response criticism. When considering a study under one or other of the headings below, therefore, its writer's principal orientation has been the guide. Second, there is bound to be anomaly. The nature and complexity of the studies varies greatly. In particular, there are two important collections of papers devoted to theoretical research and empirical enquiries in this area (Cooper 1985a; Many and Cox 1992). These are most conveniently considered between discussion of the first and second themes below to which most of their papers relate.

The discussion deals, in turn, with five themes: the process of responding; development in reading; types of reader behaviour; culturally oriented studies exploring children's attitudes; and text-oriented studies employing reader-response concepts.

The process of responding

The stances of those enquirers who have explored the response processes of young readers vary as much as those of the literary theorists, but the most common one is that of the teacher-researcher attempting to theorise classroom practice. The range and combinations of the variables in these studies are enormous: texts, contexts, readers and research methods are all divisible into subsets with seemingly infinite permutations. Among texts, short stories, poems, fairy tales and picture books are favoured, with a few studies focusing upon the novel and none on plays. Contexts, in the sense of physical surroundings, also influence response. The 'classroom' itself can mean a variety of things and clearly there are crucial differences between say, monitoring the responses of thirty children within normal lesson time and four or five children who volunteer to work outside lessons. Most studies are small-scale enquiries run by individual researchers, perhaps with a collaborative element; hence, the focus is usually narrow when selecting the number, age–level, social background, gender and literacy level of the readers. Finally, reader-response monitoring procedures are generally devised in the knowledge that the medium is the message. The ways readers are asked to present their responses are fundamental influences upon those responses; they range from undirected invitations to free association or 'say what comes into your mind as you read', through various 'prompts' or guideline questions to consider, to the explicit questionnaire. Oral, written, or graphic responses and whether the readers are recording individually or in groups all provide further dimensions to the means of monitoring and collecting response data.

Guidance through this diversity is offered by two older books already mentioned (Purves and Beach 1972; D'Arcy 1973); and, more recently, by Galda (1983) in a special issue of the *Journal of Research and Development in Education* on 'Response to literature: empirical and theoretical studies', and by Squire's chapter 'Research on reader response and the national literature initiative' in Hayhoe and Parker (Squire 1990: 13–24). What follows does not attempt to be exhaustive but briefly to indicate the main lines that process studies have taken.

The process of responding became one of the main objects of enquiry during the 1980s. Studies of children's responses to poetry began to appear in articles or booklet form: Wade (1981) adapted Squire's (1964) work on short stories to compare how a supervised and an unsupervised group of middle-school children responded to a poem by Charles Tomlinson. Dixon and Brown (1984) studied the writings of 17-year-old students in order to identify what was being assessed in their responses; Atkinson (1985) built upon Purves and Rippere's (1968) categories and explored the process of response to poems by children of different ages. Several books also focused exclusively on young readers and poetry and, either wholly or in part, concerned themselves with the response process, notably Benton (1986), Dias and Hayhoe (1988) and Benton *et al.* (1988). The work of Barnes (1976), particularly, lies behind the enquiries of Benton (1986) into small group responses to poetry by 13 to 14-year-olds. What is characterised as 'lightly-structured, self-directed discussion' is seen as the means of optimising group talk about poems and as the most appropriate way for teacher-researchers to explore the process of response. Dias and Hayhoe (1988) build upon Dias's earlier work (1986) to develop responding-aloud protocols (RAPs) which, essentially, require individual pupils to think aloud as they attempt to make sense of a poem with the help, if needed, of a non-directive interviewer. Preparatory group discussions were used to build up confidence for the individual sessions. The RAP transcripts were then analysed to see how pupils negotiated meaning. Dias and Hayhoe claim that their study is 'designed to track the process of responding as it occurs' (1988: 51) and their methodology is a significant contribution to this end.

Similarly, the work of Benton and his co-authors (1988) focuses upon process. It shows three experienced teachers exploring how their students, aged 14 and above, read and respond to poetry. Rosenblatt's transactional theory underpins the approach, especially in Teasey's work which gives the hard evidence for the reader's 'evocation' of a poem through meticulous, descriptive analyses of aesthetic reading. Bell's data shows the emphases of the response process from initial encounter through group discussion, to an eventual written account, in such a way that what in mathematics is called 'the working' can be observed – in this case, the slow evolution over time and in different contexts of how young readers make meaning. Hurst's focus is upon the whole class rather than individuals. From studying the responses of pupils in a variety of classrooms and with different teachers and texts, he develops a model of three frames (story, poet, form), derived from Barnes' and Todd's (1977) notion of the 'cycles of utterances' that characterise group talk, as a means of mapping the episodes of a group's engagement with a poem. The three enquiries are set against a critical appraisal of the main theorists in the field from Richards to Rosenblatt and all contribute to the development of a response-centred methodology.

The process of responding to fictional narrative was first examined by Squire (1964) and Purves and Rippere (1968), whose early studies provoked many adaptations of their work with students of different ages and backgrounds. These studies all tended to categorise the elements of response, with Squire's list emerging as the most commonly quoted and replicated in studies of children's responses. Squire's study of adolescents responding to short stories described the six elements of response as literary judgements, interpretational responses, narrational reactions, associational responses, self-involvement and prescriptive judgements (Squire, 1964: 17–18). He showed that the greater the involvement of readers, the stronger was their tendency to make literary judgements; and that what he termed 'happiness-binding' (41) was a characteristic of adolescent readers' behaviour. Here, as in many studies of fiction reading, there is a noticeable move towards a broadly psychoanalytical explanation for the gratifications readers seek in fiction (compare Holland 1975). More recent studies include those of Fox (1979) whose phrase 'dark watchers' (32) is a memorable description of the imaginary, spectator role that young readers often adopt during reading; and Jackson (1980) who explored the initial responses of children to fiction which later he developed more fully throughout the secondary school age range (Jackson 1983). Several books also focused wholly or in part upon young readers' response processes, notably Protherough (1983), Benton and Fox (1985), and Thomson (1986). Drawing upon enquiries he conducted in Hull, Protherough suggests that there are five major ways in which children see the process of reading fiction: projection into a character, projection into the situation, association between book and reader, the distanced viewer, and detached evaluation. There is a developmental dimension and he argues that maturity in reading is connected with the ability to operate in an increasing number of modes.

Benton and Fox address the question of what happens when we read stories and consider that the process of responding involves the reader in creating a secondary world. This concept is elaborated with reference to children's accounts of their experiences with various stories. The reading experience is then characterised in two ways: first, as a four-phase process of feeling like reading, getting into the story, being lost in the book, and having an increasing sense of an ending; and second, as an activity consisting of four elements – picturing, anticipating and retrospecting, interacting and evaluating. This latter description has been taken up by others, notably Corcoran (Corcoran and Evans, 1987: 45–51).

Thomson's work with teenage readers offers a further description of the elements of response to fiction and cross-hatches this with a developmental model. The requirements for satisfaction at all stages are enjoyment and elementary understanding. Assuming these are met, his six stages are described as: unreflective interest in action, empathising, analogising, reflecting on the significance of events and behaviour, reviewing the whole work as the author's creation, and the consciously considered relationship with the author. Thomson's is a sophisticated and detailed account, firmly rooted in young readers' fiction reading, and drawing effectively upon the theoretical literature summarised earlier in this chapter.

As can be seen from this summary, studies of the process of responding tend towards categorisation of the different psychological activities involved and towards descriptions of what constitutes maturation in reading. Two collections of papers which should contribute more than they do to our understanding of the process of responding are Cooper (1985a) and Many and Cox (1992), although in their defence it has to be said that the former has a focus upon the theories that should guide our study of readers and the research methodologies that derive from them, and the latter is primarily concerned with reader 'stance' (Rosenblatt 1978) as the discussion of types of reader below indicates. Brief comment upon these two collections is appropriate before moving on to consider reading development.

Only some of the seventeen papers in Cooper's compilation bear upon the subject of children and literature. The first of the three parts of the book is helpful in relating theoretical issues of response to practice, especially the chapters by Rosenblatt, Purves and Petrosky. In Part 2, Kintgen's piece stands out, not only because its focus is poetry (a comparative rarity in such company), but because it faces up to the problems of monitoring responses, and attempts to describe the mental activities and processes of the reader. Kintgen's subjects (as with many researchers) are graduate students but the methodology here could readily transfer to younger readers. The four contributors to the final part of the book on classroom literature, whom one might expect to deal with children and their books, studiously avoid doing so, preferring instead to discuss theoretical and methodological issues such as the need to identify response research with literary pedagogy (Bleich), the use of school surveys (Squire), and the evaluation of the outcomes of literary study (Cooper 1985b).

Many and Cox (1992) take their impetus from Cooper's book and their inspiration from Rosenblatt (1978). The first part gives theoretical perspectives on reader stance and response and includes specific consideration of readings of selected children's books (Benton: 1992b) and of young readers' responses (Corcoran). The papers in Part two focus upon students' perspectives when reading and responding and tell us more about types of readers than about process; these are dealt with below. Part three deals with classroom interactions of teachers, students and literature. Hade explores 'stance' in both silent reading and reading aloud, arguing its transactional and triadic nature in the classroom. Zancella writes engagingly about the use of biography, in the sense of a reader's personal history, in responding to literature and how this influences the teacher's methods. Zarrillo and Cox build upon Rosenblatt's efferent/aesthetic distinction and urge more of the latter in classroom teaching in the light of their empirical findings that 'elementary teachers tend to direct children to adopt efferent stances towards literature' (245). Many and Wiseman take a similar line and report their enquiries into teaching particular books (for example, Mildred Taylor's *Roll of Thunder, Hear My Cry* (1976)) with efferent and aesthetic emphases to different, parallel classes. At various points, all these studies touch upon the issue of the process of responding; but, equally, they also relate to some of the other issues that are discussed in the remainder of this chapter.

Development in reading

Of these issues, the question of how children develop as readers of literature is one of the most frequently raised. This has been approached in four main ways: personal reminiscences of bookish childhoods (Sampson, 1947; Inglis, 1981); the growth of the child's sense of story in relation to the Piagetian stages of development (Applebee 1978; Tucker 1981); the development of literacy, with the idea of matching individual and age-group needs to appropriate books (Fisher 1964; Meek 1982); and, deductions about development drawn from surveys of children's reading interests and habits (Jenkinson 1940; Whitehead *et al.* 1977). While none of these writers would see their work as necessarily falling strictly under the reader-response heading, all are in fact listening to what children as readers say about their experiences and, in more recent years, are conscious of interpreting their findings against a background of reader-response criticism. This awareness is evident, for example, in the work of Tucker (1980) who, in a paper entitled 'Can we ever know the reader's response?' argues that children's responses are different from adults' (in, say, the relative emphasis they give to the quality of the writing as opposed to the pace of the plot) before he goes on to relate their responses to intellectual and emotional development as psychologists describe it (the subject of his subsequent book (Tucker 1981)). In the highly influential work of Meek, too, from *The Cool Web* (Meek *et al.* 1977) onwards, reader-response criticism has been one of her perspectives – evident, for example, in her 'Prolegomena for a study of children's literature' (1980: 35) and in her exploration of the relationship between literacy and literature in her account of the reading lessons to be found in picture books (Meek 1988). Or again, in the discussion of their findings of children's reading preferences at 10+, 12+ and 14+, Whitehead and his team speculate about the cognitive and affective factors involved in the interaction between children and their books. All are aware that response-oriented criticism should be able to tell us more about this interaction at different ages.

Developmental stages in literary reading are outlined by Jackson (1982), Protherough (1983), and Thomson (1986) on the basis of classroom enquiries with young readers as we have already seen; and there have been some small-scale studies of reading development focused upon responses to specific books. Hickman (1983) studied three classes, totalling ninety primary school-aged children, and monitored their spontaneous responses, variations in solicited verbal responses, the implications of non-responses, and the role of the teacher in respect of two texts: Silverstein's *Where the Sidewalk Ends* (1974) and McPhail's *The Magical Drawings of Moony B. Finch* (1978). She was interested in the age-related patterns of responses and in the influences of the class teacher. Cullinan *et al.* (1983) discuss the relationship between pupils' comprehension and response to literature and report the results of a study, conducted with eighteen readers in grades, 4, 6 and 8, which focused on readings of and taped responses to Paterson's *Bridge to Terabithia* (1977) and Le Guin's, *A Wizard of Earthsea* (1968). Their data confirmed that there are clear developmental levels in children's comprehension and they claim that: 'Reader-response provides a way to look at the multi-dimensional nature of comprehension' (37). Galda (1992) has subsequently reported on a four-year longitudinal study of eight readers' readings of selected books representing realistic and fantasy fiction in order to explore any differences in responses to these two genres. The 'realistic' texts included Paterson's *Bridge to Terabithia* (1977) and S. E. Hinton's *The Outsiders* (1968); the 'fantasy' texts included L'Engle's *A Wind in the Door* (1973) and Cooper's *The Dark is Rising* (1981). She considers reading factors, such as developing analytical ability; text factors, arguing that children find it easier to enter the world of realistic fiction than they do of fantasy stories; and concludes by advocating the 'spectator role' (Harding 1937; Britton 1970) as a stance that offers readers access to both genres.

Types of reader behaviour

The third theme concerns different sorts of readers or readings. It would be too much to claim that there is an established typology of readers; there have been few studies that venture beyond generalised discussions such as that between 'interrogative' and 'acquiescent' reading styles (Benton and Fox 1985: 16–17), itself a tentative extension of Holland's (1975) notion of personal style in reading behaviour. One study that does make some clear category decisions is that of Dias and Hayhoe (1988: 52–58) in respect of 14- and 15-year-old pupils reading and responding to poems. Their 'Responding-aloud protocols' (RAPs), described earlier, revealed four patterns of reading: paraphrasing, thematising, allegorising and problem solving. They stress that these are patterns of reading not readers (57) but have difficulty throughout in maintaining this discrimination. None the less, theirs is the most sophisticated account to date of that phenomenon that most teachers and others concerned with children's books have noticed without being able to explain, namely, that individual children reveal personal patterns of reading behaviour irrespective of the nature of the book being read. The study of these four reading patterns under the sub-headings of what the reader brings to the text, the reader's moves, closure, the reader's relationship with the text, and other elements is one that needs to be replicated and developed in relation to other types of text.

Fry (1985) explored the novel reading of six young readers (two 8-year-olds; two 12-year-olds; two 15-year-olds) through tape-recorded conversations over a period of eight months. The six case studies give some vivid documentary evidence of individual responses (for example, on the ways readers see themselves in books (99)) and also raise general issues such as re-readings, the appeal of series writers like Blyton, the relation of text fiction and film fiction, and the developmental process. Many and Cox's (1992) collection of papers includes their own development of Rosenblatt's efferent/aesthetic distinction in respect of the stances adopted by a class of 10-year-olds in their responses to Byars's *The Summer of the Swans* (1970) and other stories. Enciso, in the same collection, builds upon Benton's (1983) model of the secondary world and gives an exhaustive case-study of one ten-year-old girl's reading of chapters from three stories in order to observe the strategies she uses to create her story world from these texts. Benton's development of the secondary world concept, after Tolkien (1938) and Auden (1968), is reappraised in Many and Cox (1992: 15–18 and 23–48) and has also been extended by the author to incorporate aspects of the visual arts, notably paintings and picture-books (Benton 1992). The concept as originally formulated appeared in the special issue of the *Journal of Research and Development of Education* (Agee and Galda 1983) along with several other articles that focus upon readers' behaviours. Beach (1983) looks at what the reader brings to the text and reports an enquiry aimed at determining the effects of differences in prior knowledge of literary conventions and attitudes on readers' responses through a comparison between high school and college English education students' responses to a short story by Updike. Pillar (1983) discusses aspects of moral judgement in response to fairy tales and presents the findings from a study of the responses of sixty elementary school children to three fables. The responses are discussed in terms of the principles of justice that distinguish them. This enquiry edges us towards the fourth theme, where reader-response methods are employed in culturally oriented studies.

Culturally oriented studies

Children's concepts and social attitudes have been the subject of reader-response enquiries in three complementary ways: multicultural and feminist studies, which explore how far literature can be helpful in teaching about issues of race or gender; whole-culture studies, which consider children's responses to literature in the context of the broad range of their interests; and cross-cultural studies, which compare the responses of young readers from different countries to the same texts to identify similarities and cultural differences. An article and a book about each group must suffice to indicate the emphases and the degree to which reader-response theory and practice have been influential.

Evans (1992) contains several studies with explicitly cultural concerns, among which is 'Feminist approaches to teaching: John Updike's "A & P"' by Bogdan, Millen and Pitt which sets out to explore gender issues in the classroom via Updike's short story. They quote Kolodny (in Showalter 1985: 158) in support of the shift feminist studies makes from seeing reader-response in a purely experiential dimension to a more philosophical enquiry into how 'aesthetic response is ... invested with epistemological, ethical, and moral concerns'. The feminist position is stated explicitly: 'Reading pleasure can no longer be its own end-point, but rather part of a larger dialectical process which strives for an "altered reading attentiveness" to gender in every reading act' (Evans: 151). This dialectical response model is further elaborated and augmented by specific pedagogical suggestions to help young readers towards this new attentiveness.

Within the broadly, and somewhat uncomfortably, defined field of multicultural education, the most sophisticated use of reader-response criticism and practice is Beverley Naidoo's (1992) enquiry into the role of literature, especially fiction, in educating young people about race. Working with a teacher and his class of all-white 13 to 14-year-old pupils over a period of one academic year, Naidoo introduced a sequence of four novels to their work with increasingly explicit racial issues: *Buddy* (Hinton 1983), *Friedrich* (Richter 1978), *Roll of Thunder, Hear My Cry* (Taylor 1976) and *Waiting for the Rain* (Gordon 1987). Influenced by Hollindale's (1988) notion of 'the reader as ideologist', Rosenblatt's (1978, 1985) transactional theory and Benton's ethnographic approach to reader-response enquiries (Benton *et al.* (1988), Naidoo adopted an action-researcher role to develop 'ways of exploring these texts which encouraged empathy with the perspective of characters who were victims of racism but who resisted it' (22). Written and oral responses in journals and discussion were at the centre of the procedures. Many challenging and provocative issues are examined through this enquiry, including overt and institutionalised racism, whether teaching about race challenges or merely reinforces racism, the nature of empathy and the gender differences pupils exhibited. The cultural context, especially the subculture of the particular classroom, emerged as a dominant theme. The subtle interrelatedness of text, context, readers and writers, is sensitively explored in a study that shows how reader-response methods can help to illuminate the values and attitudes that readers sometimes hide, even from themselves.

The second group of whole-culture studies tends to focus upon adolescent readers. Stories and poems, especially those encountered in school, are seen as but one aspect of the cultural context in which teenagers live and in which books are low on their agenda after television, computer games, rock music, comics and magazines. Beach and Freedman's (1992) paper, 'Responding as a cultural act: adolescents' responses to magazine ads and short stories' widens the perspective from the individual reader's 'personal' and 'unique' responses to accommodate the notion of response as a cultural practice. They discuss the cultural practices required in adolescent peer groups and note the ways in which these are derived from experiences with the mass media, with examples from adolescents' responses to magazine advertisements and short stories. Particular points of interest in the responses of these 115 8th and 11th grade pupils are the gender differences, the tendency to blur fiction and reality when talking about the advertising images, and the low incidence of critical responses.

Reader-response criticism also influences Sarland's (1991) study of young people's reading. He takes seriously both Chambers's (1977) account of the implied child reader (discussed below) and Meek's (1987) plea for an academic study of children's literature which situates it within the whole culture of young people. Building on Fry's (1985) work, he considers the popular literature that children read both in relation to a culture dominated by television and video, and in relation to the 'official' literature read in school. By eliciting and analysing students' responses to such books as King's *Carrie* (1974) and Herbert's *The Fog* (1975), Sarland draws upon response-oriented theory and practice to discuss the importance of these texts to their readers and to begin to open up a subculture of which, at best, teachers are usually only hazily aware.

Cross-cultural studies are relatively uncommon for the obvious reason that they are more difficult to set up and sustain. Bunbury and Tabbert's article for *Children's Literature in Education* (1989; reprinted Hunt 1992) compared the responses of Australian and German children to an Australian bush-ranger story, Stow's *Midnite* (1967/1982). Using Jauss's notion of 'ironic identification', where the reader is drawn in and willingly submits to the fictional illusion only to have the author subvert this aesthetic experience, the enquiry considered a range of responses; while there are interesting insights into individual readings, it none the less ends inconclusively by stating: 'The best we can say is that the capacity to experience ironic identification extends along a spectrum of reading encounters which vary in intensity' (Hunt: 124). The study is ambitious in tackling two difficult topics whose relationship is complex: children's sense of the tone of a text and the effect of translation upon the readers' responses. To begin to open up such issues is an achievement in itself.

Chapter 6 of Dias and Hayhoe's (1988) book makes explicit the international perspective on the teaching of poetry that permeates the whole of this Anglo-Canadian collaboration. Views from Australia, Britain, Canada and the USA on good practice in poetry teaching all share the same principle of developing pupils' responses. Clearly, cross-cultural influences grow more readily and are more easily monitored in English-speaking countries than elsewhere; yet there is sufficient evidence here of cultural diversity to encourage other researchers to explore the ways in which we can learn from each other about how children's responses to literature are mediated by the cultural contexts in which they occur.

Text-oriented studies

Studies of children's literature which directly parallel the work of, say, Iser (1974) or Fish (1980) in their close examination of particular texts are surprisingly rare. It is as if those who work in this field have been so concerned with pedagogy and children as readers that they have failed to exploit reader-response criticism as a means of understanding the nature of actual texts. Two concepts, however, which have received some attention are the 'implied reader' and the notion of 'intertextuality'. The first, developed by Iser (1974) after Booth (1961), for a time encouraged the search for the 'implied child reader' in children's books; the second followed from enquiries into how readers make meaning and the realisation of the complex relationships that exist between the readers, the text, other texts, other genres, and the cultural context of any 'reading'.

Although Chambers (1977/1985) and Tabbert (1980) gave the lead, the implied child reader remains a neglected figure in children's book criticism. In 'The reader in the book' Chambers takes Iser's concept and advocates its central importance in children's book criticism. He illustrates Roald Dahl's assumptions about the implied adult reader of his story 'The champion of the world' (1959) in contrast to those about the implied child reader of the rewritten version in the children's book *Danny: The Champion of the World* (1975), and argues that the narrative voice and textual features of the latter create a sense of an intimate, yet adult-controlled, relationship between the implied author and the implied child reader. He generalises from this example to claim that this voice and this relationship are common in children's books, and identifies both with the figure of the 'friendly adult storyteller who knows how to entertain children while at the same time keeping them in their place' (69). Much of the remainder of his article rests upon two further narrative features: 'the adoption of a child point of view' (72) to sustain this adult–author/child–reader relationship; and the deployment within the text of indeterminacy gaps which the reader must fill in order to generate meanings. These three characteristics – the literary relationship, the point of view, and the tell-tale gaps – are then exemplified in a critique of Boston's *The Children of Green Knowe* (1954).

Chambers's article is already regarded as a landmark in the development of criticism (Hunt 1990: 90), not least because it opened up one means of defining the singular character of a form of literature that is designated by its intended audience. That this lead has been followed so infrequently calls into question the seriousness of the whole critical enterprise in this field. Among the few who have exploited these concepts in relation to children's books is Tabbert (1980) who comments usefully on the notion of 'telling gaps' and 'the implied reader' in some classic children's texts and sees a fruitful way forward in psychologically oriented criticism, particularly in the methodology adopted by Holland. Benton (1992a) parallels the historically changing relationship between implied author and implied reader that is found in Iser's (1974) studies of Fielding, Thackeray and Joyce, with a corresponding critique of the openings of three novels by children's authors – Hughes's *Tom Brown's Schooldays* (1856), Day Lewis's *The Otterbury Incident* (1948), and Garner's *Red Shift* (1973). The emphases, however, here, are upon the nature of the collaborative relationship and upon narrative technique rather than on the implied child reader. Shavit (1983: 60–67) extends Iser's concept to embrace the notion of childhood as well as the child as implied reader. After giving a historical perspective on the idea of childhood the discussion focuses upon various versions of 'Little Red Riding Hood' in order to explore 'how far they were responsible for different implied readers' (61). In particular, she argues that prevailing notions of childhood helped determine the changing character of these texts over several centuries from Perrault's version to those of the present day.

By far the most rigorous account of the implied reader is that of Stephens (1992), given from a position that is sceptical about a mode of reading which locates the reader only within the text and ignores questions of ideology. He argues that in critical practice the being or meaning of the text is best characterised as 'a dialectic between textual discourse (including its construction of an implied reader and a range of potential subject positions) and a reader's disposition, familiarity with story conventions and experiential knowledge' (59). His account of ideology and the implied reader in two picture books (Cooper and Hutton, *The Selkie Girl*, 1986; Gerstein, *The Seal Mother*, 1986) develops this argument and leads him to take issue with Chambers's view of the implied reader on ideological grounds. He says of Chambers's account that: 'his own ideology of reading demands a reified "implicated" reader, led by textual strategies to discover a determinate meaning' (67). Stephens's conceptualisation of the implied reader is significant both of itself and in helping to explain the paucity of critical effort in this area following Chambers's article. For it tells us that criticism has moved on and, in particular, that such concepts can no longer be regarded as innocent aspects of narrative.

Stephens, too, offers the fullest account to date of intertextuality in the third chapter of his book 'Not by words alone: language, intertextuality and society' (84–119). He outlines seven kinds of relationship which may exist between a particular text and any other texts and goes on to discuss various manifestations of intertextuality in children's literature, notably in fairy tales. Agee (1983: 55–59) concentrates on the narrower focus of literary allusion and reader-response and begins to explore the intertextual patterning of such books as *Z for Zachariah* (O'Brien 1977), *Jacob I Have Loved* (Paterson 1981) and *Fahrenheit 451* (Bradbury 1967). Stephens and Agee both approach the topic exclusively through the study of texts.

Meek (1988) keeps young readers constantly in view when she draws upon the intertext of oral and written literature, together with the Iserian concepts of the implied reader and indeterminacy gaps, in her brief but widely acclaimed paper 'How texts teach what readers learn'. Her main texts are picture books: the telling gaps in *Rosie's Walk* (Hutchins 1969) and *Granpa* (Burningham 1984) and the play of intertexts in *The Jolly Postman* (Ahlberg 1986) and the short story 'William's Version' (Mark 1980) are explored with great subtlety, and display, above all, the quality that distinguishes the best sort of criticism of children's literature: the ability to listen to children's responses to a book and to 'read' these with the same effort of attention that is afforded to the text themselves. Reader-response criticism accommodates both the reader and the text; there is no area of literary activity where this is more necessary than in the literature that defines itself by reference to its young readership.

References

Abrams, M. H. (1953) *The Mirror and the Lamp: Romantic Theory and the Critical Tradition*, New York: Norton.

Agee, H. (1983) 'Literary allusion and reader response: possibilities for research', in Agee, H. and Galda, L. (eds) 'Response to literature: empirical and theoretical studies', *Journal of Research and Development in Education* 16, 3: 55–59.

—— and Galda, L. (eds) (1983) 'Response to literature: empirical and theoretical studies', *Journal of Research and Development in Education* 16, 3: 8–75.

Applebee, A. N. (1978) *The Child's Concept of Story: Ages Two to Seventeen*, Chicago and London: Chicago University Press.

Atkinson, J. (1985) 'How children read poems at different ages', *English in Education* 19, 1: 24–34.

Auden, W. H. (1968) *Secondary Worlds*, London: Faber.

Barnes, D. (1976) *From Communication to Curriculum*, Harmondsworth: Penguin.

—— and Todd, F. (1977) *Communication and Learning in Small Groups*, London: Routledge and Kegan Paul.

Beach, R. (1983) 'Attitudes, social conventions and response to literature', in Agee, H. and Galda, L. (eds) 'Response to literature: empirical and theoretical studies', *Journal of Research and Development in Education* 16, 3: 47–54.

—— and Freedman, K. (1992) 'Responding as a cultural act: adolescents' responses to magazine ads and short stories', in Many, J. and Cox, C. (eds) *Reader Stance and Literary Understanding: Exploring the Theories, Research and Practice*, Norwood, NJ: Ablex.

Benton, M. (1983) 'Secondary worlds', in Agee, H. and Galda, L. (eds) 'Response to literature: empirical and theoretical studies', *Journal of Research and Development in Education* 16, 3: 68–75.

—— (1992a) *Secondary Worlds: Literature Teaching and the Visual Arts*, Milton Keynes: Open University Press.

—— (1992b) 'Possible worlds and narrative voices', in Many, J. and Cox, C. (eds) *Reader Stance and Literary Understanding: Exploring the Theories, Research and Practice*, Norwood, NJ: Ablex.

—— and Fox, G. (1985) *Teaching Literature 9–14*, Oxford: Oxford University Press.

—— Teasey, J., Bell, R. and Hurst, K. (1988) *Young Readers Responding to Poems*, London: Routledge.

Benton, P. (1986) *Pupil, Teacher, Poem*, London: Hodder and Stoughton.

Bleich, D. (1985) 'The identity of pedagogy and research in the study of response to literature', in Cooper, C. R. (ed.) *Researching Response to Literature and the Teaching of Literature: Points of Departure*, Norwood, NJ: Ablex.

Bogdan, D., Millen, K. J. and Pitt, A. (1992) 'Feminist approaches to teaching: John Updike's "A & P"' in Evans, E. (ed.) *Young Readers, New Readings*, Hull: Hull University Press.

Booth, W. C. (1961) *The Rhetoric of Fiction*, Chicago: University of Chicago Press.

Britton, J. N. (1970) *Language and Learning*, London: Allen Lane and The Penguin Press.

Bunbury, R. and Tabbert, R. (1978) 'A bicultural study of identification: readers' responses to the ironic treatment of a national hero', *Children's Literature in Education*, 20, 1: 25–35.

Chambers, A. (1977) 'The reader in the book', *Signal* 23: 64–87.

Cooper, C. R. (ed.) (1985a) *Researching Response to Literature and the Teaching of Literature: Points of Departure*, Norwood, NJ: Ablex.

—— (1985b) 'Evaluating the results of classroom literary study', in Cooper, C. R. (ed.) *Researching Response to Literature and the Teaching of Literature: Points of Departure*, Norwood, NJ: Ablex.

Corcoran, B. (1992) 'Reader stance: from willed aesthetic to discursive construction', in Many, J. and Cox, C. (eds) *Reader Stance and Literary Understanding: Exploring the Theories, Research and Practice*, Norwood, NJ: Ablex.

—— and Evans, E. (eds) (1987) *Readers, Texts, Teachers*, Milton Keynes: Open University Press.

Cox, C. B. (1989) *English for Ages 5–16*, London: HMSO.

Culler, J. (1975) *Structuralist Poetics: Structuralism, Linguistics and the Study of Literature*, London: Routledge and Kegan Paul.

Cullinan, B. E, Harwood, K. T. and Galda, L. (1983) 'The reader and the story comprehension and response', in Agee, H. and Galda, L. (eds) 'Response to literature: empirical and theoretical studies', *Journal of Research and Development in Education* 16, 3: 29–38.

D'Arcy, P. (1973) *Reading For Meaning*, vol. 2, London: Hutchinson.

Dias, P. (1986) 'Making sense of poetry', *English and Education*, Sheffield: NATE, 20(2).

—— and Hayhoe, M. (1988) *Developing Response to Poetry*, Milton Keynes: Open University Press.

Dixon, J. and Brown, J. (1984) *Responses to Literature: What is Being Assessed?* London: Schools' Council Publications.

Encisco, P. (1992) 'Creating the story world', in Many, J. and Cox, C. (eds) *Reader Stance and Literary Understanding: Exploring the Theories, Research and Practice*, Norwood, NJ: Ablex.

Evans, E. (ed.) (1992) *Young Readers, New Readings*, Hull: Hull University Press.

Fish, S. (1980) *Is There a Text in this Class?*, Cambridge, MA: Harvard University Press.

Fisher, M. (1964) *Intent Upon Reading*, London: Brockhampton Press.

Fox, G. (1979) 'Dark watchers: young readers and their fiction', *English in Education* 13, 1: 32–35.

Freund, E. (1987) *The Return of the Reader: Reader-Response Criticism*, London: Methuen.

Fry, D. (1985) *Children Talk About Books: Seeing Themselves as Readers*, Milton Keynes: Open University Press.

Galda, L. (1983) 'Research in response to literature', *Journal of Research and Development in Education* 16: 1–7.

—— (1992) 'Evaluation as a spectator: changes across time and genre', in Many, J. and Cox, C. (eds) *Reader Stance and Literary Understanding: Exploring the Theories, Research and Practice*, Norwood, NJ: Ablex.

Hade, D. D. (1992) 'The reader's stance as event: transaction in the classroom', in Many, J. and Cox, C. (eds) *Reader Stance and Literary Understanding: Exploring the Theories, Research and Practice*, Norwood, NJ: Ablex.

Harding, D. W. (1937) 'The role of the onlooker', *Scrutiny* 6: 247–258.

—— (1962) 'Psychological processes in the reading of fiction', *The British Journal of Aesthetics* 2, 2: 113–147.

Hayhoe, M. and Parker, S. (eds) (1990) *Reading and Response*, Milton Keynes: Open University Press.

Herbert, J. (1975) *The Fog*, London: New English Library.

Hickman, J. (1983) 'Everything considered: response to literature in an elementary school setting', in Agee, H. and Galda, L. (eds) 'Response to literature: empirical and theoretical studies', *Journal of Research and Development in Education* 16, 3: 8–13.

Hinton, N. (1983) *Buddy*, London: Heinemann Educational.

Hinton, S. E. (1968) *The Outsiders*, New York: Dell.

Holland, N. N. (1968) *The Dynamics of Literary Response*, New York: Norton.

—— (1973) *Poems in Persons*, New York: Norton.

—— (1975) *Five Readers Reading*, New Haven and London: Yale University Press.

Hollindale, P. (1988) 'Ideology and the children's book', *Signal* 55: 3–22.

Holub, R.C. (1984) *Reception Theory*, London: Methuen.

Hunt, P. (ed.) (1990) *Children's Literature: The Development of Criticism*, London: Routledge.

—— (ed.) (1992) *Literature for Children: Contemporary Criticism*, London: Routledge.

Inglis, F. (1981) *The Promise of Happiness*, Cambridge: Cambridge University Press.

Iser, W. (1974) *The Implied Reader*, Baltimore: Johns Hopkins University Press.

—— (1978) *The Act of Reading: A Theory of Aesthetic Response*, Baltimore: Johns Hopkins University Press.

Jackson, D. (1980) 'First encounters: the importance of initial responses to literature', *Children's Literature in Education* 11, 4: 149–160.

—— (1982) *Continuity in Secondary English*, London: Methuen.

—— (1983) *Encounters With Books: Teaching Fiction 11–16*, London: Methuen.

Jefferson, A. and Robey, D. (1986) *Modern Literary Theory*, 2nd edn, London: Batsford.

Jenkinson, A. J. (1940) *What Do Boys and Girls Read?* London: Methuen.

Kintgen, E. R. (1985) 'Studying the perception of poetry', in Cooper, C. R. (ed.) *Researching Response to Literature and the Teaching of Literature: Points of Departure*, Norwood, NJ: Ablex.

Lerner, L. (ed.) (1983) *Reconstructing Literature*, Oxford: Blackwell.

Many, J. and Cox, C. (eds) (1992) *Reader Stance and Literary Understanding: Exploring the Theories, Research and Practice*, Norwood, NJ: Ablex.

—— and Wiseman, D. (1992) 'Analysing versus experiencing: the effects of teaching approaches on students' responses', in Many, J. and Cox, C. (eds) *Reader Stance and Literary Understanding: Exploring the Theories, Research and Practice*, Norwood, NJ: Ablex.

Meek, M. (1980) 'Prolegomena for a study of children's literature', in Benton, M. (ed.) *Approaches to Research in Children's Literature*, Southampton: Department of Education, Southampton University.

—— (1982) *Learning to Read*, London: Bodley Head.

—— (1987) 'Symbolic outlining: the academic study of children's literature', *Signal* 53: 97–115.

—— (1988) *How Texts Teach What Readers Learn*, South Woodchester: Thimble Press.

—— Warlow, A. and Barton, G. (eds) (1977) *The Cool Web*, London: Bodley Head.

Naidoo, B. (1992) *Through Whose Eyes? Exploring Racism: Reader, Text and Context*, London: Trentham Books.

Petrosky, A. R. (1985) 'Response: a way of knowing', in Cooper, C. R. (ed.) *Researching Response to Literature and the Teaching of Literature: Points of Departure*, Norwood, NJ: Ablex.

Pillar, A. M. (1983) 'Aspects of moral judgement in response to fables', in Agee, H. and Galda, L. (eds) 'Response to literature: empirical and theoretical studies', *Journal of Research and Development in Education* 16, 3: 39–46.

Protherough, R. (1983) *Developing Response to Fiction*, Milton Keynes: Open University Press.

Purves, A. C. (1985) 'That sunny dome: those caves of ice', in Cooper, C. R. (ed.) *Researching Response to Literature and the Teaching of Literature: Points of Departure*, Norwood, NJ: Ablex.

—— and Beach, R. (1972) *Literature and the Reader*, Urbana, IL: NCTE.

—— and Rippere, V. (1968) *Elements of Writing About a Literary Work*, Research Report No. 9, Champaign, IL: NCTE.

Richards, I. A. (1924) *Principles of Literary Criticism*, London: Routledge and Kegan Paul.

—— (1929) *Practical Criticism*, London: Routledge and Kegan Paul.

Rosenblatt, L. (1938/1970) *Literature as Exploration*, London: Heinemann.

—— (1978) *The Reader, The Text, The Poem: The Transactional Theory of the Literary Work*, Carbondale, IL: Southern Illinois University Press.

—— (1985) 'The transactional theory of the literary work: implications for research', in Cooper, C. R. (ed.) *Researching Response to Literature and the Teaching of Literature: Points of Departure*, Norwood, NJ: Ablex.

Sampson, G. (1947) *Seven Essays*, Cambridge: Cambridge University Press.

Sarland, C. (1991) *Young People Reading: Culture and Response*, Milton Keynes: Open University Press.

Scholes, R. (1985) *Textual Power: Literary Theory and the Teaching of English*, New Haven and London: Yale University Press.

Shavit, Z. (1983) 'The notion of childhood and the child as implied reader', in Agee, H. and Galda, L. (eds) 'Response to literature: empirical and theoretical studies', *Journal of Research and Development in Education* 16, 3: 60–67.

Showalter, E. (ed.) (1985) *The New Feminist Criticism: Essays on Women, Literature and Theory*, New York: Pantheon.

Squire, J. R. (1964) *The Responses of Adolescents While Reading Four Short Stories*, Research Report No. 2, Champaign, IL: NCTE.

—— (1985) 'Studying response to literature through school surveys', in Cooper, C. R. (ed.) *Researching Response to Literature and the Teaching of Literature: Points of Departure*, Norwood, NJ: Ablex.

—— (1990) 'Research on reader response and the National Literature initiative', in Hayhoe, M. and Parker, S. (eds) *Reading and Response*, Milton Keynes: Open University Press.

Stephens, J. (1992) *Language and Ideology in Children's Fiction*, London: Longman.

Suleiman, S. R. and Crosman, I. (eds) (1980) *The Reader in the Text*, Princeton, NJ: Princeton University Press.

Tabbert, R. (1980) 'The impact of children's books: cases and concepts', in Fox, G. and Hammond, G. (eds) *Responses to Children's Literature*, New York: K. G. Saur.

Thomson, J. (1986) *Understanding Teenagers Reading: Reading Processes and the Teaching of Literature*, Sydney: Methuen.

Tolkien, J. R. R. (1938) *Tree and Leaf*, London: Unwin Books.

Tompkins, J. P. (1980) *Reader-Response Criticism: From Formalism to Post-Structuralism*, Baltimore: Johns Hopkins University Press.

Tucker, N. (1980) 'Can we ever know the reader's response?', in Benton, M. (ed.) *Approaches to Research in Children's Literature*, Southampton: Department of Education, Southampton University.

—— (1981) *The Child and the Book*, Cambridge: Cambridge University Press.

Wade, B. (1981) 'Assessing pupils' contributions in appreciating a poem', *Journal of Education for Teaching* 7, 1, 40–49.

Wellek, R. and Warren, A. (1949) *Theory of Literature*, London: Cape.

Whitehead, F. *et al.* (1977) *Children and their Books*, London: Macmillan.

Wimsatt, W. K. and Beardsley, M. (1954/1970) *The Verbal Icon: Studies in the Meaning of Poetry*, London: Methuen.

Zancella, D. (1992) 'Literary lives: a biographical perspective on the teaching of literature', in Many, J. and Cox, C. (eds) *Reader Stance and Literary Understanding: Exploring the Theories, Research and Practice*, Norwood, NJ: Ablex.

Zarillo, J. and Cox, C. (1992) 'Efferent and aesthetic teaching', in Many, J. and Cox, C. (eds) *Reader Stance and Literary Understanding: Exploring the Theories, Research and Practice*, Norwood, NJ: Ablex.

8 Reading the Unconscious: Psychoanalytical Criticism

Hamida Bosmajian

Editor's introduction

A lot of what is written about children's literature is implicitly concerned with the psychology of the reader, the writer, and the characters in the books. However, as Hamida Bosmajian points out, very often this criticism relies on 'the informal developmental psychological knowledge of the interpreter without reference to any specific theory'. This chapter provides a lucid guide to the key writers and thinkers in this field, from Freud and Jung to the highly influential contemporary work of Lacan.

P. H.

Because the child and childhood hold a privileged position in most psycho-analytical theories, the elective affinity between children's literature and psychological criticism seems even more natural than the affinity between psychology and literature in general. Psychoanalytic theory adds to the literary text a 'second dimension – unfolding what might be called the unconscious content of the work' (Holland 1970: 131), but the condensations and displacements at work in the author–text–reader relation are problematised in children's literature because of the double reader: adult/child.

Children's fiction might be impossible because it rests on the assumption that there is a child who can be addressed when, in actuality, 'children's fiction sets up the child as an outsider to its own process, and that aims, unashamedly, to take the child in' (Rose 1984: 2). The implied author, even in first-person narration by a child character, is a displacement of the contexts of personal and collective values and neuroses. Furthermore, while the analyst is supposedly the most reliable reader-interpreter of stories told in a psychoanalytic dialogue by the analysand-author, the reader of adult literature may or may not be a reliable interpreter of the text. In children's literature the implied reader is, moreover, highly unreliable and, therefore, most easily 'taken in'. Thus, the authorial self is in a sense liberated, in that the textual strategies and gaps that constitute the subtext of the work escape the implied reader, the child. The author can experience therapeutic release without anxieties over the scrutiny of an adult's psychoanalytical critique.

The nemesis for the projection of the naïve implied reader is the adult reader as psychoanalytic critic of children's literature who exposes the gaps, substitutions and displacements of the author and appropriates the author's text as a symptom of individual or cultural neuroses that underlie and undermine values associated with growth and development. While psychoanalytic critics of adult literature amplify the reader's appreciation of the text, those same critics will, in the case of children's literature, conceal their interpretation from the child and, therewith, both censor and protect the author. The child may be imaged as myth of origin – as father of the man and mother of the woman – but in children's literature the adult is in control.

The correspondences between author–text–reader and analysand–psycho-analytic dialogue-analyst break down, for author–reader are not in a dialogical relation, no matter how intensely the reader *responds*, nor can the critic-interpreter make enquiries of a character in a narrative, as an analyst can in the psychoanalytic situation. While critics act as if one could ask about Alice's relation with her parents as she develops from pawn to queen in *Through the Looking Glass*, they forget that she is a linguistic construct, a trope for the unresolved problems of her author (Greenacre 1955). It is important that psychoanalytic critics are aware of the ambivalences inherent in their method and do not seize one aspect of a psychoanalytical theory as a tool for interpretation, thereby reducing the text to universals about human development (compare Hogan 1990; Knoepflmacher 1990; Phillips and Wojcik-Andrews 1990; Steig 1990; Zipes 1990).

The following discussion will focus on defining those psychoanalytic theories that have influenced the criticism of children's literature. Frequently such criticism relies on the informal developmental psychological knowledge of the interpreter without reference to any specific theory. This is especially true of realistic narratives for young adults. The strongest psychoanalytic tradition of criticism can be found in the interpretation of folktales and *märchen* and, to a lesser extent in fantasy literature. While Freud, Jung and their disciples have been important in interpretations of children's literature, the poststructuralist influence has not been as prevalent. Quite dominant, however, is the influence of psychological criticism that relates the development of the child character to the social context depicted in psychologically realistic narratives. Perhaps because of the deep issues involved in psychoanalytic criticism, critics of children's literature occasionally seem to screen discussions of psychoanalytical issues with analyses of social contexts, even where the topic is announced as being psychoanalytical (Smith and Kerrigan 1985).

Freudian Criticism

Classical Freudian criticism interprets the work as an expression of psychopatho-graphy, as a symptom whose creation provided therapeutic release for the author. In 'The relation of the poet to daydreaming' (1908), Freud saw the crucial relationship between child–play/poet–language: 'every child at play behaves like an imaginative writer, in that he creates a world of his own or, more truly, he arranges the things of this world and orders it in a new way that pleases him better ... Language has preserved this relationship between children's play and poetic creation' (1908/1963 9: 144), just as it does between dream and text.

Freud assumed that all psychoneurotic symptoms are generated by psychic conflicts between a person's sexual desires and the strictures of society. The conflict is expressed through substitutions and displacements, just as in literature a metaphor's tenor and vehicle condense two disparate ideas into one image that hides and reveals what is not articulated. Similarly, displacement substitutes socially acceptable modes for desires that are forbidden. Substitutions thus function as censors in dreams and daydreams, in play and in texts. Freud's first triad of unconscious, pre-conscious and conscious defines the unconscious as a non-verbal, instinctual and infantile given and as dominated by the pleasure principle. The desires and conflicts (oral, anal, oedipal) of childhood persist throughout the adult's life and can be made conscious only by being first raised to the level of the pre-conscious which facilitates the dynamic of consciousness and repression through condensation and displacement. Freud later modified his first triad with the paradigm of id, ego and superego, in part because he suspected a greater simultaneity in the dynamics of the psyche. The revised triad places the embattled ego between the deterministic forces of the id and the internalised strictures of society. It is here where we find the cause of the pessimism in Freudian psychoanalytic theory: the ego's inevitable discontent.

Crucial for Freudian critics of children's literature is the importance Freud gave to the child in the psychoanalytic process. Though the Oedipus complex has been accepted as part of child development, Freud's insistence on the polymorphous sexuality of the infant (1962/1975: 39–72) is somewhat more troubling for most critics of children's literature, for if such sexuality is displaced in the text but communicates itself sub-textually to the child-reader, then the author has transferred his infantile sexuality and communicates it to the child. Texts such as Dahl's *Charlie and the Chocolate Factory* (see Bosmajian 1985), Sendak's *In the Night Kitchen* might fall into this category.

Freud's profound appreciation of the psychological importance of language was bound to lead him not only to interpretations of everyday language phenomena in the processes of repression and substitution, but also to interpretations of major authors of European literature. In 'The occurrence in dreams of materials from fairy tales', Freud notes that fairy tales have such an impact on the mental life of the child that the adult will use them later as screen memories for the experiences of childhood (1913/1963: 59).

'The serious study of children's literature may be said to have begun with Freud', acknowledges Egan in his discussion of *Peter Pan* (1982: 37). Psycho-analysts have indeed been the precursors of the study of children's literature, which explains the powerful but dubious influence of Bruno Bettelheim's *The Uses of Enchantment* (1975), a discussion of familiar tales along infantile and adolescent psychosexual development. Bettelheim sees the child's libido as a threat to both a meaningful life and the social order; therefore, the child needs fairy tales to order his inner house by acquiring a moral education through the tales (5), for, as the stories unfold, they 'give conscious credence and body to the id pressures and show ways to satisfy these that are in line with ego and superego' (6). Literary critics have strongly critiqued Bettelheim not only for his a-historicality and reduction-ism of Freud's theories (Zipes 1979), but also for his punitive pedagogy, for being 'oddly accusatory towards children' (Tatar 1992: xxii) and for displacing his 'own real life fantasies, particularly of the dutiful daughter who takes care of her father's needs' (xxv) into his interpretative work.

Jungian Criticism

Jungian criticism discovers archetypes that are the basis for the images in a text. Pre-consciously, or consciously, the author connects with archetypal patterns of which the narrative becomes a variable whose content will somehow relate to the issue of the ego's integration with the self. Jung's concept of the therapeutic process begins with the recognition of the loss of an original wholeness, possessed by every infant, a wholeness lost through self-inflation and/or alienation of the ego. On a mythic level, the ego would experience a dark night of the soul followed by a breakthrough that establishes, not an integration with the self, but a connection with the transpersonal self. The end of Jungian analysis is not a complete individuation of the ego, but rather the analysand's recognition that growth is a life-long process, a quest, during which conscious and unconscious connect primarily through symbols and archetypes.

Jung assumed a personal unconscious consisting of memories and images gathered during a life-time, for the archetypes, as experienced by the individual, are in and of the world. This personal unconscious is raised to consciousness when the analysand connects the personal with the collective unconscious. The collective unconscious is an *a priori* existence of 'organising factors', the archetypes understood as inborn modes of functioning, rather like a grammar that generates and structures the infinite variables of symbol formations whose recurrence is to be understood again as archetypal (Jung 1964: 67). Archetypes are 'without known origin; and they reproduce themselves in any time or any part of the world – even where transmission by direct descent or "cross-fertilisation" through migration must be ruled out' (69). Jung, too, believed that dreams are meaningful and can be understood (102) as their specific images connect with archetypes whose force can suddenly overwhelm the dreamer. Such an experience contrasts with the conscious use of representing archetypes through culturally defined images and motifs. Jung's own metaphoric use of archetypal images such as shadow, anima or animus and self, blurred the distinction between archetype as a grammar and archetype as symbol.

Jung, whose theory has been criticised for demanding a vast amount of knowledge of myth, did not perceive the unconscious as an instinctual and libidinal battleground, although he posited a 'primitive psyche' in the child which functions in dreams and fantasies comparable to the physical evolution of mankind in the embryo (1964: 99). In Jung's 'Psychic conflicts in a child' (1946/1954: 8–46), the child-patient, obsessed with the origin of babies, fantasised that she would give birth if she swallowed an orange, similar to women in fairy tales whose eating of fruit leads to pregnancy. The child-patient was eventually enlightened by her father, but Jung concludes that, while false explanation are not advisable, no less inadvisable is the insistence on the right explanation, for that inhibits the freedom of the mind's development through concretistic explanations which reduce the spontaneity of image-making to a falsehood (34).

Because the essential nature of all art escapes our understanding, Jung did not perceive literature as psychopathography. We can interpret only 'that aspect of art which consists in the process of artistic creation' (1931/1966: 65). While he admits that literary works can result from the intentionality of the author, they are also those that 'force themselves on the author', reveal his inner nature, and overwhelm the conscious mind with a flood of thoughts and images he never intended to create: 'Here the artist is not identical with the process of creation; he is aware that he is subordinate to his work or stands outside it, as though he were a second person' (73). An author may, for a time, be out of fashion when, suddenly, readers rediscover his work, because they perceive in it archetypes that speak to them with renewed immediacy (77). We can, therefore, only discuss the psychological phenomenology in a work of literature.

It is evident how readily children's literature, especially when it has components of fantasy, connects with Jungian theories. Marie Louise von Franz (1977, 1978) has written comprehensive studies of fairy tales which the Jungian critic tends to see as 'allegories of the inner life' that meet 'the deep-seated psychic and spiritual needs of the individual' (Cooper 1983: 154). The problem with such criticism is that it reduces images in fairy tales to fixed allegorical meanings without regard for historical and social contexts, as the Jungian critic basically explains metaphor with metaphor. Northrop Frye's discussion of archetypes in terms of convention and genre is an attempt to avoid such reductionism (1957). What makes the Jungian approach attractive to interpreters of children's literature is that the theory assumes an original wholeness that can be regained after alienation is overcome. This coincides with the comic resolution of so many narratives for children and young adults.

In Jungian literary criticism children's literature is often seen as privileged, just as the 'primitive psyche' of the child is in Jungian psychoanalysis. 'Children's literature initiates us into psychic reality, by telling about the creatures and perils of the soul and the heart's possibilities of blessing in images of universal intelligibility' (Hillman 1980: 5). At its best Jungian criticism is able to integrate the author's and the reader's needs as exemplified in Lynn Rosenthal's interpretation of Lucy Boston's *The Children of Green Knowe* (1980).

Ego Psychology and Object Relations Theories

The generation of psychoanalysts that was influenced by, reacted against and revised Freud, distinguishes itself by overcoming Freud's pessimism regarding the ego's inevitable discontent. While the new focus does not deny the existence of the unconscious, it emphasises the possibility of healthy growth and development in the ego's self-realisation in relation to its environment. Karen Horney and Abraham Maslow, Melanie Klein and Donald Winnicott describe possibilities for growth through constructive management of the id's pressures. Each insists that the developing psyche of the child responds to environmental conditions with a positive urge to self-actualisation that is thwarted only by hostile environments. From the perspective of ego psychology, author and reader participate in a shareable fantasy that constructively breaks down 'for a time the boundaries between self and other, inner and outer, past and future, and ... may neutralise the primal aggressions bound up in those separations' (Holland 1968: 340). Psychoanalytic literary critics have, however, also been concerned that ego psychology tends to be in one direction only, 'namely from the ego as a publicly adjusted identity' (Wright 1984: 57).

Karen Horney and Abraham Maslow

According to Horney, the goal of psychoanalysis is the patient's discovery of the possibility of self-realisation and the recognition that good human relations are an essential part of this, along with the faculty for creative work and the acceptance of personal responsibility (1950: 334). Persistent denial of childhood conflicts and their screening with defensive self-delusions block self-realisation. Irrational expectations or 'neurotic claims' such as self-idealisation obscure not only self-hate, but also 'the unique alive forces' that each self possesses and that are distorted by the self-illusions. The therapeutic process weakens the obstructive forces so that the constructive forces of the real self can emerge (348). The constructive forces in ego psychology become known as the 'Third Force'.

Bernard Paris has applied 'Third Force' psychology to several canonical novels whose self-alienating characters fit Horney's descriptions of neurotic styles, while self-activating characters express their 'Third Force' as defined by Maslow (Paris 1974: 29). For Maslow, the 'Third Force' is our 'essentially biologically based inner nature', unique to the person but also species-wide, whose needs, emotions and capacities are 'either neutral, pre-moral or positively good' (1968: 3). Neuroses result when our hierarchically organised basic needs are not met (21). When one level of needs is satisfied, the needs of another level emerge as persons define themselves existentially. During that process the person has 'peak experiences', epiphanic moments that afford glimpses into the state of being fully actualised and can have the effect of removing symptoms, of changing a person's view of himself and the world, of releasing creativity and generally conveying the idea that life is worth living in spite of its difficulties (101). Maslow admits that not all peak experiences are moments of 'Being recognition' (100), but he insists that people are 'most their identities in peak experiences' (103) where they feel most self-integrated.

The development of the ego as self-reliant and socially accepted is perhaps most evident in the young adult novel whose comic resolution integrates the young person with socially acceptable norms. Frequently such narratives include the figure of the social worker or therapist who aids the process, or the young protagonist plans to become a therapist so as to 'help kids in trouble'. Such problem narratives are accessible to young readers through stories that occasionally seem like case studies. The young adult novel that projects the genuine misfit as a worthwhile subject is a rarity. The largely middle-class context of young adult novels generally furthers the optimism implied in ego psychology.

Melanie Klein and D. W. Winnicott

According to Klein, because the ego is not fully integrated at birth, it is subject to splitting and fragmentation as it projects states of feeling and unconscious wishes on objects or absorbs qualities of the object through introjection where they become defined as belonging to the ego.

Like Freud, Klein saw the 'exploration of the unconscious [as] the main task of psycho-analytic procedure, and that the analysis of transference [was] the means of achieving this' (1955/1975a: 123). Her analysands were primarily children whose inability to freely associate verbally led Klein to develop the psychoanalytic play technique already begun by Anna Freud (1925/1975b: 146).

The use of simple toys in a simply equipped room brought out 'a variety of symbolical meanings' bound up with the child's fantasies, wishes and experiences. By approaching the child's play in a manner similar to Freud's interpretation of dreams, but by always individualising the child's use of symbols, Klein felt she could gain access to the child's unconscious (1975a: 137). She discovered that the primary origin of impulses, fantasies and anxieties could be traced back to the child's original object relation – the mother's breast – even when the child was not breastfed (138).

In commenting on the influence of Klein on literary theory, Elizabeth Wright regrets that Klein's demonstration of fantasy as a precondition of any engagement with reality has been neglected by literary critics who have instead focused on the aesthetic of ego psychology (1984: 83–84). It is through the structure of fantasy that the child acts out not only real or imagined damage, but also the desire for reparation. Klein saw the monsters and menacing figures of myths and fairy tales as parent displacements exerting unconscious influences on the child by making it feel threatened and persecuted, but such emotions 'can clear our feelings to some extent towards our parents of grievances, we can forgive them for the frustrations we had to bear, become at peace with ourselves' so that 'we are able to love others in the true sense of the word' (1975b: 343).

In criticisms of children's literature, Klein's approach can reveal how the text enables the actualisation of the ego intentionally or how it falls short of it. For example, an interpretation of Bianco's *The Velveteen Rabbit* reveals it as a fantasy of unresolved ambivalence between the need to be loved and becoming independent, that is, real. Because 'the story never acknowledges the Rabbit's desire to grow away from the object of his attachment, and hence never acknowledges the basis for his entry into the depressive position, it cannot credit him with working through it' (Daniels 1990: 26). The Kleinian perspective also offers insight into the relation of fantasy to guilt and reparation as exemplified in White's *Charlotte's Web* (Rustin 1987: 161).

While Klein focused on play as a means to the end of the therapeutic process, D. W. Winnicott saw play as intrinsically facilitating healthy development and group relationships. Even psychoanalysis is an elaborate playing 'in the service of communication with oneself and others' (1971: 41). In his studies of babies and children, Winnicott retained the psychoanalytic attention to inner reality along with an emphasis on the child's cultural and social context. Crucial in his discovery is the concept of the 'transitional object': 'one must recognise the central position of Winnie-the-Pooh' (xi). By transitional object and transitional space Winnicott designates the intermediate area of experience between the thumb and the teddy bear, between oral eroticism and true object relationships. Identifying the mother's breast as part of itself, the baby must develop the ability of the 'not me' through substitutions which are transitions between the illusion of identification and the acceptance of the 'not me'. The baby's relationship with the transitional object has special qualities: the infant assumes right but not omnipotence over the object which can be loved and changed, even mutilated by the infant. Gradually, the infant will be able to detach itself from the object which becomes consigned to a limbo, rather than being introjected by the infant (1–5). The object is not a signifier for some hidden unconscious content, but a crucial partner in the game of intersubjectivity as the playing infant tests out the me/not me.

Winnicott's concept of the transitional object not only lends itself to the interpretation of content images in narratives, but also to the text itself. Both author and reader can claim the text as transitional object. Small children do indeed appropriate a book as object – loving it, adding to it, mutilating it. An especially Winnecottian book would be Margaret Wise Brown's *Good Night Moon*, which has been cited as an example of child's having just learned the distinction between animate and inanimate objects. 'Good night, bears' (toys) and 'good night, kittens' is acceptable, but saying good night to chairs and mittens provokes shrieks of laughter in the child (Applebee 1978: 41) who does not yet accept the object 'bear' as inanimate. *Good Night Moon* is, for a certain age, a transitional object containing many transitional objects that assuage bedtime anxieties as the child connects with all of them, thus assuring itself of the 'me' before the lights go out at bedtime.

Jacques Lacan: The Return to Freud Through Language

For Freud the subconscious is the irreducible radical of the psyche, its universal, whose paradox it is that nothing raised from it remains unconscious: we can only be conscious of *something*. Thus the unconscious is replaced by the comprehensible mental acts of the ego, be they dreams, symbolisation's or linguistic utterances. As Wright points out, for Jacques Lacan 'the dictum "the unconscious is structured like a language" ' is borne out in that 'every word indicates the absence of what it stands for, a fact that intensifies the frustration of this child of language, the unconscious, since the absence of satisfaction has not to be accepted. Language imposes a chain of words along which the ego must move while the unconscious remains in search of the object it has lost' (Wright 1984: 111). The unconscious as a language allows Lacan to revise Freud's self-sufficiency of the unconscious with social interaction. How this comes about through the development of the infant and how this relates to the perception of the text as psyche – a major shift away from the author's or reader's psyche – has special relevance to interpreters of children's literature.

Lacan distinguishes three stages in the infant's development: the imaginary, the symbolic and the real. In the imaginary or mirror stage, which can happen at the age of six months, the infant receives the *imago* of its own body (*Ecrits*, 1977: 3). Having seen itself only as fragmentary, the infant perceives in the mirror a symbolic 'mental permanence of the I', but this perception prefigures alienation, for the mirror stage is a spatial illusion of totality (4), an imaginary identification with reflection. The mirror stage, which is pre-verbal, conveys the illusion that the image will respond to the child's wishes, as did the mother–breast–infant identification. The symbolic stage is the stage of language, a stage that will form the subject henceforth only in and as dialogue. The implied assumption that language may have definitive authority is undermined or deconstructed by Lacan's argument that every utterance is permeated by the unconscious in the sense that wholeness, meaning, and gratification of wishes are perpetually deferred. The real, not to be confused with 'external reality', describes what is lacking in the symbolic – 'it is the residue of articulation or the umbilical cord of the symbolic' (ix-x) (translator's note).

The literary text, then, is an image of the unconscious structured like a language. 'The lure of all texts', comments Wright, 'lies in a revelation, of things veiled coming to be unveiled, of characters who face shock at this unveiling' (1984: 121). When this phenomenon is given utterance in the reader-interpreter's language, meaning is inevitably deferred. In contrast to Freudian interpretation, we have here no unearthing of authorial neuroses. The Lacanian consequences for reader and text is the realisation that

> the selves we see ourselves as being are as fictional [made up of language] as the stories of written fiction – limited images like those we see in mirrors when we first became conscious of our separateness – so fiction can be read in terms of the way it echoes our basic human activity of inventing ourselves and becoming conscious of the limitation of our invention. All we usually call reality is in fact fiction, and always less complete than the actual real world outside our consciousness.
>
> Nodelman 1992: 93–94

Perry Nodelman discusses how Cinderella becomes a fixed subject at the end of the story rather than the multifaceted one she was. As she completes her stage of becoming, she has actually lost wholeness in her state of being (94). An analysis of *Charlotte's Web* shows how Lacan's imaginary and symbolic stage work through the 'Miracle of the web' in that Wilbur perceives himself and is perceived as transformed through the ability of words to reorient desire by demonstrating 'that things are desirable because they are signified and, therefore, significant' in and through language (Rushdy 1991: 56). Another Lacanian interpretation applies the concept of the subject being created by disjunction and discontinuity to Russell Hoban's *The Mouse and His Child* where the mouse child, submerged to the bottom of a pond, is jubilant when it sees itself reflected in the labelless Bonzo dog food can: 'He sees himself suddenly whole, apparently co-ordinated and in control' (Krips 1993: 95). The directive 'be happy' is in *The Mouse and His Child* as authoritative as Charlotte's five single word texts in the web, in that it creates the illusion of desire fulfilled, even as desire is deferred.

Psychoanalytic Theory and the Feminist Critique

The patrimony psychoanalytic criticism received from Freud has exerted a deep 'anxiety of influence' on the feminist critic (Gilbert and Gubar 1979: 45–92; Gallop 1982), primarily because of Freud's definition of female sexuality and his centring of the male myth of Oedipus, both of which reduce the female to an addendum. Revisionary readings of Freud, particularly those by French feminists influenced by Lacan, both appropriate and retain his powerful influence. Feminist readings of Jung underwent less radical revisions (Lauter and Rupprecht 1985). Even without specific reference to ego-relations and object psychology, the feminist critic, by delineating the struggle of the female in a patriarchially constructed world, finds in the concept of self-actualisation an ally in her attempt at social transformation.

While not denying the existence of the subconscious, feminist psychoanalytic criticism, including the feminist criticism of children's literature, privileges the concept of social construction in the development of the female. Nancy Chodorow's *The Reproduction of Mothering* has been especially influential in its synthesis of psychoanalysis and the sociology of gender where 'the reproduction of mothering occurs through social structurally induced psychological processes' and is 'neither a product of biology nor of intentional role training' (1978: 7). Here the critic of children's literature finds a female focus, especially for the mother–daughter relation (Barzilai 1990; Murphy 1990; Natov 1990). The focus on the body–self relations allows the feminist critic to explore unique female experiences that have been neglected in the study of literature. The focus on the social construction of female and male children, especially since the nineteenth-century middle-class self-definition of gender roles and the family, has guided feminists to valuable contextual insights into the history of children's literature and its readers.

A major issue in feminist criticism is the problematics of the female writer's precursors which has led Gilbert and Gubar to revise Bloom's 'anxiety of influence' (Bloom 1973) with 'anxiety of authorship' by which the female writer questions her claim to be a writer (Gilbert and Gubar 1979: 48–49). It remains to be seen if the important role of female writers in children's literature and the status of children's literature as a field of study might be understood as defences against the pressures of the male dominated literary and critical tradition.

Conclusion

The revisions and transformations by which psychoanalytical theories and criticisms continue to construct themselves have retained so far the concept of the unconscious and its powerful influence on the ego's development and struggle in the world. Children's literature, whose language signifies the substitutions and displacements necessitated in that struggle, intimates and makes acceptable the dream of desire. It is a great irony of our psychoanalytic age that the psychological self-help narratives for young readers abandon consideration of the powers of the id in favour of the social adjustment of the young ego and that they do so, usually, in the language of low mimetic accessibility where the mode of romance and poetry is gone. That phenomenon is itself worthy of psychoanalytical interpretations of authors, texts and readers.

References

Applebee, A. N. (1978) *The Child's Concept of Story*, Chicago: University of Chicago Press.
Barzilai, S. (1990) 'Reading 'Snow White': the mother's story', *Signs* 15, 3: 515–534.
Bettelheim, B. (1976) *The Uses of Enchantment*, New York: A. A. Knopf.
Bloom, H. (1973) *The Anxiety of Influence*, New York: Oxford University Press.
Bosmajian, H. (1985) '*Charlie and the Chocolate Factory* and other excremental visions', *The Lion and the Unicorn* 9: 36–49.
Chodorow, N. (1978) *The Reproduction of Mothering. Psychoanalysis and the Sociology of Gender*, Berkeley: University of California Press.

Cooper, J. C. (1983) *Fairy Tales: Allegories of the Inner Life*, Wellingborough: Aquarian Press.

Daniels, S. (1990) '*The Velveteen Rabbit*: a Kleinian perspective', *Children's Literature* 18: 17–30.

Egan, M. (1982) 'The neverland of id: Barrie, *Peter Pan*, and Freud', *Children's Literature* 10: 37–55.

Franz, M.-L. von (1977) *Individuation in Fairy Tales*, Zurich: Spring.

—— (1978) *An Introduction to the Psychology of Fairy Tales*, Irving, TX: Spring.

Freud, S., (1908/1963) 'The relation of the poet to daydreaming', *Character and Culture*, trans. J. Strachey, New York: Macmillan.

—— (1913/1958) 'The occurrence in dreams of material from fairy tales', *Character and Culture*, trans. J. Strachey, New York: Macmillan.

—— (1962/1975) *Three Essays on the Theory of Sexuality*, trans. J. Strachey, New York: Harper Collins.

Frye, N. (1957) *Anatomy of Criticism*, Princeton: Princeton University Press.

Gallop, J. (1982) *The Daughter's Seduction: Feminism and Psychoanalysis*, Ithaca, NY: Cornell University Press.

Gilbert, S. and Gubar, S. (1979) *The Madwoman in the Attic: The Woman Writer and the Nineteenth Century Literary Imagination*, New Haven: Yale University Press.

Greenacre, P. (1955) *Swift and Carroll: A Psychoanalytic Study of Two Lives*, New York: International Universities Press.

Hillman, J. (1980) 'The children, the children!' *Children's Literature* 8: 3–6.

Hogan, P. (1990) 'What's wrong with the psychoanalysis of literature?', *Children's Literature* 18: 135–140.

Holland, N. (1968) *The Dynamics of Literary Response*, New York: Oxford University Press.

—— (1970) 'The 'unconscious' of literature: the psychoanalytic approach', in Bradbury, N. and Palmer, D. (eds) *Contemporary Criticism*, Stratford-upon-Avon Series 12, New York: St Martin's.

Horney, K. (1950) *Neurosis and Human Growth: The Struggle Toward Self-Realization*, New York: Norton.

Jung, C. G. (1931/1966) 'On the relation of analytical psychology to poetry', *The Spirit in Man, Art, and Literature. Collected Works* vol. 15, trans. R. F. C. Hull, New York: Random House.

—— (1946/1954) 'Psychic conflicts in a child', *The Development of Personality. Collected Works* vol. 17, trans. R. F. C. Hull, New York: Random House.

—— (1964) 'Approaching the unconscious', *Man and His Symbols*, New York: Doubleday.

Klein, M. (1975a) *Envy and Gratitude*, New York: Delacorte.

—— (1975b) *Love, Guilt and Reparation*, New York: Delacorte.

Knoepflmacher, U. C. (1990) 'The doubtful marriage: a critical fantasy', *Children's Literature* 18: 131–134.

Krips, V. (1993) 'Mistaken identity: Russell Hoban's *Mouse and His Child*', *Children's Literature* 21: 92–100.

Lacan, J. (1977) *Ecrits*, trans. Alan Sheridan, New York: W. W. Norton.

Lauter, E. and Rupprecht, C. S. (1985) *Feminist Archetypal Theory. Interdisciplinary Revisions of Jungian Thought*, Knoxville: University of Tennessee Press.

Maslow, A. (1968) *Toward a Psychology of Being*, New York: D. Van Nostrand.

Murphy, A. (1990) 'The borders of ethical, erotic, and artistic possibilities, *Little Women*', *Signs* 15, 3: 562–585.

Natov, R. (1990) 'Mothers and daughters: Jamaica Kincaid's pre-oedipal narrative', *Children's Literature* 18: 1–16.

Nodelman, P. (1992) *The Pleasures of Children's Literature*, New York: Longman.

Paris, B. J. (1974) *A Psychological Approach to Fiction*, Bloomington: Indiana University Press.

Phillips, J. and Wojcik-Andrews, I. (1990) 'Notes toward a Marxist critical practice', *Children's Literature* 18: 127–130.

Rollin, L. (1990) 'The reproduction of mothering in *Charlotte's Web*', *Children's Literature* 18: 42–52.

Rose, J. (1984) *The Case of Peter Pan, or the Impossibility of Children's Fiction*, London: Macmillan.

Rosenthal, L. (1980) 'The development of consciousness in Lucy Boston's *The Children of Green Knowe*', *Children's Literature* 8: 53–67.

Rushdy, A. H. A. (1991) ' "The Miracle of the Web": community, desire and narrativity in *Charlotte's Web*', *The Lion and the Unicorn* 15, 2: 35–60.

Rustin, M. and Rustin, M. (1987) *Narratives of Love and Loss: Studies in Modern Children's Fiction*, New York: Verso.

Segel, E. (1986) ' "As the Twig Is Bent ...", gender and childhood reading', in Flynn, E. A. and Schweikart, P. (eds) *Gender and Reading*, Baltimore: Johns Hopkins University Press.

Smith, J. and Kerrigan, W. (1985) *Opening Texts: Psychoanalysis and the Culture of the Child*, Baltimore: Johns Hopkins University Press.

Steig, M. (1990) 'Why Bettelheim? A comment on the use of psychological theories in criticism', *Children's Literature* 18: 125–126.

Tatar, M. (1992) *Off with Their Heads! Fairy Tales and the Culture of Childhood*, Princeton: Princeton University Press.

Winnicott, D. W. (1971) *Playing and Reality*, New York: Tavistock/Routledge.

Wright, E. (1984) *Psychoanalytic Criticism*, New York: Methuen.

Zipes, J. (1979) *Breaking the Magic Spell: Radical Theories of Folk and Fairy Tales*, Austin: University of Texas Press.

—— (1990) 'Negating history and male fantasies through psychoanalytic criticism', *Children's Literature* 18: 141–143.

Further Reading

Bloch, D. (1978) *'So the Witch Won't Eat Me' Fantasy and the Child's Fear of Infanticide*, New York: Grove Press.

Byrnes, A. (1995) *The Child: An Archetypal Symbol in Literature for Children and Adults*, New York: Peter Lang.

Cech, J. (1995) *Angels and Wild Things: The Archetypal Poetics of Maurice Sendak*, Pennsylvania: Pennsylvania State University Press.

Jung, C. G. (1964) *Man and His Symbols*, New York: Doubleday.

Tucker, N. (1981) *The Child and the Book: A Psychological and Literary Exploration*, New York: Cambridge University Press.

9 From Sex-Role Stereotyping to Subjectivity: Feminist Criticism

Lissa Paul

Editor's introduction

'There is', Lissa Paul has written, 'good reason for appropriating feminist theory to children's literature. Both women's literature and children's literature are devalued and regarded as marginal or peripheral by the literary and educational communities...'. At the turn of the millenium, the pattern changes. Feminist criticism has taught readers to see and hear the stories of women and children in ways not understood before. This chapter tracks the history of that re-visioning.

P. H.

'A Cinderella story: research on children's books takes on new life as a field of literary study': that was the headline for an article on the rise of academic children's literature criticism, published 13 February 1991, in the *Chronicle of Higher Education* (the newspaper for American universities, similar to the *Times Higher Educational Supplement* in Britain). Although the article, by Ellen K. Coughlin, nicely sketches several of the current poststructuralist, including feminist, lines in children's literature criticism, it is the headline that is arresting. The teasing, metaphoric association with the rags-to-riches image of Cinderella stories inadvertently discloses the uneasy relations between children's literature, feminist theory and the academy.

Cinderella herself is, after all, the subject of a great deal of feminist critique. Most of us – women, children and feminist critics, I imagine – don't want to be seen valuing riches. Or princes for that matter. The implication in the Cinderella reference in the headline is that as 'the province of library schools and education departments' (Coughlin 1991: 5), children's literature criticism ranks low on the academic hit parade. Now associated with high-order poststructuralist theory and with English departments, children's literature criticism moves up in the respectability ratings.

If the destabilisation of hierarchical orders is one of the mobilising features of feminist theory then there is probably something hypocritical and arrogant about disenfranchising librarians, teachers – and children – from the ranks of stakeholders in the field of children's literature studies. It is not coincidental that librarians and teachers tend to be women and that the education of young children is not regarded as the serious business of scholars (a hold over from the New Criticism).

A pair of articles in *Orana*, an Australian children's literature journal, neatly problematise the gender equity issues as raised often by critics from education, library science and psychology. In 'Sexism and children's literature: a perspective for librarians' (1981), Christine Nicholls recognises that 'sexism is a type of colonialism', but she then goes on to suggest that solutions to the problem include the use of 'white out' and the abandonment of books no longer in accord with contemporary definitions of gender equity. Hugh Crago (a psychologist and a fine children's literature critic) offers a sensitively worked out corrective. In 'Sexism, literature and reader-response: a reply to Christine Nicholls', he reminds Nicholls (and the rest of us) that responses to texts are subject to large fluctuations, especially in fluid forms like fairy tales where versions, translations and illustrations all contribute to shaping the interpretative possibilities of texts. He also foregrounds the idea there is really no such thing as 'the one-way cause and effect relationship' (Crago 1981: 161) between reader and text – something implicit in the Nicholls article and in a great many like it.

There are two points worth foregrounding here. One is that the emphasis on sex-role stereotyping and sexism found most often in education and library science journals is connected with an honest front-line attempt to create a more female-friendly climate, especially in schools. That connection between theoretical change and political change is true to the roots of feminist theory in the women's movements of the 1970s. To dismiss librarians and teachers as the 'rags' phase of the Cinderella story is to participate in a hierarchical ordering of critical values. As a feminist critic, I don't want to do that.

The other point worth keeping in mind is that current poststructuralist discussions, especially those on semiotics, deconstruction, ideology and sub-jectivity, make it possible to develop language and strategies that speak – to borrow a phrase from Carol Gilligan – 'in a different voice'. As an academic feminist children's literature critic, feminist admonitions to remember our histories and value members of our communities constantly sound in my mind.

Children's literature offers to children the promise of inclusion in a literate community (something regarded as culturally valuable, at least nominally). The critical apparatus surrounding children's books offers an intellectual under-standing of what inclusion means and how it might be achieved. In an ideal world anyway. What feminist theory has done for children's literature studies – and for all fields of literary study – is to insist on the right to be included, but not just as honorary white men. As a result, not only have our interpretations of texts changed, but also our production of them and our access to them – as I'll try to demonstrate throughout this article.

The current wave of academic children's literature criticism rose in the early 1970s at the same time as the rise of what is known as the 'second wave' of feminist theory in this century. In the 1990s both feminist criticism and children's literature criticism are established participants in the academy with all the requisite structures in place to support establishment status – refereed journals, professional associations, graduate degree programmes.

Signs of the common ground between children's literature criticism and feminist theory are marked in two special issues of children's literature journals. The *Children's Literature Association Quarterly* ran a special section, edited by

Anita Moss, in the Winter 1982 edition: 'Feminist criticism and the study of children's literature'. In that early collection of essays there were several reviews of books of feminist literary criticism, each sketching possible critical lines children's literature critics might find worth exploring. Virginia Wolf, for instance, writes about alternatives to the heroic quest in science fiction; and Lois Kuznets about texts that value communities rather than kingdoms.

In December 1991, *The Lion and the Unicorn* published an issue called 'Beyond sexism: gender issues in children's literature'. By this time the lessons of feminist theory are internalised, and critics are actively constructing a feminist tradition in children's literature (see especially essays by Judith John, W. Nikola-Lisa, Lynne Vallone and the essay by Lois Kuznets discussed below). Note the switch, incidentally, from 'feminist criticism' to 'gender' studies. That shift marks the subtle inclusion of gay and lesbian studies into the fray. It also marks the popular use of a code word to try prevent feminist studies from becoming a pink-collar ghetto. And it hints at the speed with which feminist theory is changing – something I'll try to track.

In keeping with feminist critic Jane Gallop's cryptic caution to remember that 'history is like a mother' (1992: 206–239), I'm going to focus on three broad areas of academic children's literature criticism influenced (unanxiously) by feminist theory: the rereading of texts for previously unrevealed interpretations; the reclaiming of texts that had been devalued or dismissed; and the redirection of feminist theory into providing a welcoming climate for texts by people marginalised by patriarchal colonial societies. The titles in each of my three sections in this essay, 'Rereading', 'Reclaiming' and 'Redirection' take their cue from Adrienne Rich's ideas that feminist poetics are about 'revision' (Rich 1976).

Rereading

The desire for feminist rereading comes from an understanding of the ways ideological assumptions about the constitution of good literature (or criticism for that matter) work. By the early 1970s, feminist critics like Kate Millett had made it common knowledge that assumptions about good literature had been predicated on the belief that the adult white male was normal, while virtually everyone else was deviant or marginal. And so was born a critical desire to see if a feminine literary tradition, and feminine culture could be made visible. By using techniques from deconstruction (derived largely from Derrida) and from contemporary discussions of ideology (from Althusser and Pierre Bourdieu) and subjectivity (largely derived from Lacan), feminist critics began to look at the ways ideological assumptions are played out in the text. They searched for a feminine tradition of 'other' stories: mother, daughter, sister stories (Chodorow, Hirsch); a preference for survival tactics over honour (Gilligan); a search for a 'both/and' feminine plot rather than an 'either/or' oedipal plot (Hirsch); a preference from multiplicity, plurality, jouissance and a valuing of pro-creations, recreations and new beginnings (Cixous, Gallop, Rich). Feminist children's literature critics also participate in this recovery of a female literary tradition (Paul 1987/1990; 1990). The following small sketches of reinterpretation, rehabilitation and re-creation demonstrate the range of ways in which that tradition is being revealed.

Reinterpretation

Feminist reinterpretations of familiar classics like *The Secret Garden* and *Little Women* turn stories we thought were about struggles to conform to the social order into stories about women's healing and successful communities of women (Bixler, Nelson, Auerbach). *Little Women* – as read by Edward Salmon (a nineteenth-century authority on children's literature) in his 1888 obituary of Alcott in *Atalanta* – is a story about instructing girls to be 'the proper guardians of their brothers' and to be 'all-powerful for good in their relations with men' (449). But for Nina Auerbach, in *Communities of Women* (1978), it is the story of 'the formation of a reigning feminist sisterhood whose exemplary unity will heal a fractured society' (37). The critical rereading turns it from a story about women learning how to serve men into a story of women supporting each other.

Rehabilitation

The rehabilitation of works by Mary Wollstonecraft, Maria Edgeworth and other 'lady moralists' of the Georgian and Romantic periods, is one of the major success stories of academic feminist children's literature criticism. Although I am going to focus on criticism by Mitzi Myers, credit also goes to Anita Moss and Lynne Vallone.

As Mitzi Myers pointedly states, texts by Georgian 'lady' moralists as rendered in standard overviews of children's literature, suffer from 'something like the critical equivalent of urban blight' (Myers 1986: 31). John Rowe Townsend dismisses these women as ranging 'from the mildly pious to the sternly moralistic' (1974: 39). Harvey Darton refers to 'the truculent dogmatic leanings of Mrs Sherwood and Mrs Trimmer' and the 'completely dogmatic' Mary Godwin (1982: 156, 196).

Myers offers different readings. She participates in what feminist critic Elaine Showalter calls 'gynocriticism', that is, criticism that attends to 'the woman as producer of textual meaning, with the history, themes, genres, and structures of literature by women' (Showalter 1985: 128). What Myers asks is how those Georgian women found autonomy and influence in a world where those freedoms were denied. Her answers transform lady moralists scorned for their conformity, into the founding mothers of a feminist pedagogical tradition.

In Georgian England, where there were few roles for (upper class) women except as wives, mothers and governesses, Mary Wollstonecraft, Maria Edgeworth and other women like Mrs Trimmer and Mrs Sherwood transformed their roles. They constructed 'an almost unrecognised literary tradition', one that 'accepts and emphasises the instructive and intellectual potential of narrative' (Myers 1986: 33). Maria Edgeworth, for example, creates female protagonists as 'desiring' subjects, not just objects of desire. And Mary Wollstonecraft, in her 'Mrs Mason' stories, redefines power in unpatriarchal terms 'as pedagogic and philanthropic power' (43).

The autonomy, creativity and integrity of those Georgian women would not have been possible without the eyes of Mitzi Myers and her knowledge of feminist theory. They would have remained in the footnotes of what is now beginning to look like a masculinist tradition of children's literature.

Re-creation

Although I've focused so far on the way academic critics construct feminist traditions in children's literature, I'm mindful of the ways authors living through the second wave of feminism are changing what we read. Author Ursula Le Guin chronicles the change most dramatically. In *Earthsea Revisioned* (1993), the published version of lecture she gave in Oxford in 1992, Le Guin records the influence of gender politics on her *Earthsea* quartet. The first three *Earthsea* novels published between 1968 and 1972, are in the genre of the traditional heroic fantasy, something Le Guin defines as 'a male preserve: a sort of great game-park where Beowulf feasts with Teddy Roosevelt, and Robin Hood goes hunting with Mowgli, and the cowboy rides off into the sunset alone' (Le Guin 1993: 5).

Le Guin does not apologise for the male-order, hierarchical world in the first three novels. But twenty years after their publication she recognises things about that world that she didn't understand when she made it. With the insights of contemporary feminist theory, she understands that at the time, she was 'writing partly by the rules, as an artificial man, and partly against the rules, as an inadvertent revolutionary' (7). In her revolutionary mode, in a partly conscious attempt to create a hero from a visible minority, Le Guin made Ged and all the good guys in the *Earthsea* books black, and the bad guys white. Nevertheless, the good guys were standard male-order heroes anyway. They lived lives of 'continence; abstinence; denial of relationship' (16). And they worked in a world predicated on 'power as domination over others, unassailable strength, and the generosity of the rich' (14).

But in *Tehanu*, the fourth and final *Earthsea* book, published seventeen years after the third, Le Guin scraps male-order heroism. She creates Tenar, a feminist pro-creative, recreative hero: 'All her former selves are alive in her: the child Tenar, the girl priestess Arha ... and Goha, the farmwife, mother of two children. Tenar is whole but not single. She is not pure' (Le Guin 1993: 18). The traditional male hero, the dragonslayer and dragonlord, marked by his capacity to defeat evil, to win, and to receive public adoration and power, is nowhere in sight. In the new mythology Le Guin creates, the dragon is transformed into a familiar, a guide for a new female hero: 'The child who is our care, the child we have betrayed, is our guide. She leads us to the dragon. She is the dragon'. Le Guin moves out of the hierarchical ordering of the heroic world, and into a new world where the search is for wildness, a 'new order of freedom' (26).

The feminist tradition created in the span that includes Mitzi Myers's rereading Wollstonecraft, and Le Guin revisioning *Earthsea*, is one that celebrates maternal pedagogies, disorder, wildness, pro-creation, re-creation and multi-plicity: a large cultural shift in a short space of time.

Reclaiming

One of the most significant feminist projects of the last twenty-five years has been the reissuing of long out-of-print books by women authors. Many have been gathering dust on library shelves for dozens, sometimes hundreds of years. Most had long since ceased to make any money for anyone. But Virago and other feminist presses that grew up with the second wave of feminism, have put many of these books back into circulation. Now easily available in good quality paperback editions they are read for pleasure, not just among scholars, though scholars were often the first to create the demand for these books by finding them, writing about them and bringing them to university course lists and to public attention.

Though there is no exactly comparable resurrection of authored fiction in children's literature (Angela Brazil is as unlikely to be reissued as Talbot Baines Reed), there is one class of texts enjoying a new lease on life as a direct result of the second wave of feminism: fairy tales. In fact, the shift in fairy tale fashions over the last twenty-five years provides a virtual paradigm for shifts in feminist poetics.

In the 1970s, with the rise of the second wave of feminist theory, there was increasing discomfort with the gender dynamics in popular Grimm, Andersen and Perrault fairy tales (though Simone de Beauvoir had already drawn attention to passive Grimm heroines twenty years earlier in *The Second Sex*). Girls and women play dead or doormats (as in 'Snow White', 'Cinderella', and 'Sleeping Beauty') or are severely mutilated (as in 'The Little Mermaid').

The move was on for female heroes (I'll use the term in preference to 'heroines' – who tend to wait around a lot). Unfortunately, the female heroes of the early 1970s tended not to be of a different order, as is Tenar in Le Guin's *Tehanu*. They tended to be more like men tricked out in drag. The stories were the same as those with male heroes in them. But instead of being about boys seeking adventure, profit, and someone to rescue, girls were in the starring roles. They rescued instead of being rescued. Like television situation comedies that colour middle-class families black, most of those tales died natural deaths. *The Paper Bag Princess* by Robert Munsch is a dubious exception. It is still in print, and the princess uses the feminist tactic of deceit to defeat the dragon and rescue the prince. But as the prince suffers from the traditionally feminine vice of vanity, s/he is essentially rejected for a lack of machismo.

When revisionist tales virtually disappeared in the late 1970s, reclaimed tales looked like a more viable alternative. But in the first collections of reclaimed tales, the preference for male characteristics in female heroes was still much in evidence. In the introduction to *Tatterhood and Other Tales*, for example, Ethel Johnston Phelps states a preference for stories with 'active and courageous girls and women in the leading roles', ones who are 'distinguished by extraordinary courage and achievements' (1978: vx). In other words, she prefers the same old male type, who, as Valerie Walkerdine suggests, is 'gender-neutral, self-disciplined, and active' (120). That is, the preferred hero is still a man.

The one voice that begs to differ belongs Angela Carter. Her two collections of reclaimed fairy tales for Virago are so good they are difficult to put down. She doesn't just present tales about the unrelieved glory of women – a male-order project anyway. Instead, she tries 'to demonstrate the extraordinary richness and diversity of responses to the same common predicament – being alive – and the richness and diversity with which femininity, in practice is represented in "unofficial" culture: its strategies, its plots, its hard work' (Carter 1991: xiv). One of her favourite stories from this collection was apparently 'Tongue meat', a Swahili story that tells of a languishing queen who only revives when fed 'tongue meat', something that turns out to be a metaphor for stories. The tales of girls and women that Angela Carter revives are exactly that kind of 'tongue meat'. They establish an alternative feminist tradition – one that hadn't been visible before.

While it is true that fairy tales seem to have enjoyed the most dramatic revival as a result of twinned interests in women's studies and children's literature studies, other reclamation projects are also taking place. The texts being rediscovered by feminist critics are important because they provide a historical context for our own ideological assumptions about gender, about what constitutes good literature, and about what is worth remembering, circulating and retaining for study.

One of the most compelling studies of women's texts lost and found is, 'Lost from the nursery: women writing poetry for children 1800–1850', by Morag Styles (1990). Styles came to write the article because she casually noticed how few women were represented in poetry anthologies for children, especially poets who published before 1900. As she began to explore, she discovered consistent patterns working to obliterate women poets from the record.

In early anthologies Styles found that poems which had quickly become popular in their own time, like 'Twinkle twinkle little star', or 'Mary had a little lamb', rapidly became separated from their authors as they entered anthologies. They were usually attributed to the anonymous authors of oral tradition. So while generations of children learned to say 'Twinkle twinkle little star', few knew it was by Jane Taylor, or that Sara Hale wrote 'Mary had a little lamb', or that 'The months of the year' was by Sara Coleridge.

The systematic exclusion of these women from the children's literature canon accords precisely with the ideological reasons for their exclusion from the literary canon – and from positions of power and influence. Styles explains that 'the colloquial domestic writing of some women whose concern in literature for children (and often for adults) is with relationships, affection, friendship, family life often located in the small-scale site of the home' (Styles 1990: 203) was devalued, lost and forgotten in a world where large scale adventures and public rhetoric were valued. So the voices of Jane and Anne Taylor 'talking lovingly and naturally' in their poetry collections were lost. And Dorothy Wordsworth, with her 'private, colloquial and domestic' poetry (202), was relegated to a footnote in her brother's life.

By bringing the domestic cadences of women 'lost from the nursery', to our eyes and ears again, Styles provides a climate that warms to the domestic scene and to the softer, more direct, colloquial cadences of the female voice. She teaches us to listen with different ears to the different voice of women's poetry for children.

Although I've focused on two specific feminist reclamation efforts, fairy tales and poetry, both are part of a much larger feminist agenda, and I don't want to leave this section without mentioning other ways in which feminist children's literature critics are gradually recovering a female literary tradition.

By revealing the constructions of gendered patterns of childhood reading, academic feminist critics are beginning to locate the origins of ideological constructions of gender. Two studies of nineteenth-century girls' books and boys' books were published within a year of one another: *Girls Only?: Gender and Popular Children's Fiction in Britain, 1880–1910*, by Kimberley Reynolds in 1990, and *Boys will be Girls: The Feminist Ethic and British Children's Fiction, 1857–1917*, by Claudia Nelson in 1991. The sudden focus on that late nineteenth- and early twentieth-century time period is more than coincidental. It marks a critical recognition of that period as the time when colonial and patriarchal values were being actively inscribed in the culture. In widely circulating publications like the *Girl's Own Paper*, girls were apparently encouraged to accept simultaneously characteristics gendered feminine – 'purity, obedience, dependence, self-sacrifice and service' – and, an 'image of feminine womanhood ... expanded to incorporate intelligence, self-respect, and ... the potential to become financially dependent'. The result was a set of 'contradictory tendencies characteristic of femininity: reason and desire, autonomy and dependent activity, psychic and social identity' (Nelson 1991: 141). Those contradictions still haunt women today.

Other critics participate in the recovery of more recent histories of the relations between gender and reading. Lois Kuznets, in 'Two Newbery Medal winners and the feminine mystique: *Hitty, Her First Hundred Years*' and *Miss Hickory* (1991) looks at how two doll stories reflect the shifting ideological values of their times: *Hitty*, the 1930 winner, reflects the valuing of the independent woman who flourished in the 1920s; while *Miss Hickory*, the 1947 winner, reflects the post-war 'feminine mystique', something we now read as revealing a sadly repressed woman.

Relations between public success and childhood reading are being recounted in several reading memoirs published in the late 1980s and early 1990s. The women writing them at the height of, or late in, their professional careers seem to be offering clues that might be of use to librarians and teachers interested in creating a more supportive academic environment for girls. In *My Book House as Bildung*, Nancy Huse reconstructs her childhood reading of Olive Miller's *My Book House* as a way of establishing a maternal pedagogical line that influenced her choice of an academic career. And in the children's literature journal, *Signal*, Nancy Chambers has published several reading memoirs by well-known women who are active in a range of children's literature fields. Among them are ones by children's book editor Margaret Clark; author Jane Gardam; and Susan Viguers writing about her children's literature expert mother. All reveal how childhood reading enabled them to enter public worlds of letters on bridges built from private, domestic literate environments.

The tunes – to borrow a phrase from Margaret Meek (1992) – of women's texts are different from the ones established in the canon as being of value. What feminist theory has revealed, especially in reconstructions of a female literary tradition, is that the disproportionate emphasis placed on adventure, power, honour and public success squeezed out feminine valuing of maternal, domestic voices, ideas of sisterhood and stories about the lives of women. While only the feminist fairy tales may have found popular readership, scholarship teaches us to value domestic scenes and colloquial voices, and to remember our histories. It enables us to make familiar the new texts that come our way. The scholarship enables us to appreciate their difference.

Redirection

The second wave of feminism began in the late 1960s when a whole generation of white, well-educated 'baby-boomer' women found that they were still relegated to making the coffee and stuffing envelopes. They were still excluded from the dominant discourses. The consciousness-raising groups of the 1970s began as means of mobilising collective voices in order to gain inclusion.

The right to be included: that became a basic tenet of feminist theory. So feminist theory changed to become increasingly inclusive: the feminist studies of the 1970s grew into gender studies in the 1980s. In the 1990s another change is happening as gender studies become aligned with post-colonial and cultural studies. Critics like Gayatri Spivak and Tinh T. Minh-ha, recognising the similarities between political power plays and gender power plays, have helped feminist criticism shed its Eurocentric, middle-class look. For children's literature critics, there is an increased awareness of the way primitives and children are frequently (t)roped together. In keeping with feminist agendas, this new theoretical line is changing both the readings and the text.

It is true that there is nothing in children's literature or children's literature criticism as yet that is as dramatic as the acknowledgement in Marina Warner's novel *Indigo*, that it was a work of post-colonial theory, *Colonial Encounters* by Peter Hulme, that spurred her to write the novel. But there are changes, as children's literature increasingly includes the images and voices of people of colour. I'm thinking especially of writers for children like John Agard, Grace Nichols, James Berry and Joy Kogawa who probe at the ways patriarchal powers have screwed up, how they've ruined the environment in favour of profit, and how they locked-up people designated as 'other' on the grounds that if they were foreign they were dangerous.

The unpicking of the child/primitive trope is also the subject of academic study. Stephen Slemon and Jo-Ann Wallace, professors at the University of Alberta in Canada taught a graduate course together called, 'Literatures of the child and the colonial subject: 1850–1914'. In an article they wrote together about their experience 'Into the heart of darkness? Teaching children's literature as a problem in theory' (1991), they discuss their struggle with the construction of the child in pedagogical and institutional terms. They write about the child who, like the 'primitive' is treated, 'as a subject-in-formation, an individual who often does not have full legal status and who therefore acts or who is acted against in ways that are not perceived to be fully consequential' (20). Post-colonial discourse illuminates ways in which authority over the 'other' is achieved in the name of protecting innocence. The ideological assumption is that primitives and children are too naïve (or stupid) to look after themselves so need protecting – like rain-forests.

The critical lessons in feminist/post-colonial theory increasingly have to do with ideology and with constructions of the subject. That's quite different from what used to be the common feature of children's literature and children's literature criticism – the notion of the identity quest, with its attendant assumption that there was such a thing as a stable identity. Instead, contemporary critical emphasis is on the ways we are constructed by the socialising forces pressuring us in all aspects of our lives: relationships with parents and families, class, gender and cultural patterns and expectations.

The implications for the unpicking of the child/primitive trope are part of something provoking a new crisis of definition in children's literature and children's literature criticism and teaching. While children's literature is predicated on the notion that children are essentially blank or naïve and in need of protection and instruction, then issues of suitability or unsuitability are important. But as children become differently constructed in the light of feminist and post-colonial theory, so does children's literature. Distinctions between them and us no longer become categorising features and suitability recedes as an issue.

The effects of this ideological shift begin to become apparent in criticism and in texts. Critics who work in feminist theory, post-colonial studies and children's literature all find themselves interested in common grounds: in the dynamics of power, in ideology, in the construction of the subject. And authors produce texts in which child/adult categories are no longer the significant ones. Jane Gardam's books, for example, appear in Abacus editions that don't make adult/child distinctions. And Angela Carter's Virago fairy tales are catalogued in the library not with children's literature or women's literature – but as anthropology.

The second wave of feminist theory has profoundly changed what we read and how we read. New texts and reclaimed texts have changed the canon so that more people are included and the 'dead white male' is less dominant. There is an increased awareness and valuing of maternal pedagogies and traditions of women's writing. Tastes have developed for colloquial, domestic voices pitched in higher registers and speaking in other cadences.

It is true that by the time this text is in print, the second wave of feminist theory will be long over. But it has created something else, something not fully defined yet. An article on feminist theory and children's literature written in 2006 would look radically different from this one – perhaps closer to the wild world of Le Guin's imaginings.

References

Auerbach, N. (1978) *Communities of Women: An Idea in Fiction*, Harvard: Harvard University Press.

Beauvoir, S. de (1953) *The Second Sex*, New York: Random House.

'Beyond sexism: gender issues in children's literature' (1991), *The Lion and the Unicorn* 15, 2.

Bixler, P. (1991) 'Gardens, houses, and nurturant power in *The Secret Garden*', in McGavran, J. (ed.) *Romanticism and Children's Literature in Nineteenth Century England*, Athens, GA: University of Georgia Press.

Carter, A. (ed.) (1991) *The Virago Book of Fairy Tales*, London: Virago.

—— (1992) *The Second Virago Book of Fairy Tales*, London: Virago.

Chodorow, N. (1978) *The Reproduction of Mothering: Psychoanalysis and the Sociology of Gender*, Berkeley, CA: University of California Press.

Cixous, H. (1991) *Coming to Writing and Other Essays*, Cambridge MA: Harvard.

Clark, M. (1991) 'Early to Read', *Signal* 65: 112–119.

Coughlin, E. K. (1991) 'A Cinderella story: research on children's books takes on new life as a field of literary study', *Chronicle of Higher Education* 13 February: 5–7.

Crago, H. (1981) 'Sexism, literature and reader-response: a reply to Christine Nicholls', *Orana* 17, 4: 159–162.

Darton, F. J. H. (1982) *Children's Books in England: Five Centuries of Social Life*, 3rd edn, rev. B. Alderson, Cambridge: Cambridge University Press.

'Feminist criticism and the study of children's literature' (1982), special section of *Children's Literature Association Quarterly* 7, 4.

Gallop, J. (1992) *Around 1981: Academic Feminist Literary Theory*, New York: Routledge.

Gardam, J. (1991) 'A writer's life and landscape', *Signal* 66: 179–194.

Gilligan, C. (1982) *In a Different Voice: Psychological Theory and Women's Development*, Cambridge MA: Harvard University Press.

Hirsch, M. (1989) *The Mother/Daughter Plot: Narrative, Psychoanalysis, Feminism*, Bloomington: Indiana University Press.

Hulme, P. (1986) *Colonial Encounters: Europe and the Native Caribbean, 1492–1797*, New York: Methuen.

Huse, N. (1988) *'My Book House as Bildung'*, *Children's Literature Association Quarterly* 13, 3: 115–121.

John, J. G. (1990) 'Searching for great-great grandmother: powerful women in George MacDonald's fantasies', *The Lion and the Unicorn* 15, 2: 27–34.

Kuznets, L. (1982) 'Defining full human potential: *Communities of Women, An Idea in Fiction*, and *Toward a Recognition of Androgyny'*, *Children's Literature Association Quarterly* 7, 4: 10.

—— (1991) 'Two Newbery Medal winners and the feminine mystique: *Hitty, Her First Hundred Years* and *Miss Hickory'*, *The Lion and the Unicorn* 15, 2: 1–14.

Le Guin, U. K. (1993) *Earthsea Revisioned*, Cambridge: Children's Literature New England in association with Green Bay Publications.

Meek, M. (1992) 'Transitions: the notion of change in writing for children', *Signal* 67: 13–32.

Millett, K. (1977) *Sexual Politics*, London: Virago.

Moss, A., 1988) 'Mothers, monsters, and morals in Victorian fairy tales', *The Lion and the Unicorn* 12, 2: 47–59.

Munsch, R. (1980) *The Paper Bag Princess*, Toronto: Annick Press.

Myers, M. (1986). 'Impeccable governesses, rational dames, and moral mothers: Mary Wollstonecraft and the female tradition in Georgian children's books', *Children's Literature* 14: 31–59.

Nelson, C. (1991) *Boys Will Be Girls: The Feminine Ethic and British Children's Fiction, 1857–1917*, New Brunswick: Rutgers.

Nicholls, C. 'Sexism and children's literature: a perspective for librarians', *Orana* 17, 3: 105–111.

Nikola-Lisa, W. (1991) 'The cult of Peter Rabbit: a Barthesian analysis', *The Lion and the Unicorn* 15, 2: 61–66.

Paul, L. (1987/1990) 'Enigma variations: what feminist theory knows about children's literature', in Hunt, P. (ed.) *Children's Literature: The Development of Criticism*, London: Routledge.

—— (1990) 'Escape claws: cover stories on *Lolly Willowes* and *Crusoe's Daughter'*, *Signal* 63: 206–220.

Phelps, E. J. (1978) *Tatterhood and other Tales*, New York: The Feminist Press.

Reynolds, K. (1990) *Girls Only? Gender and Popular Children's Fiction in Britain, 1880–1910*, New York: Harvester Wheatsheaf.

Rich, A. (1976) 'When we dead awaken: writing as re-vision', *On Lies, Secrets, and Silence: Selected Prose 1966–1978*, New York: Norton.

Salmon, E. (1888) 'Miss L. M. Alcott', *Atalanta* 1, 8: 447–449.

Showalter, E. (1985) 'Toward a feminist poetic', *Feminist Criticism: Essays on Women, Literature, and Theory*, New York: Pantheon.

Slemon, S. and Wallace, J. (1991) 'Into the heart of darkness? Teaching children's literature as a problem in theory', *Canadian Children's Literature*, 63: 6–23.

Styles, M. (1990) 'Lost from the nursery: women writing poetry for children 1800 to 1850', *Signal* 63: 177–205.

Townsend, J. R. (1974) *Written For Children: An Outline of English-language Children's Literature*, Harmondsworth: Penguin.

Vallone, L. (1990) 'Laughing with the boys and learning with the girls: humor in nineteenth-century American juvenile fiction', *Children's Literature Association Quarterly*, 15, 3: 127-30.

—— (1991) ' "A humble spirit under correction": tracts, hymns, and the ideology of evangelical fiction for children, 1780–1820', *The Lion and the Unicorn* 15, 2: 72–95.

Viguers, S. T. (1988) 'My mother, my children, and books', *Signal* 55: 23–32.

Walkerdine, V. (1990) *Schoolgirl Fictions*, London: Verso.

Warner, M. (1992) *Indigo: or Mapping the Waters*, London: Chatto and Windus.

Wolf, V. (1982) 'Feminist criticism and science fiction for children', *Children's Literature Association Quarterly* 7, 4: 13–16.

Further Reading

Auerbach, N. and Knoepflmacher, U. C. (1992) *Forbidden Journies: Fairy Tales and Fantasies by Victorian Women Writers*, Chicago: University of Chicago Press.

Barrs, M. and Pidgeon, S. (1993) *Reading the Difference: Gender and Reading in Primary School*, London: Centre for Language in Primary Education.

Clark, B. and Higonnet, M. (1999) *Girls, Boys, Books, Toys: Gender, Culture, Children's Literature*, Maryland: Johns Hopkins University Press.

Hooks, B. (1992) 'Representing whiteness in the black imagination', in Grossman, L., Nelson, C. and Treichler, P. (eds) *Cultural Studies*, New York: Routledge.

Miller, J. (1990) *Seduction: Studies in Reading and Culture*, London: Virago.

Paul, L. (1998) *Reading Otherways*, Stroud: The Thimble Press.

Trites, R. S. *Waking Sleeping Beauty: Feminist Voices in Children's Novels*, Iowa City, IA: University of Iowa Press.

Warhol, R. and Herndl, D. P. (1991) *Feminisms: An Anthology of Literary Theory and Criticism*, Rutgers University Press.

Warner, M. (1994) *Managing Monsters: Six Myths of Our Time*, The Reith Lectures, London: Vintage.

Zipes, J. (1997) *Happily Ever After: Fairy Tales, Children and the Culture Industry*, London: Routledge.

10 Inspecting the Foundations: Bibliographical Studies

Peter Hunt

Editor's introduction

For good criticism, it is sometimes said, you need good texts to criticise. Many classic (and not so classic) children's books exist in corrupt versions. There are hundreds of substantial collections of children's books around the world, which could yield invaluable information on the history of children's literature – and history in general – and yet they remain largely uninvestigated. The complex history of publishing for children is only beginning to be unravelled. This chapter reviews recent work on these fascinating areas.

P. H.

In 1975, Brian Alderson, in a paper presented before The Bibliographical Society, made the following observations:

> Although in the past this Society has enjoyed one or two addresses on detailed aspects of children's books ... there has been little attempt ... to put forward a rationale of the bibliographer's role in the study of books for this large section of the reading public ... Now while I do not wish to suggest that a more professional grasp of bibliographical skills will itself enable the study of children's books to gain greater maturity, there can be no doubt that scientific bibliography is able to play as important a role in supporting the very varied activity that is taking place among children's books as it does in the field of literary studies elsewhere ... Implicit in all that I have been saying so far is the contention that, at the nuts-and-bolts level, there is much elementary bibliographical work still to be done.
>
> Alderson 1977: 203

Twenty years later, in a review in the *Children's Books History Society Newsletter* of what he dismissed as 'sub-critical ego-trips' which characterise 'much professorial or assistant professorial writing', he lamented, 'Oh dear, so much bibliographical groundwork to be done, and all we get is floss' (Alderson 1995: 17).

The impression that little has been achieved in the bibliography of children's literature in twenty years is undoubtedly false, although the fact that *comparatively little* has been achieved in the context of other aspects of critical and practical activity surrounding children's books is undoubtedly true. However, this is a characteristic of all literary studies, as John Harwood pointed out in his swingeing attack on the literary-theoretical/critical establishment, *Eliot to Derrida: The Poverty of Interpretation*:

> Few in the field of literary studies question the value of good biography, or a scholarly edition of a writer's works, letters, manuscripts or diaries. We are not constantly assailed by warnings that the demise of editing or bibliography will bring about the end of civilisation as we know it. In contrast, doubts about the value of theory and interpretation are endemic in the profession, and it is these activities which are characteristically satirised by sceptical outsiders. Despite the efforts of some theorists to problematise them, the 'service industries' seem remarkably crisis-free. In the mid-1980s, theorists were talking about a 'return to history' as if no one had done any historical work since the advent of Derrida.) Literary works, manuscripts, letters and diaries are better edited than ever before ...
>
> Harwood 1995: 25–26

In the case of children's literature, resources are, of course, directed towards education and librarianship as well as literary and bibliographical studies; consequently the resources available to bibliography is disproportionately small for both the influence of the subject, and the amount of work which could be done. A good deal of work, then has been the result of privately financed enterprise, or has been supported by the major research collections (see Chapter 47). Juvenile bibliography might thus seem to be a poor relation, a paradox compounded by the flourishing collector's market for children's books.

The 'core' books in the area are ageing, and increasingly in need of revision as detailed bibliographical work changes the historical map. However, nothing has been published that matches the work of Darton (1932/1982), Muir (1954), Thwaite (1963/1972) or the specifically bibliophile, but widely available, 'collector's guides' of Quayle (1971; 1983) (as against the avalanche of theory and 'popular' history). (One attempt to supplement them has been Mary V. Jackson's *Engines of Instruction, Mischief and Magic: Children's Literature in England from its Beginning to 1839* (1990), which was not critically well-received.)

F. J. Harvey Darton's *Children's Books in England* (1932/1982) laid an important foundation (although its organisation may seem somewhat arcane to the lay reader), and the revised edition contains extensive bibliographies, from fables to magazines (these may be supplemented by Thwaite 1963/1972: 283–313).

Similarly, no series has emerged to replace the Oxford University Press Juvenile Library, which produced facsimiles of, for example, Sarah Fielding's *The Governess* (ed. Jill E. Grey 1968), Isaac Watts's *Divine Songs* (ed. J. H. P. Pafford 1971) and John Newbery's *A Little Pretty Pocket Book* (ed. M. F. Thwaite 1966).

The journal that most seriously addressed scholarly concerns, *Phaedrus* (which began as a Newsletter in 1973 and ended as an International Annual) did not survive the 1980s (it merged with *Die Schiefertafel* in 1989), and even by 1977 its editor, James Fraser, was lamenting his disillusion with the fact that the 'groundswell of serious discussion and superior research' had not been stimulated. (Fraser 1977: 2). The most 'respectable' of children's literature journals, the Yale annual *Children's Literature*, although rarely concerned with children, has published, in the most liberal definition, two articles which have a primarily bibliographic approach in the last ten years.

While the situation is better in the USA, in Britain the establishment of major collections, notably the Opie Collection in the Bodleian Library, Oxford, and the Renier Collection of Historical and Contemporary Children's Books at the Bethnal Green Museum of Childhood in London has not been backed up by the funding necessary to adequately document them, or to provide a viable research base. None the less, Tessa Chester of the Renier Collection has produced a number of valuable 'Occasional Lists' of different types and genres of books (the first was on Struwwelpeter (Chester 1987)). An interesting article on Peter Opie's accession diaries by Clive Hurst appears in Avery and Briggs's *Children and their Books: A Celebration of the Work of Iona and Peter Opie* (1989: 19–44).

However, the major world collections are being documented: important contributions have been Gerald Gottlieb's *Early Children's Books and their Illustrators* (1975), and the catalogue of the Osborne Collection in Toronto (St John 1975); others include Florida State University's catalogue of the *Shaw Childhood in Poetry Collection* (1967).

Equally, there has been a steady output of historical and bibliographically orientated work, both within such specialist journals as *The Library*, *The Book Collector*, *Bodleian Library Record*, *Papers of the Bibliographical Society of America*, *Antiquarian Book Monthly* and *The Private Library* and elsewhere. In Britain, the Children's Book History Society began a series of occasional papers with *After Henry*, an exploration of English ABCs (Garrett 1994), while the Provincial Booksellers Fairs Association's catalogue of an exhibition mounted at Oxford, *Childhood Re-Collected* (Alderson and Moon 1994) is characteristic of some high-quality work on the scholarly/commercial border. Many other exhibitions of early books have been mounted by individual collectors and societies, but most of the catalogues, booklets and articles associated with them are available through only the most specialist of outlets.

In the USA, the UCLA Occasional Papers have included work on children's literature, such as Alderson's description of an eighteenth-century collection from Warwickshire (1989) and Andrea Immel's *Revolutionary Reviewing: Sarah Trimmer's 'Guardian of Education' and the Cultural Politics of Juvenile Literature* (1990). The Lilly Library has, similarly, produced catalogues of exhibitions, such as Linda David's *Children's Books Published by William Darton and his Sons* (1992), and of material from the Jane Johnson nursery collection (Johnson 1987). The burgeoning de Grummond Collection of Children's Literature at the University of Southern Mississippi, Hattiesburg, occasionally includes scholarly articles in its journal, *Juvenile Miscellany*. A major step forward in work on American children's literature has been Gillian Avery's *Behold the Child: American Children and their Books 1621–1922* (1994).

There is much work to do unravelling the intricacies of the early book trade, but progress is being made. Booksellers who have been examined include Joseph Cundall (McLean 1976), James Lumsden (Roscoe and Brimmell 1981); James Burns (Alderson 1994), William Godwin (William St Clair, 'William Godwin as children's bookseller' in Avery and Briggs 1989: 165–179) and John Newbery (Townsend 1994; Roscoe 1973). Outstanding have been Marjorie Moon's work on

Tabart and Harris: *Benjamin Tabart's Juvenile Library: A Bibliography of Books for Children Published, Written and Sold by Mr Tabart 1801–1920* (1990), and *John Harris's Books for Youth 1801–1843* (1992).

Some authors, such as Beatrix Potter (Linder 1971) and Carroll (Guiliano 1981) have been well served bibliographically; others, such as Arthur Ransome, are just beginning to have their work explored in detail (for example, Wardale 1995). Other studies include work on George MacDonald (Shaberman 1990) and Richmal Crompton (Schutte 1993; and see also Cadogan with Schutte 1990), while Hans Andersen's *Eventyr* have been explored by Alderson (1982). A wider range of reference is found in Robert Kirkpatrick's *Bullies, Beaks and Flannelled Fools: An Annotated Bibliography of Boys' School Fiction 1742–1990* (1990).

However, it is clear that, despite the occasional specialist work, such as Dennis Butt's study of Mrs Hofland (Butts 1992) or M. Nancy Cutt's on Mrs Sherwood (Cutt 1974), there are vast tracts of the history of children's literature untouched by bibliographers.

The same is true of illustration, although there are some excellent outlines of its history, notably by Whalley and Chester with their *A History of Children's Book Illustration* (1988) (and also Muir, 1971/1985; Whalley 1974; Ray 1976; Martin 1989), while *The Dictionary of 20th Century British Book Illustrators* (Horne 1994) is a standard work. There are useful volumes on American (Mahoney *et al.* 1947 *et seq.*), and Australian art (Muir, 1982). There have also been individual bibliographical studies of Thomas Bewick (Roscoe 1953), the Brocks (Kelly 1982) Heath Robinson (Lewis 1973), William Nicholson (Campbell 1992) and many others.

The same principle, of excellent work in some areas and much that could be explored, could be extended to other types and genres. Thus in folklore, Neil Philip's exemplary editing and work on sources and analogues in *The Penguin Book of English Folktales* (1992) could well be extended. Similarly, book collectors have been served by Joseph Connolly's *Modern First Editions: Their Value to Collectors* (1988).

In 1966, Fredson Bowers wrote in his book *Textual and Literary Criticism*: 'I could wish that critics knew more, and knowing would care more, about the purity of the texts they use' (7). This is an even more unfashionable view now, among theorists, than it was then. Bibliographers may well see their work as fundamental to the whole project of children's literature studies, in establishing the true history, and in establishing the true texts – and it is a position difficult to argue with if one wants children's literature to stand beside other literatures. None the less, bibliographical studies often sit uneasily with the other disciplines involved with children's literature: on the one hand they seem to be concerned with irrelevant minutiae; on the other to be linked to a particularly solipsistic and monetarily oriented trade – book collecting. And if theory has not sufficiently taken on board bibliographical concerns, then the reverse seems equally to be true.

However, it is clear that in academic, historical, and bibliographical terms there is an immense amount of work to be done, in collecting, clarifying, and documenting the often bewildering output of children's literature. How successful the bibliographers are in this endeavour may well provide an accurate barometer for the progress and status of children's literature studies as a whole.

References

Alderson, B. (1977) *Bibliography and Children's Books: The Present Position*, London: The Bibliographical Society, reprinted from *The Library* 32, 3: 203–213.

—— (1982) *Hans Christian Andersen and his 'Eventyr' in England*, Wormley: Five Owls Press for International Board on Books for Young People, British Section.

—— (1989) *The Ludford Box and 'A Christmass Box': their Contribution to Our Knowledge of Eighteenth Century Children's Literature*, UCLA Occasional Papers 2, Los Angeles, UCLA.

—— (1994) 'Some notes on James Burns as a publisher of children's books', in Blamires, D. (ed.) *Bulletin of the John Rylands University Library of Manchester*, 76, 3: 103–126.

—— (1995) 'A widish, widish world', *Children's Books History Society Newsletter* 51: 17.

—— and Moon, M. (1994) *Childhood Re-Collected: Early Children's Books from the Library of Marjorie Moon*, Royston: Provincial Book Fairs Association.

Avery, G. (1994) *Behold the Child: American Children and Their Books 1621–1922*, London: Bodley Head.

—— and Briggs, J. (1989) *Children and their Books. A Celebration of the Work of Iona and Peter Opie*, Oxford: Clarendon Press.

Bowers, F. (1966) *Textual and Literary Criticism*, Cambridge: Cambridge University Press.

Butts, D. (1992) *Mistress of Our Tears: A Literary and Bibliographical Study of Barbara Hofland*, Aldershot: Scolar Press.

Cadogan, M. with Schutte, D. (1990) *The William Companion*, London: Macmillan.

Campbell, C. (1992) *William Nicholson: The Graphic Work*, London: Barrie and Jenkins.

Chester, T. R. (1987) *Occasional List no. 1: Struwwelpeter*, London: The Renier Collection of Historic and Contemporary Children's Books, Bethnal Green Museum of Childhood.

Connolly, J. (1988) *Modern First Editions: Their Value to Collectors*, London: Macdonald Orbis.

Cutt, M. N. (1974) *Mrs Sherwood and her Books*, London: Oxford University Press.

Darton, F. J. H. (1932/1982) *Children's Books in England: Five Centuries of Social Life*, 3rd edn, rev. B. Alderson, Cambridge: Cambridge University Press.

David, L. (1992) *Children's Books Published by William Darton and his Sons*, Bloomington, IN: The Lilly Library.

Florida State University (1967) *Shaw Childhood in Poetry Collection*, 5 vols., Detroit: Gale Research.

Fraser, J. (1977) 'Editor's comment', *Phaedrus* 4, 2: 3.

Garrett, P. (1994) 'After Henry', Children's Books History Society, Occasional Paper 1, London: Children's Books History Society.

Gottlieb, G. (1975) *Early Children's Books and their Illustrators*, New York: Pierpont Morgan Library.

Guiliano, E. *Lewis Carroll. An Annotated International Bibliography 1960–77*, Brighton: Harvester Press.

Harwood, J. (1995) *Eliot to Derrida: The Poverty of Interpretation*, London: Macmillan.

Horne, A. (1994), *The Dictionary of 20th Century British Book Illustrators*, Woodbridge: Antique Collectors' Club.

Immel, A. (1990) *Revolutionary Reviewing: Sarah Trimmer's 'Guardian of Education' and the Cultural Politics of Juvenile Literature*, UCLA Occasional Papers 4, Los Angeles: UCLA.

Jackson, M. V. (1990) *Engines of Instruction, Mischief and Magic: Children's Literature in England from its Beginning to 1839*, Aldershot: Scolar Press.

Johnson, E. L. (1987) *For Your Amusement and Instruction: the Elizabeth Ball Collection of Historical Children's Materials*, Bloomington, IN: The Lilly Library.

Kelly, C. M. (1975) *The Brocks: A Family of Cambridge Artists and Illustrators*, London: Skilton.

Kirkpatrick, R. (1990) *Bullies, Beaks and Flannelled Fools: An Annotated Bibliography of Boys' School Fiction 1742–1990*, privately published.

Lewis, J. (1973) *Heath Robinson, Artist and Comic Genius*, London: Constable.

Linder, L. (1971) *A History of the Writings of Beatrix Potter*, London: Warne.

McLean, R. (1976) *Joseph Cundall: A Victorian Publisher*, Pinner: Private Libraries Association.

Mahoney, B. E. *et al.* (1947/1958/1968/1978) *Illustrators of Childrens Books 1744–1945* (and supplements to 1978), Boston: The Horn Book.

Martin, D. (1989) *The Telling Line: Essays on Fifteen Contemporary Book Illustrators*, London: MacRae.

Moon, M. (1990) *Benjamin Tabart's Juvenile Library: A Bibliography of Books for Children Published, Written and Sold by Mr Tabart 1801–1920*, Winchester: St Paul's Bibliographies.

—— (1992) *John Harris's Books for Youth 1801–1843*, rev. edn, Folkstone: Dawson.

Muir, M. (1982) *A History of Australian Children's Book Illustration*, Melbourne: Oxford University Press.

Muir, P. (1954) *English Children's Books, 1600–1900*, London: Batsford.

—— (1971/1985) *Victorian Illustrated Books*, London: Batsford.

Philip, N. (1992) *The Penguin Book of English Folktales*, London: Penguin.

Quayle, E. (1971) *Collector's Book of Children's Books*, London: Studio Vista.

—— (1983) *Early Children's Books. A Collector's Guide*, Newton Abbott: David and Charles.

Ray, G. N. (1976) *The Illustrator and the Book in England from 1790 to 1914*, New York: Pierpont Morgan Library.

Roscoe, S. (1953) *Thomas Bewick: A Catalogue Raisonné*, Oxford: Oxford University Press.

—— (1973) *John Newbery and his Successors, 1740–1814: A Bibliography*, Wormley: Five Owls Press.

—— and Brimmell, R. A. (1981) *James Lumsden and Son of Glasgow, their Juvenile Books and Chapbooks*, Pinner: Private Libraries Association.

St. John, J. (1975) *The Osborne Collection of Early Children's Books, 1476–1910*, Toronto: Toronto Public Library.

Schutte, D. (1993) *William: The Immortal: An Illustrated Bibliography*, privately published.

Shaberman, R. (1990) *George MacDonald: A Bibliographical Study*, Winchester: St Paul's Bibliographies.

Thwaite, M. F. (1963/1972) *From Primer to Pleasure in Reading*, 2nd edn, London: Library Association.

Townsend, J. R. (1994), *Trade & Plumb-Cake for Ever, Huzza! The Life and Work of John Newbery 1713–1767*, Cambridge: Colt Books.

Wardale, R. (1995) *Ransome at Sea: Notes from the Chart Table*, Kendal: Amazon Publications.

Whalley, J. I. (1974) *Cobwebs to Catch Flies: Illustrated Books for the Nursery and Schoolroom, 1700–1900*, London: Elek.

—— and Chester, T. R. (1988) *A History of Children's Book Illustration*, London: John Murray with the Victoria and Albert Museum.

11 Relating Texts: Intertextuality

Christine Wilkie

Editor's introduction

Texts do not mean in isolation: there is a continuous interplay between them. Consciously or unconsciously, writers add to the range and depth of their work by allusion, reference, and quotation. Christine Wilkie shows how subtle these interactions can be, and how they operate in children's literature.

P. H.

The term 'intertextuality' is now common in literary discourse. It is used most often and most simply to refer to literary allusions and to direct quotation from literary and non-literary texts. But this is only one small part of the theory, which has its origins in the work of Julia Kristeva (1969) and Mikhael Bakhtin (1973).

Kristeva (1969: 146) coined the term 'intertextuality' when she recognised that texts can only have meaning because they depend on other texts, both written and spoken, and on what she calls the intersubjective knowledge of their interlocutors, by which she meant their total knowledge – from other books, from language-in-use, and the context and conditions of the signifying practices which make meanings possible in groups and communities (Kristeva 1974/1984: 59–60). The literary text, then, is just one of the many sites where several different discourses converge, are absorbed, are transformed and assume a meaning because they are situated in this circular network of interdependence which is called the intertextual space.

Kristeva was keen to point out that intertextuality is not simply a process of recognising sources and influences. She built on the work of Bakhtin, who had identified the word as the smallest textual unit, situated in three coordinates: of the writer, the text and exterior texts. For the first time in literary history, the literary text (the word) took on a spatial dimension when Bakhtin made it a fluid function between the writer/text (on the horizontal axis) and the text/context (on the vertical axis). This idea replaced the previous, Formalist notion that the literary text was a fixed point with a fixed meaning. Bakhtin described this process as a dialogue between several writings, and as the intersection of textual surfaces: 'any text is a mosaic of quotations; any text is the absorption and transformation of another' (in Kristeva 1980/1981: 66).

The theory of intertextuality has also been refined and extended by Jonathan Culler (1981), and by Roland Barthes (1970/1975), who have included the reader as a constituent component of intertextuality. Culler described intertextuality as the general discursive space in which meaning is made intelligible and possible (1981: 103), and Barthes invented the term 'infinite intertextuality' to refer to the intertextual codes by which readers make sense of literary works which he calls a 'mirage of citations'. They dwell equally in readers and in texts but the conventions and presuppositions cannot be traced to an original source or sources. 'The "I" which approaches the texts [says Barthes] is already a plurality of other texts, of infinite, or more precisely, lost codes (whose origins are lost)' (Barthes 1975/1976: 16).

The idea that texts are produced and readers make sense of them only in relation to the already embedded codes which dwell in texts and readers (and in authors too, since they are readers of texts before they are authors), has ramifications which challenge any claim to textual originality or discrete readings. In this sense, then, all texts and all readings are intertextual. This brings us close to Genette's use of the term 'transtextuality' (1979: 85–90), by which he is referring to *everything* that influences a text either explicitly or implicitly.

This dynamic model of intertextuality has peculiar implications for an intertextuality of children's literature because the writer/reader axis is uniquely positioned in an imbalanced power relationship. Adults write for each other, but it is not usual for children to write literature for each other. This makes children the powerless recipients of what adults choose to write for them and, *de facto*, children's literature an intertextual sub-genre of adult literature. The writer/ reader relationship is also asymmetric because children's intersubjective know- ledge cannot be assured. A theory of intertextuality of children's literature is, therefore, unusually preoccupied with questions about what a piece of writing (for children) presupposes. What does it assume, what *must* it assume to take on significance? (See Culler 1981: 101–102.) For these reasons the interrelationship between the components of intertextuality, of writer/text/reader – text/reader/ context, are quite special when we are addressing a theory of intertextuality of children's literature.

By now it should be clear that the theory of intertextuality is a dynamic located in theories of writing, reader-response theory and the production of meaning, and intersubjectivity (the 'I' who, is reading is a network of citations). It is also a theory of language inasmuch as Bakhtin had identified the word as the smallest textual link between the text and the world, and because the reading subject, the text and the world are not only situated in language, they are also constructed by it. So, not only do we have a notion of all texts being intertextual, they become so because they are dialectically related to, and are themselves the products of, linguistic, cultural and literary practices; and so too are readers and writers.

Culler (1975: 139), has described the urge towards integrating one discourse with another, or several others, as a process of *vraisemblance*. It is the basis of intertextuality. Through this process of *vraisemblance* we are able to identify, for example, the set of literary norms and the salient features of a work by which to locate genre, and also to anticipate what we might expect to find in fictional worlds. Through *vraisemblance* the child reader has unconsciously to learn that the fictional worlds in literature are representations and constructions which refer to other texts that have been normalised, that is: those texts that have been absorbed into the culture and are now regarded as 'natural'.

At the level of literary texts (the intertext) it is possible to identify three main categories of intertextuality: (1) texts of quotation: those texts which quote or allude to other literary or non–literary works; (2) texts of imitation: texts which seek to paraphrase, 'translate' and supplant the original and to liberate their readers from an over-invested admiration in great writers of the past, and which often function as the pre-text of the original for later readers (Worton and Still 1990: 7); and (3) genre texts: those texts where identifiable, shared, clusters of codes and literary conventions grouped together in recognisable patterns which allow readers to expect and locate them, and to cause them to seek out like texts.

Texts of quotation are probably the simplest level at which child readers can recognise intertextuality. Examples are works such as Janet and Allan Ahlberg's *The Jolly Postman* (1986), John Prater's *Once Upon a Time* (1993), Jon Scieszka's *The Stinky Cheese Man* (1992) and his *The True Story of the 3 Little Pigs!* (1989), and Roald Dahl's *Revolting Rhymes* (1987). All these fictions are characterised by their allusive qualities. They make explicit assumptions about previously read fairytales: 'Everyone knows the story of the Three Little Pigs. Or at least they think they do' (Scieszka 1989: first opening), and 'I guess you think you know this story. You don't, the real one's much more gory' (Dahl 1987: 5). So, as well as assuming familiarity with an 'already read' intertext the 'focused texts' are at the same time foregrounding their own authenticity; that is, they purport to be more authoritative than the texts they are quoting and are thereby undermining the 'truth' of their pre-texts. They cleverly destabilise the security of their readers by positioning them ambivalently in relation to (1) what they think they know already about the fairy tales and (2) the story they are now reading. At the discursive level, then, these particular examples of texts of quotation are doing much more than simply alluding to other texts; they are challenging their readers' 'already read' notions of the reliable narrator by an act of referring back which says it was all a lie. And *The Jolly Postman* is, at the very least, breaking readers' 'already read' boundary of fictionality by presenting them with a clutch of touchable, usable, readable literary artefacts from and to characters of fiction, which are themselves facsimile versions of their real-life counterparts.

Every text of quotation which relocates the so-called primary text in a new cultural and linguistic context must be by definition a parody and a distortion. All the examples I have given parody the telling of traditional tales: *Once Upon a Time* (Prater 1993), 'Once upon a time' (Scieszka 1992: passim), and 'Once upon a bicycle' (Ahlberg 1986: first opening). But the challenge to authority and problems of authenticity for these quotation texts of fairy tales lies in the fact that the tales themselves are a collage of quotations, each of which has assumed a spurious 'first version' authenticity but for which the ur-text does not exist, or at least, cannot be located. The situation of fairy tales in contemporary culture is analogous to Barthes's notion of 'lost codes'. The tales are intelligible because they build on already embedded discourses which happened elsewhere and at another time; they are part of the sedimented folk memory of discourse and they function now by the simple fact that other tales like them have already existed.

Children's exposure to other media such as film, television animations, and video, means increasingly, that they are likely to encounter these media adaptations of a children's fiction before they encounter the written text and to come to regard it as the 'original' from which to approach and on which to base, their (later) reading of the written version. This has particular implications for a theory of intertextuality because it raises questions about whether the nature of the later reading is qualitatively and experientially different if the ur-text happens to have been a Disney cartoon version of, say, 'Snow White'. Children's intertextual experience is peculiarly achronological, so the question about what sense children make of a given text when the intertextual experience cannot be assumed, is important.

Disney adaptations of fairy tales are particularly interesting to an intertextuality of children's literature because, as touchstones of popular culture, they reflect the way in which each generation's retellings have assumed and foregrounded the dominant socio-linguistic and cultural codes and values at a particular moment in history: for example Disney's foregrounding Snow White's good looks over qualities of moral rectitude and goodness claimed for her by earlier, written versions.

But it is not only the stories which change in the repeated intertextual quotations – the intertextual context of the reading and their reception also changes. For example, contemporary, feminist, post-Freudian readings of Carroll's *Alice's Adventures in Wonderland* (1866), or Hodgson Burnett's *The Secret Garden* (1911), make them different kinds of texts from what was previously possible. Similarly, a contemporary child reader's readings of, say, a modern reprint of the original tales of Beatrix Potter will be quite different from that of its intended readers. In their reading of *Jemima Puddle-Duck* (1908), for example, today's child readers are less likely than child readers from the earlier part of the century to recognise the ingredients of duck stuffing for what they are. This is not because, like Jemima, they are simpletons, but because their stuffing today is more likely to be from a packet. Their probable inability to recognise the ingredients of duck stuffing removes an opportunity to anticipate Jemima's fate well in advance of narration. And, not only do contemporary-child readers have an intertextual familiarity with Beatrix Potter's character, Jemima Puddle-Duck and her Potter co-star, Peter Rabbit, from a proliferation of non-literary artefacts, including video adaptations, they can also now read about them in series adaptations in Ladybird books (1992). Ladybird has developed a very powerful position in Britain as a publisher of low-priced, hardback, formula books – especially retellings of traditional tales – with simplified language and sentence constructions. They are a good example of the texts of imitation I described earlier. For some children in Britain they will be the only written version of traditional tales they have encountered. Comparison between the Ladybird and original versions of *Jemima Puddle-Duck* reveals linguistic and syntactic differences that make assumptions about their respective implied readers; and there are other syntactic, micro-discursive and linguistic differences which encode different socio-linguistic climates and – by extension – imply different language-in-use on the parts of their respective readerships. What we see in operation in these two texts is the tension and interplay between two idiolects and two sociolects: the uses of language in each text and their situation in, and reception by their respective socio-historic contexts and readers. Each is operating as a textual and intertextual paradigm of its time, but the first-version text can only be 'read' through a network of late-twentieth-century intertexts.

Susan Cooper's *The Dark is Rising* quintet (1966–1977), and Alan Garner's *The Owl Service* (1967), are texts which rely for their fullest reading on a reader's knowledge of Arthurian and Celtic myth, especially of the *Mabinogion*. Together these texts are examples of the type of two-world fantasy genre where child readers can come to recognise, and to expect, such generic conventions as character archetype, stereotype and the archetypal plot structures of quest and journeys. The novels allude only obliquely to their mythical sources, even though myth is integral to their stories. So, even in readings that do not rely on knowledge of the myth, readers might intuit the echoes of myth as they read and absorb the novels' more subtle messages and connections.

Similarly, Robert Cormier's *After the First Death* (1979), and Jill Paton Walsh's novels *Goldengrove* (1972) and *Unleaving* (1976), allude to lines from Dylan Thomas's poem 'A refusal to mourn the death, by fire, of a child in London' (After the first death, there is no other) and Gerard Manley Hopkins's 'Spring and fall' (Márgarét, áre you grieving/Over Goldengrove unleaving?). In each case, a perfectly coherent reading of the text is possible without the reader's knowledge of the intertextual poetic allusions; but the potential for a metaphoric reading is enhanced by the reader's previous knowledge of them. In the case of Paton Walsh's *Goldengrove*, for example, the metaphor for metaphysical transience first mooted by Hopkins in his image of the Goldengrove unleaving, is employed again by Paton Walsh as the name of the fictional house, 'Goldengrove', from which the book takes its title. This is the place of symbolic and literal change where the two teenage characters spend their (significantly) late-summer vacation of maturation and realisation. The image is extended in numerous other references: changing body-shapes, changed sleeping arrangements, changed attitudes to each other, and not least, in repeated references to the falling leaves of late summer. It also invokes and parodies the style and content of Virginia Woolf's *To The Lighthouse* (1927), with a polyphony which moves effortlessly between several viewpoints, and positions its readers accordingly. This polyphonic, multilayered structure, which is also a feature of the Cormier novel, is particularly interesting to an intertextuality of children's literature because it breaks the intertextual discursive codes and conventions of the single viewpoint and linear narrative that are usually typical of the genre.

Young readers who come to these novels by Cooper, Garner, Cormier and Paton Walsh with an explicit knowledge of their intertexts will have a markedly different experience of reading. They will experience what Barthes has described as the 'circular memory of reading' (Barthes 1975: 36). This describes a reading process where the need consciously to recall and to refer back to specific, obligatory intertexts now being quoted as metaphor and/or metonymy in the focused texts, restricts the reader's opportunity for free intertextual interplay at the point of reading. The reading experience is, therefore, simultaneously centrifugal and centripetal as the reader seeks to refer to the 'borrowing' and at the same time to integrate it into a new context. It is the essence of this kind of reading to deny readers an opportunity for linear reading as they move in and out of the text to make connections between it and the intertext(s).

Another Paton Walsh novel, *A Parcel of Patterns* (1983), is a fictionalised account of the bubonic plague's destruction of the inhabitants of the Derbyshire village of Eyam. It uses many secondary signals to ground the events in their historic context and to ensure that readers locate the events in these pretextual happenings by, for example, the use of paratextual devices such as the words of the publisher's introduction:

> Eyam (pronounced Eem) is a real village in Derbyshire and many of the events in this evocative novel are based on what actually happened there in the year of the Plague.
>
> Paton Walsh 1983

Another example is the use of direct quotation from historic artefacts, not least, from the inscription of the great bell of Eyam 'SWEET JESU BE MY SPEDE' (54). The book reinforces the historic authenticity of its subject matter by a consistent capitalisation throughout of the word Plague, and by use of an invented dialect which pastiches what we know about the dialect of sixteenth-century Derbyshire.

In contrast, Robert Westall's novel *Gulf* (1992), is embedded in the events of the 1991 Gulf War which began after the Iraqi invasion of Kuwait and the retaliation by the United Nations. *Gulf*, unlike *A Parcel of Patterns*, assumes (for its Western readers) a shared, contemporary, intertextual experience. This makes recovery of the pre-text more likely and it therefore calls for little explanation and contextualisation. But the novel's foregrounded meaning centres on the need for its readers to see the connection between the out-of-body experiences of the narrator's younger brother, Figgis, and the experiences of a young Iraqi boy soldier whose life he shares. The detail of the geography and history of Iraq is an intertextual experience that cannot be assumed; so the narrative deals with it by way of explanation, 'I looked up Tikrit in our atlas; it was north of Baghdad. Then I read in the paper it was where Saddam Hussein himself came from' (Westall 1992: 47). This is an example of the way in which texts written for children sometimes have a felt need to be overreferential; the need to fill intertextual gaps to mobilise a positive reading experience in its young readers.

Literature for children has to tread a careful path between a need to be sufficiently overreferential in its intertextual gap filling so as not to lose its readers, and the need to leave enough intertextual space and to be sufficiently stylistically challenging to allow readers free intertextual interplay. It is on the one hand a formally conservative genre that is charged with the awesome responsibility to initiate young readers into the dominant literary codes of the culture. On the other hand, the genre has seen the emergence of what we now confidently call the 'new picture books' and the 'new young adult' novel. Picture book writers such as John Scieszka, Maurice Sendak, the Ahlbergs, Ruth Brown, David McKee, Anthony Browne, John Burningham; young adult writers like Robert Cormier, Aidan Chambers and Peter Hunt, and books like Gillian Cross's *Wolf* (1990), Berlie Doherty's *Dear Nobody* (1991), Nadia Wheatley's *The Blooding* (1988), Aidan Chambers's *Breaktime* (1978), and Geraldine McCaughrean's *A Pack of Lies*

(1988), are challenging conventional literary forms of children's literature and breaking the codes.

A theory of intertextuality of children's literature points the way forward for a genre that acknowledges the lost codes and practices and underlying discursive conventions by which it functions and is defined, and urges the breaking of ranks. Some of the children's writers I have mentioned here have demonstrated how this is beginning to happen. They have been prepared to take risks with their writing and with their young readers. Some of these books, such as Scieszka's *The Stinky Cheese Man*, Chambers's *Breaktime*, Cormier's, *After the First Death*, and *Fade* (1988), and McCaughrean's *A Pack of Lies*, have a metafictional dimension which causes readers to pay attention to the fabric and artifice of these texts as works of literature, and to the textuality of the world to which they allude; it also causes readers to recognise how they are being (have been) textually constructed in and by this intertextual playground. Since both using codes and breaking codes are sites for intertextual interplay, the work of these writers is a legitimate site on which to mobilise the construction of a child-reader intersubjectivity that is intertextually aware.

References

Bakhtin, M. (1973) *Problems of Dostoevsky's Poetics*, trans. R. W. Rostel, Ann Arbor, MI: Ardis.
Barthes, R. (1970/1975) *S/Z*, trans. R. Miller, London: Cape.
—— (1975/1976) *The Pleasure of the Text*, trans. R. Miller, London: Cape.
Culler, J. (1975) *Structuralist Poetics: Structuralism, Linguistics and the Study of Literature*, London: Routledge and Kegan Paul.
—— (1981) *The Pursuit of Signs: Semiotics, Literature, Deconstruction*, London: Routledge and Kegan Paul.
Dahl, R. (1987) *Revolting Rhymes*, London: Jonathan Cape.
Genette, G. (1979) *The Architext: An Introduction*, trans. J. E. Lewin, Berkeley and Los Angeles: University of California Press.
Kristeva, J. (1969) *Semiotiké*, Paris: Editions du Seuil.
—— (1974/1984) *Revolution in Poetic Language*, trans. M. Waller, New York: Columbia University Press.
—— (1980/1981) *Desire In Language: A Semiotic Approach to Literature and Art*, trans. T. Gora, A. Jardine, and L. Roudiez, Oxford: Blackwell.
Paton Walsh, J. (1983) *A Parcel of Patterns*, Harmondsworth: Kestrel (Penguin).
Prater, J. (1993) *Once Upon a Time*, London: Walker.
Scieszka, J. (1989) *The True Story of the 3 Little Pigs!*, New York: Viking.
—— (1992) *The Stinky Cheese Man*, New York: Viking.
Worton, M. and Still, J. (eds) (1990) *Intertextuality*, Manchester: Manchester University Press.

Further Reading

Ahlberg, J. and Ahlberg, A. (1985) *The Jolly Postman*, London: Heinemann.
Bloom, H. (1975) *A Map of Misreading*, New York: Oxford University Press.
Hunt, P. (1988) 'What do we lose when we lose allusion? Experience and understanding stories', *Signal* 57: 212–222.

Riffaterre, M. (1984) 'Intertextual representation: On Mimesis as interpretive discourse', *Critical Inquiry* 11, 1: 141–162.

Stephens, J. (1990) 'Intertextuality and the wedding ghost', *Children's Literature in Education* 21, 1: 23–36.

—— (1992) *Language and Ideology in Children's Fiction*, London: Longman.

Valdes, M. J. (ed.) (1985) *Identity and the Literary Text*, Toronto: University of Toronto Press.

12 Very Advanced Texts: Metafictions and Experimental Work

Robyn McCallum

Editor's introduction

It is very difficult to isolate theory from practice in the study of children's literature: the need to consider the relationship between author and audience in a complex way has led, directly or indirectly, to some innovative writing for children. While much of children's literature tends to be controlled by, and to reinforce, the dominant ideology, nevertheless its cultural marginalisation has allowed it to be one of the most experimental and creative areas of the arts. Robyn McCallum looks at the ways in which highly self-conscious writers for children have manipulated the form, and demonstrates how such texts can be analysed.

P. H.

The term 'metafiction' is used to refer to fiction which self-consciously draws attention to its status as text and as fictive. It does this in order to reflect upon the processes through which narrative fictions are constructed, read and made sense of and to pose questions about the relationships between the ways we interpret and represent both fiction and reality (Waugh 1984: 2). Although they are not interchangeable, there is considerable overlap between contemporary categories of metafiction and experimental fiction. Texts which are experimental are often also metafictive, and vice versa. As categories of fiction both are, to some extent, context bound, definable in relation to other forms of narrative fiction – the category 'experimental' changes through time, socio–historical context, and critical conceptions of what constitutes the mainstream. With children's literature this category can shift between 'literary' and popular, neither of which is exempt from experimentation, depending on which aspects of a text are the focus of attention: the discursive and stylistic techniques, narrative technique and structures, content, social, ideological, intellectual and moral concerns and so on.

A key distinction between metafictive and experimental texts and the majority of fiction written for children lies in the kinds of narrative and discursive techniques used to construct and inscribe audience positions within texts. Briefly, the narrative modes employed in children's novels tend to be restricted to either first person narration by a main character or third person narration with one character focaliser (Stephens 1991: 63). Texts tend to be monological rather than dialogical, with single-stranded and story-driven narratives, closed rather than open endings, and a narrative discourse lacking stylistic variation (Moss 1990;

Hunt 1988). These are strategies which function to situate readers in restricted and relatively passive subject positions and to implicitly reinforce a single dominant interpretive stance. Restrictions on narrative point of view in particular frequently have the effect of restricting the possible interpretive positions available to implied readers (Stephens 1991: 63; 1992b: 27).

Metafictive and experimental forms of children's writing generally use a broader range of narrative and discursive techniques: overly obtrusive narrators who directly address readers and comment on their own narration; disruptions of the spatio-temporal narrative axis and of diegetic levels of narration; parodic appropriations of other texts, genres and discourses; typographic experimentation; mixing of genres, discourse styles, modes of narration and speech representation; multiple character focalisers, narrative voices, and narrative strands and so on. These are strategies which distance readers from a text and frequently frustrate conventional expectations about meaning and closure. Implied readers are thereby positioned in more active interpretive roles. By foregrounding the discursive and narrative structuring of texts, metafictions can show readers how texts mean and, by analogy, how meanings are ascribed to everyday reality.

Metafiction and Readers

Although the use of metafictive and experimental narrative forms in children's fiction has recently received positive criticism (Moss 1985; Lewis 1990; Moss 1990, 1992; Hunt 1992; Stephens 1991, 1992b, 1993; Mackey 1990), the genre can still generate resistance and scepticism. A common response is that it is too difficult for children. Metafictive texts often draw attention to their own artifice through the parody or inversion of other texts, genres and discourses. These strategies depend upon a reader's recognition of the parodied text, genre, or discourse, and hence assume certain levels of literary and interpretive competence. As inexperienced readers, children may not have learned the cultural and literary codes and conventions necessary to recognise metafictive devices. However, as Hunt has observed 'it may be correct to assume that child-readers will not bring to the text a complete or sophisticated system of codes, but is this any reason to deny them access to texts with a potential of rich codes?' (1991: 101). Furthermore, Mackey argues that metafictive children's texts can 'foster an awareness of how a story works' and implicitly teach readers how texts are structured through specific codes and conventions (1990: 181).

The instructive potential of metafiction has been emphasised by many theorists (of both adult and children's texts). Hutcheon's description of the activity of a reader of metafiction also aptly describes the activity of an inexperienced child reader: that is, 'one of learning and constructing a new sign-system, a new set of verbal relations' (1980: 19). By involving readers in the production of textual meanings, metafictions can implicitly teach literary and cultural codes and conventions, as well as specific interpretive strategies, and hence empower readers to read more competently: more explicit forms often seek to teach readers conventions and strategies with which to interpret metafictions as well as other more closed texts.

There are two main aspects of metafiction which are important for reading development. First, developmental studies suggest that mature readers 'read with a more reflective and detached awareness of how the processes of fiction are operating as they read' (Mackey 1990: 179). Metafictive narratives construct a distance between an audience and the represented events and characters and can potentially foster such an awareness (Stephens 1991: 75). Second, there is a demonstrated relationship between play-oriented activities, such as verbal puns, jokes and rhymes, role play and story-telling, and the acquisition of language and of complex cognitive and social skills (Vygotsky 1934/1962; Britton 1970/1972). Underlying much metafiction for children is a heightened sense of the status of fiction as an elaborate form of play, that is a game with linguistic and narrative codes and conventions. Janet and Allan Ahlberg exemplify this kind of writing for quite young children, by producing narratives which are parodic reversions of familiar childhood texts (for example Allan Ahlberg's *Ten in a Bed* (1983)).

A second objection to metafiction (for children and adults) is that as a radically self-reflexive and playful genre it is ultimately self-indulgent and solipsistic. To assume that fiction can be self-reflexive in any simple way, however, is to confuse the signifying and referential functions of the linguistic signs that constitute a text – that is, it is indicative of a failure to distinguish between signs and things. It is precisely this distinction that theorists such as Britton see as important in the encouragement of an 'openness to alternative formulations of experience' associated with the move out of egocentricism (1970/1972: 86), and which metafictions frequently foreground and exploit. We use language and narrative to represent, mediate and comprehend reality, as well as to construct fictions. By 'laying bare' the artifice through which fictional texts mean, metafictions can also lay bare the conventions through which what we think of as 'reality' is represented and ascribed with meanings.

Defining Metafiction

Metafiction tends to be defined in two main ways: as a distinctive sub-genre of the novel, defined in opposition to literary realism; or as an inherent tendency of the novelistic genre (Ommundsen 1989: 266). Waugh (1984) and Lewis (1990) both stress the relation between metafiction and the classic realist text. Metafictions appropriate and parody the conventions of traditional realism in order to construct a fictional illusion and simultaneously expose the constructedness of that illusion (Waugh 1984: 6). Our understanding of a metafiction will depend to some extent upon the conventions and intertexts which it parodies, but more specifically upon assumptions about the verbal sign inscribed within these conventions. The narrative conventions of realist fiction work to mask the gap between linguistic signs and their fictive referents and to construct an illusion of an unmediated relation between signs and things. In doing so, these conventions obscure the fictionality of referents and imply a reading of fiction as if it were 'real'. In metafiction, however, the ontological gap between fiction and reality is made explicit; that is, the fictionality of the events, characters and objects referred to is foregrounded.

While the relations between metafiction and literary realism are important, to define one in opposition to the other excludes from consideration a vast number of (often ostensibly 'realist') texts which have self-reflexive elements but which are not 'systematically self-conscious' (Ommundsen 1989: 265), as well as early forms of metafictive writing. Hutcheon has stressed that the use of self-reflexive narrative strategies is part of a long novelistic tradition: 'Art has always been "illusion" and it has often, if not always, been self-consciously aware of that ontological status' (1980: 17). Anita Moss's (1985) inclusion of early writers such as Nesbit and Dickens acknowledges this tradition in children's literature.

Much of the critical discourse around children's metafiction has been situated within a theoretical frame which opposes metafiction and realism and has focused on recent and unambiguously 'metafictive' examples. However, an approach which proceeds from an opposition between mainstream children's writing and 'counter texts' – texts which don't fit unproblematically into the category of children's literature – excludes all but the most explicitly self-conscious forms and, by implication, suggests a simplistic correlation between metafiction and subversion (for example, Moss 1990: 50). On the other hand, to over-emphasise the novelistic potential for self-reflexivity at the expense of specific identifiable metafictive narrative techniques and discursive strategies is to reduce the possibilities of critical insight and analysis. In other words, both aspects need to be taken into account: the specific strategies through which metafictions play with literary and cultural codes and conventions, and the historicity and conventionality of these metafictive textual practices.

Postmodernism, metafiction and experimental picture books

Metafiction is a mode of writing which has recently flourished within a broader cultural movement referred to as postmodernism (Waugh 1984: 21) with which it shares some common features: narrative fragmentation and discontinuity, disorder and chaos, code mixing and absurdity of the kind which appears in the picture books of John Burningham, Chris Van Allsburg, Anthony Browne, David Wiesner, David Macaulay and the novels of William Mayne and Terry Pratchett.

Two recent studies have focused on postmodern features of contemporary picture books (Lewis 1990; Moss 1992). The tendency toward parody, playfulness and openness in many recent picture books constitutes a metafictive potential: picture books comprise two inherently different modes of representation – verbal and visual – the relations between which are always to some extent more or less dialogical. Words and pictures interact so as to construct (and defer) meanings, rather than simply reflecting or illustrating each other. The visual and verbal components of a picture book can thus imply a dialogue between text and picture and readers – for example, Burningham's Shirley books or Van Allsburg's *The Mysteries of Harris Burdick*.

The combination of two sign systems clearly provides a way of problematising the representational function of visual and verbal signs and of foregrounding the ways in which the relations between signs and things are structured by culturally inscribed codes of representation and signification. The extent to which meanings are socially and culturally constructed, and hence open to challenge, is a concern addressed in many of Browne's picture books, for example *A Walk in the Park* (1977) or *Willie the Wimp* (1984). Browne characteristically uses surrealist visual elements to foreground the gap between signs and things (for example, his construction of settings out of pieces of fruit and other odd objects). Similarly, Wiesner's pictures in *Tuesday* (1991) are constructed out of a bricolage of visual quotations. Van Allsburg uses realist pictorial conventions to represent fantastical situations, blurring textual distinctions between the fantasy and reality.

Metafictive and Experimental Narrative Techniques

Though we can make broad distinctions between implicit and explicit forms of metafiction and between texts which reflect on their own narrative processes and those which reflect on their linguistic construction, metafictive strategies tend to be used in combination, which means that individual texts have a curious habit of refusing classification. For this reason, rather than attempting to classify texts, I have organised the discussion which follows around specific metafictive and experimental strategies.

Intertextuality and parody

The term intertextuality covers the range of literary and cultural texts, discourses, genres and conventions used to construct narrative fictions. In metafictions these are often foregrounded so as to heighten their conventionality and artifice. Intertexts include specific literary texts, as well as generic and discursive conventions – such as Leon Garfield's parody of nineteenth-century narrative genres in *The Strange Affair of Adelaide Harris* (1971) – and cultural texts and discourses – such as Terry Pratchett's parodic appropriations of department store jargon in *Truckers* (1989). The relationship between the focused text and its intertexts in metafiction is frequently parodic, though not always – for example, references to the work of John Fowles in Caroline Macdonald's *Speaking to Miranda* (1990) indicate interpretive possibilities to readers (McCallum 1992). A common metafictive strategy is the production of a re-version of a specific text – such as Jan Needle's *Wild Wood* (1981), a re-version of *The Wind in the Willows* – or of well-known fairy stories, or folk-tales. Overt forms of intertextuality have three main effects: they foreground the ways in which narrative fictions are constructed out of other texts and discourses; they work to indicate possible interpretive positions for readers, often distancing readers from represented events and characters; and they can enable the representation within a text of a plurality of discourses, voices and meanings.

Narratorial and authorial intrusions

There is a strong tradition of intrusive narrators who by drawing attention to their story-telling function seek to validate the status of their narrative as 'truth'. A common self-reflexive narrative strategy is to use narratorial intrusions to comment on the processes involved in story-telling and to implicitly or explicitly foreground the fictionality of the narrative. In implicit forms of metafiction, such as Edith Nesbit's *The Story of the Treasure Seekers* (1899) the narrator draws attention to the act of narration through direct address to readers, discussion of narrative choices about material, tone, register, diction and order, self-conscious parody of conventionalised narrative discourses, and references to the relations between 'life' and fiction. Anita Moss (1985) argues on these grounds that the novel is an explicit form of metafiction. However, although the narrative is self-reflective and readers may go on to infer the status of Nesbit's text as a literary artefact, this is not a position constructed within the text. More explicit forms of metafiction, such as Terry Jones's *Nicobobinus* (1985) Gene Kemp's *Jason Bodger and the Priory Ghost* (1985) or Aidan Chambers's *Breaktime* (1978) overtly parody the intrusive narrator so as to break the fictional illusion. In the final paragraph of *Nicobobinus* the narrator, Basilcat, discloses that the whole narrative – including himself – is a fiction. Anachronistic narratorial intrusions in *Jason Bodger* also break the fictional frame by alerting readers to the gap between the time of narration and the time of the story.

In experimental fictions narratorial and authorial intrusions often function quite overtly to position readers in relation to a text. An authorial note at the end of Kemp's *I Can't Stand Losing* (1987/1989) almost demands that readers take a moral stance in relation to the text. Kemp morally censures the behaviour of the main character, thereby confirming the implied reader position constructed through the novel and implicitly undermining the contrived fictionality of the ending of the novel. Jan Mark's *Finders Losers* opens with a note addressed to a narratee which describes the relationship between the narrative and the narratee (and by analogy the text and its readers) in terms which constitute the story and its meanings as being constructed by the narratee rather than as being artefacts of the text: 'By the time you have read all six [stories] you will know exactly what happened on that day, and why, but you'll be the only one who does' (1990: 6). The second person pronoun usually refers to a narratee, but is also used to directly address an implied reader (as in 'choose your own adventure' novels). When it is used more extensively – as it is in Peter Dickinson's *Giant Cold* (1984) and the opening of Peter Hunt's *Backtrack* (1986) – its referential function can be more ambiguous, having a disruptive effect on the relations between text and reader.

Narrative forms: mystery, fantasy, games and readers

Hutcheon describes specific narrative forms which can function as internalised structuring devices to represent reading positions and strategies (1980: 71–86). The mystery is a common device whereby a character's quest to solve a central mystery is represented as analogous to a reader's struggle with the text (Stephens 1993: 102). Combined with an extensive use of character focalisers whose viewpoints are limited, partial and selective and who consistently misinterpret events, this strategy can be used to construct implied readers in a position of superior knowledge, as in Garfield's parody of Conan Doyle in the character Selwyn Raven, in *The Strange Affair of Adelaide Harris*. Further, Stephens has shown how Mayne uses these strategies in *Salt River Times* (1980) and *Winter Quarters* (1982) to express an 'analogy between interpreting human situations and reading fictions' (1993: 102). A variation on this structuring device is the construction of a mystery which remains unsolved, for example Hunt's *Backtrack* or Gary Crew's *Strange Objects* (1990). The focus becomes, not so much the mystery itself, but the interpretive processes and discourses through which characters attempt to produce solutions.

Fantasy and game genres are also used as internalised structuring devices which point to the self-referentiality of a text. A fantasy text constructs an autonomous universe with its own rules and laws. Metafictive fantasies draw attention to the temporal and spatial structuration of this world – its geography, history, culture – and the role of readers in the act of imagining it and giving shape to the referents of words (Hutcheon 1980: 76). In this way, the reading of metafictive fantasies is 'emblematic' of the reading of fiction in general (81).

The 'choose your own adventure' novel is a relatively recent popular genre which explicitly constructs readers as 'players' in a fictional game and as active participants in the construction of the story. Readers construct characters from an assortment of traits and roles, and at each narrative juncture readers are offered a choice, usually from two or three possible narrative paths leading to a range of possible endings – see for example Steve Jackson's and Ian Livingstone's *The Warlock of Firetop Mountain* (1982). This is a highly conventionalised and codified genre, which can potentially teach its readers specific narrative conventions, as well as implicitly reinforce social codes. It is not, in itself, particularly metafictional, though it does clearly have a metafictive potential which has been exploited by writers such as Gillian Rubinstein and Pratchett. In *Beyond the Labyrinth* (1988) Rubinstein's main character attempts to transpose the rules and conventions of the Fighting Fantasy fiction which he is reading on to life. In *Only You Can Save Mankind* (1992) Pratchett inverts and parodies the conventions of computer games. Both writers are concerned with the interrelationships between the ways in which we perceive, think and behave in game fictions and in life. Pratchett's novel implicitly suggests that the modes of action and interpretation used in both fiction and life are very similar; Rubinstein makes more clear-cut distinctions between them.

Narrative disruptions and discontinuities

Disruptions to the causal, logical or linear relationships between narrative events, characters and narrators, and between primary and secondary narratives have the effect of foregrounding the narrative structuring of texts. There are two main strategies for disrupting narratives: narrative metalepsis, and the representation of heterotopias. Metalepsis refers to the transgression of logical and hierarchical relations between different levels of narration (Genette 1980: 234–235; McHale 1987/1989: 119); heterotopias are fictional 'spaces in which a number of possible orders of being can coincide' (Stephens 1992a: 52).

A classic example of narrative metalepsis occurs in Browne's *Bear Hunt* (1979). By literally drawing his way out of each predicament, Bear functions as both a character constructed within the text and as an authorial figure who actively creates and changes the discourse of the text. By transgressing his narrative function, Bear disrupts the conventional hierarchy of relations between character, narrator and author. A more subtle use of metalepsis occurs in Diana Wynne Jones's *The Spellcoats* (1979) where through the process of narrating her story, Tanaqui realises that the act of narration is itself a performance which can influence events in the world. Implicit here is an awareness that any narration of a past simultaneously re-constructs (and fictionalises) that past, but Tanaqui's narratorial role literally shifts from scribe to that of author. What begins as retrospective narration of past events (that is a secondary narrative) becomes a narrative which simultaneously shapes and changes events in the present (that is a primary narrative).

The relationships between authors, primary narrators, secondary narrators and characters are usually hierarchical. By inverting or transgressing these hierarchical relations, metalepsis can be used to articulate questions about authority, power, and freedom, such as who has control of the story and its characters – the narrator, her narratees, an author, his readers, or the socio-cultural context within and through which stories are told, heard, interpreted and appropriated. In *A Step off the Path* (1985) Hunt makes extensive use of metalepsis to articulate complex concerns with forms of textual and cultural appropriation and displacement. This is a multistranded novel, in which a story told by a character (Jo) in one narrative strand is a version of events occurring in another strand. The story concerns a group of knights (descendants of their Arthurian namesakes) who exist on the margins of mainstream society and culture. The novel hinges on a discrepancy between these knights, and their 'fictional' counterparts represented in the popular medieval romance fictions of mainstream culture, out of which Jo's narrative is constructed. Furthermore, these fictions also inform and obscure the perceptions and interpretations of other characters in the primary narrative. The point is that by appropriating the stories and culture of one social group and re-writing it as 'romance' (that is, fiction or myth), the dominant culture effectively writes this group out of 'history' and out of the present. With his representation of the knights, then, Hunt inverts the usual direction of metaleptic transgression, so that the primary narrative disrupts and transgresses the secondary narrative.

Fantastic children's literature is characterised by widespread representation of heterotopias (Stephens 1992a: 52). Diana Wynne Jones and Peter Hunt both construct temporal heterotopias in which a number of possible time zones co-exist in order to overtly play with the relations between history and the temporal structuring of narrative. Jones's *Witch Week* is premised on the possibility that parallel alternative worlds are constructed through spatio-temporal divergences which occur at decisive points in history – for example events such as battles, 'where it is possible for things to go two ways' (1982/1989: 171). This works self-reflectively to represent the kinds of narrative choices which writers make in constructing fictions (Waterhouse 1991: 5). In *The Maps of Time* (1983) Hunt takes this idea a step further: narrative paths diverge as characters perceive and imagine events as occurring differently.

Macaulay's picture books quite overtly play with narrative and temporal linearity. He uses a recursive narrative structure in *Why the Chicken Crossed the Road* (1991). *Black and White* (1990) is an elaborate play with perception, representation and interpretation. It consists of four narrative strands. Each is represented using different narrative and pictorial techniques, and they become visually mixed in the latter part of the text as the visual frames are broken by images which mirror and spill over into adjacent frames. The four narratives are linked by repeated images and 'story' elements, which imply that the four stories might constitute aspects of the same story. However, readers' attempts to construct a single logical chronological narrative are frustrated through the confusion of logical, temporal and causal relations between the four strands. Ultimately the text refuses interpretive closure. What we get is layering of different but similar fictions, interwoven into and endlessly reflecting each other.

Mise en abyme *and self-reflective devices*

The term *mise en abyme* refers to a representation or narrative segment, which is embedded within a larger narrative, and which reflects, reproduces or mirrors an aspect of the larger primary narrative (Prince 1987/1988: 53; McHale 1987/1989: 124–125; Hutcheon 1980: 54–56). It usually functions to indicate ways in which 'the larger narrative might be interpreted' (Stephens 1993: 105). Narrative aspects which might be reflected include: the story or themes of the primary narrative; its narrative situation – such as the relationship between the narrator and narratee; or the style of the primary narrative text (McHale 1987/1989: 124–125).

In realist novels a story, photo, painting or drawing will often function as a *mise en abyme* to reflect the thematic concerns of the primary narrative. For example, in Zibby Oneal's *The Language of Goldfish* the main character, Carrie, executes a series of abstracted drawings based on 'the idea of making patterns in which the real object disappeared' (1980/1987: 31), descriptions of which are analogous with Carrie's experience of a dissolution of selfhood which she both desires and fears as she retreats from adolescence and growing up. Lois Lowry also uses this device in *A Summer to Die* (1977). Self-reflective visual images, such as mirrors, paintings and intertextual quotations are also a common metafictive strategy in the picture books of Browne and Van Allsburg, where they work to foreground the nature of the text as representation, and to blur the distinctions between textual fantasy and reality.

Stories narrated within the primary narrative by a character or a secondary narrator which reflect the story or themes of the primary frame-narrative can also function as *mise en abyme* devices. For example, in Paula Fox's *How Many Miles to Babylon?* (1967) the stories which James tells reflect larger thematic concerns with the role of story-telling in the recuperation of the past and the construction of a subjectivity. Russell Hoban plays with the recursiveness of the 'story-within-story-within-story' structure in repeated descriptions of 'Bonzo Dog Food' labels in *The Mouse and His Child* (1967). Stephens has discussed the use of *mise en abyme* in three of Mayne's novels *Salt River Times*, *Drift* (1985) and *Winter Quarters*, where he sees the device as functioning to replicate the relations between reader and text (1993: 108). Similarly, the representation of relations between a narrator and her narratees in Hunt's *A Step off the Path* replicates a range of text/reader relations.

Self-reflective images are also used to mirror the narrative processes in texts. Thus the narrator of Price's *The Ghost Drum* (1987) is a cat chained to a pole around which it walks, telling stories, winding up the chain (that is, the story) as it goes. Similarly, the image of story-telling as 'weaving' is represented literally in *The Spellcoats* where the narrator's story is literally woven into a coat.

The linguistic construction of texts and the world

There are four main strategies whereby metafictive novels can be self-conscious about their existence as language: parodic play on specific writing styles; thematised wordplay, such as puns, anagrams, clichés; variation of print conventions and the use of marginalia, footnotes and epigraphs – strategies which draw attention to the physicality of texts; and deliberate mixing of literary and extra-literary genres, such as the journal, letter, newspaper items, historical documents, and so on.

Pratchett's *Truckers* is a metafictive fantasy novel about a group of 'nomes' who live under the floorboards of a large department store. Their social system, culture and religion is a bricolage of appropriated signs and discourses associated with department stores, mixed with parodic forms of Biblical and religious discourse. Pratchett constantly plays on the slippage between signifiers and signifieds, foregrounding the gap between signs and things (in the meanings the nomes ascribe to 'Bargains Galore' for instance). By foregrounding the construction of the represented world and, hence, the construction of the text, Pratchett also draws attention to the ways in which representations of the world outside the text are similarly constructed and ascribed with meanings. The stories in Alhberg's *The Clothes Horse* (1987) are constructed out of a play with the literal meanings of commonplace figures of speech, such as 'clothes horse' or 'jack pot'.

The combination of typographical experimentation and overt genre mixing is widespread in recent popular children's fiction, but as Stephens has suggested, 'seems to be settling into its own formulaic conventions: two or three clearly delineated genres or modes ... are juxtaposed in order to suggest restricted perspective and to complicate otherwise flat, everyday surfaces' (1992a: 53). In novels such as Libby Gleeson's *Dodger* (1990) or Aidan Chambers's *The Toll Bridge* (1992) the metafictive and experimental potential of genre mixing is repressed through the combination of these strategies with an implicit authorial position and with realist conventions. The discourse is treated as a transparent medium which simply conveys information, rather than as a specific linguistic code which constructs and inscribes this information with meaning. Novels such as Hunt's *Backtrack*, Chambers's *Breaktime* or Crew's *Strange Objects* consistently foreground their own textuality. Extra-literary genres and discourses are combined so as to effect abrupt shifts in the diegetic levels of narration, disrupt relations between fiction and reality within the textual frame, and draw attention to the discursivity of extraliterary genres.

Multistranded and polyphonic narratives

Two common experimental strategies which can also be used metafictionally are multistranded and polyphonic narration. Multistranded narratives are constructed of two or more interconnected narrative strands differentiated by shifts in temporal or spatial relationships, and/or shifts in narrative point of view (who speaks or focalises). In polyphonic narratives events are narrated from the viewpoints of two or more narrators or character focalisers. These are strategies which enable the representation of a plurality of narrative voices, social and cultural discourses, perceptual, attitudinal and ideological viewpoints. In doing so they can work to efface or destabilise a reader's sense of a single authoritative narratorial position, and thereby situate readers in more active interpretive positions. These are not in themselves metafictive strategies though they can be used as such, particularly in texts which use multiple narrators or focalisers to represent different versions of the same events, such as Mayne's *Drift*.

One of the most common narrative structures used is interlaced dual narration. The narratives of two narrators or character focalisers are represented as two parallel strands interlaced together in alternating chapters or segments. This can work to overtly structure a novel as a 'dialogue' between two social, cultural, historical or gendered positions, as in Hunt's *Going Up* (1989), Caroline Macdonald's *The Lake at the End of the World* (1988), Jenny Pausacker's *What Are Ya?* (1987), Jan Mark's *The Hillingdon Fox* (1991) or Dickinson's *A Bone from a Dry Sea* (1992). However, like typographic and generic forms of experimentation, interlaced dual narration has also settled into its own formulaic conventions and is frequently structured so as to privilege one dominant authoritative position.

These narrative forms are at their most innovative when combined with other experimental narrative features, such as intertextuality, complex shifts in narrative point of view, and indirect and effaced modes of narration (see Stephens 1992b and Hunt 1991: 100–117). Two of the most sophisticated examples of polyphonic multistranded narration to date are Alan Garner's *Red Shift* (1973) and Jill Paton Walsh's *Unleaving* (1976).

Postmodernist historiographic metafictions

Historiographic metafiction refers to novels which self-reflexively mix fictive and historical modes of representation so as to pose questions about the relationships between fiction, history and reality (Hutcheon 1989: 50). Represented historical material may refer to either actual or fictive events – the texts and documents represented in Hunt's *Backtrack* are almost entirely fictional, whereas those in Crew's *Strange Objects* are a mixture of actual and fictive. It is the physical incorporation of the discursive style of history writing, rather than their actual historicity, that is characteristic.

Intellectual historians such as White (1987) and LaCapra (1980) have focused on the relations between representation, in particular narrative representation, and our capacity to know and understand the past. To the extent that the past is only accessible via its documents, archives and artefacts, our knowledge of that past is always mediated and determined by prior textualisations or representations. Potentially the past is, therefore, only knowable as text, and is thereby always already implicated in problems of language, discourse and representation. Historiographic metafictions highlight concerns with interpretation and representation by incorporating 'historical' texts and discursive conventions. For example, Hunt plays with the conventional historicist assumption that the closer an account of an event is to that event in time, the more accuracy and credibility it has, by including a transcript of an Inquest Report in which he steadfastly refuses to disclose information, thereby drawing attention to the discursive strategies which structure the report. The primary narrative of *Backtrack* centres on two characters, Jack and Rill, who attempt to solve a mysterious train crash which occurred seventy years earlier. The mystery remains unsolved and the lack of narrative resolution draws attention to the discourses whereby the mystery is constructed and whereby Jack and Rill attempt to solve it: namely, historical research, conjecture and reconstruction, and conventionalised generic narrative codes – the espionage plot, and the crime of passion plot. A subsequent blurring of the status of these discourses, as fiction and/or history, foregrounds their conventionality and the extent to which fiction and history are both culturally inscribed categories of discourse and not always easily distinguishable from each other. The narrative forms for representing and structuring events are common to both history writing and fiction, and that these are forms which impart meaning as well as order (Hutcheon 1989: 62). The possibility remains that the act of narration, in either fictive or historical writing, might construct and thereby construe its object.

Conclusions

An increasingly noticeable phenomena has been the appropriation of experimental and metafictive narrative techniques into mainstream children's literature, an occurrence which blurs the distinctions between experimental and non-experimental, between the mainstream and the marginal. However, a key distinction between experimental and non-experimental writing for children lies in the audience positions constructed within texts. As experimental and metafictive features become more superficial aspects of a texts construction, and hence more conventionalised and formulaic, the range of interpretive positions inscribed in texts become increasingly restricted. Many of the techniques and strategies which I have described are not in themselves 'experimental' or 'metafictive', though they have the capacity to function in these ways when used in combination either with each other, or with particular discursive and narrational modes. Metafictive and experimental forms of children's writing generally utilise a wide range of narrative and discursive strategies which distance readers from texts, and construct implied readers who are more actively involved in the production of meanings. By drawing attention to the ways in which texts are structured and to how they mean, metafictions can potentially teach readers specific codes and conventions and interpretive strategies with which to read and make sense of other, more closed, fictions. Furthermore, to the extent that we use language and narrative to represent and comprehend reality, as well as to construct fictions, metafictions can, by analogy, show readers how representations of reality are similarly constructed and ascribed with meanings.

References

Britton, J. (1970/1972) *Language and Learning*, Harmondsworth: Penguin.
Genette, G. (1980) *Narrative Discourse*, Oxford: Blackwell.
Hunt, P. (1988) 'Degrees of control: stylistics and the discourse of children's literature', in Coupland, N. (ed.) *Styles of Discourse*, London: Croom Helm.
—— (1991) *Criticism, Theory and Children's Literature*, Oxford: Blackwell.

—— (ed.) (1992) *Literature for Children: Contemporary Criticism*, London: Routledge.

Hutcheon, L. (1980) *Narcissistic Narrative: The Metafictional Paradox*, New York: Methuen.

—— (1989) *The Politics of Postmodernism*, London: Routledge.

Jones, D. W. (1982/1989) *Witch Week*, London: Mammoth.

Kemp, G. (1987/1989) *I Can't Stand Losing*, Harmondsworth: Penguin.

LaCapra, D. (1980) 'Rethinking intellectual history and reading texts', *History and Theory* 19, 3, 245–276.

Lewis, D. (1990) 'The constructedness of texts: picture books and the metafictive', *Signal* 61, 131–146.

McCallum, R. (1992) '(In)quest of the subject: the dialogic construction of subjectivity in Caroline Macdonald's *Speaking to Miranda*', *Papers: Explorations into Children's Literature* 3, 3: 99–105.

McHale, B. (1987/1979) *Postmodernist Fiction*, London: Routledge.

Mackey, M. (1990) 'Metafiction for beginners: Allan Ahlberg's *Ten in a Bed*', *Children's Literature in Education* 21, 3, 179–187.

Mark, J. (1990) *Finders Losers*, London: Orchard Books.

Moss, A. (1985) 'Varieties of children's metafiction', *Studies in the Literary Imagination* 17, 2: 79–92.

Moss, G. (1990) 'Metafiction and the poetics of children's literature', *Children's Literature Association Quarterly* 15, 2: 50–52.

—— (1992) 'Metafiction, illustration, and the poetics of children's literature', in Hunt, P. (ed.) *Literature for Children: Contemporary Criticism*, London: Routledge.

Ommundsen, W. (1989) 'Narrative navel gazing: or how to recognise a metafiction when you see one', *Southern Review* 22, 3: 264–274.

Oneal, Z. (1980/1987) *The Language of Goldfish*, London: Gollancz.

Prince, G. (1987/1988) *A Dictionary of Narratology*, Aldershot: Scolar.

Stephens, J. (1991) 'Did I tell you about the time I pushed the Brothers Grimm off Humpty Dumpty's wall? Metafictional strategies for constituting the audience as agent in the narratives of Janet and Allan Ahlberg', in Stone, M. (ed.) *Children's Literature and Contemporary Theory*, Wollongong: New Literatures Research Centre.

—— (1992a) 'Modernism to postmodernism, or the line from Insk to Onsk: William Mayne's *Tiger's Railway*', *Papers: Explorations into Children's Literature* 3, 2: 51–59.

—— (1992b) *Language and Ideology in Children's Fiction*, London: Longman.

—— (1993) 'Metafiction and interpretation: William Mayne's *Salt River Times, Winter Quarters* and *Drift*', *Children's Literature* 21: 101–117.

Vygotsky, L. S. (1934/1962) *Thought and Language*, ed. and trans. E. Hanfmann and G. Vakar, Cambridge, MA: MIT Press.

Waterhouse, R. (1991) 'Which way to encode and decode fiction', *Children's Literature Association Quarterly* 16, 1: 2–5.

Waugh, P. (1984) *Metafiction: The Theory and Practise of Self-Conscious Fiction*, London: Methuen.

White, H. (1987) *The Content of the Form: Narrative Discourse and Historical Representation*, Baltimore: Johns Hopkins University Press.

13 Children Becoming Readers: Reading and Literacy

Geoffrey Williams

Editor's introduction

One of the major concerns of those who work with children and books is literacy, and it may seem obvious that children's literature can be an important tool in the acquisition and use of language. However, both the theory and the practice are complex and continually developing; Geoffrey Williams's discussion looks both at children's books and at classroom work, drawing together many of the critical and theoretical issues of other chapters in this book.

P. H.

Introduction

Over the past decade or so children's literature has assumed a new status in the teaching of reading in the first years of school. Previously, though enthusiastic teachers read to children during story time, actual instruction in reading 'skill' was largely carried out through specially written materials, in the form of reading schemes and comprehension exercises. The result was that for very many children Janet and John, Dick and Jane were more familiar figures of fiction than Rosie, Alfie or Tom Long. There have, of course, always been teachers who understood that the texts through which children learned to read were important for the kinds of readers they became, but these exceptions were the more remarkable because the dominant practices were so strong.

Some features of recent changes in literacy pedagogy which give children's literature a new status in reading pedagogy are explored in this chapter. There are two aspects of particular interest: appreciation of the significance of the semiotic patterning of literary texts; and explorations of effects of ways of talking about literary texts. Certain ways of talking about narrative in some families have profoundly influenced the teaching of reading, but these pedagogic strategies rest on specific images of relations between home and school reading practices, which it is therefore important to examine closely. In particular, the metaphor of an essential partnership between home and school literacy practices will be under focus. The chapter also considers different forms of classroom work which develop through the metaphors of personal response to, and collaborative exploration of, literary text, and concludes with an image of a class of 11-year-old children using metasemiotic tools, in this case linguistic tools, to talk about a book they enjoyed greatly. For reasons of space the discussion is restricted to the early periods of children's literacy development in primary school, a selection which is perhaps justified by the fact that far greater critical attention is usually given to adolescents' reading.

Texts in Reading Development

When children learn to read, they do so by reading *something*, texts, in fact. Despite this truism the effects of texts have been very little studied in reading pedagogy. A typical formulation is that 'Children learn to read', and it is the agent 'children' and the process 'read' which have attracted most attention from analysts. Even when children have been studied, it has typically not been children in some actual context of lived experience but individual, displaced acts of perception and cognition which experimenters have probed. Margaret Meek comments, on the basis of a lifetime's interest in children's literature and reading development,

> In all of the books I have read about reading and teaching reading there is scarcely a mention about what is to be read. Books are, as the saying goes, taken as read in the discussions about reading teaching. The reading experts, for all their understanding about 'the reading process', treat all text as the neutral substance on which the process works, as if the reader did the same thing with a poem, a timetable, a warning notice.
>
> Meek 1988: 5

Only in the last decade has a different formulation, 'Texts construct children's reading', entered discussions about how children learn to read, although understanding of the agency of texts in the making of readers has now become an important aspect of the children's literature field. Scholars such as Meek and Nodelman (1988) cross the established boundaries of academic disciplines to develop their accounts of the subtlety and significances of literary texts written for children, often surprising readers by how transdisciplinary the reach of such work is, and needs must be. Such studies draw on research in semiotics, socio-cultural theories of children's mental development, histories of literacy and, increasingly, anthropological and sociological studies of cultural differences in narrative practices.

Meek writes in particular of the 'untaught lessons' in reading, those which readers experience only through deep involvement in what they read and through sharing readings with others (1988: 7). These accounts of untaught reading lessons rest on the textuality of the literature children read, and they therefore require careful investigation of how meanings are built up by the patterning of visual and linguistic elements of individual texts. It is worth taking a few moments with the detail so that the specific resources for these signifying practices are made visible.

Since *Where the Wild Things Are* (Sendak 1970) counts as an example of a text which many children become deeply involved with, it is a useful 'test case' for the argument. Some economy can be achieved by asking a specific question about children's reading of narrative: how does a child reader learn about the development of plot from the semiotic patterning of this text? This is surely one crucial aspect of being able to read like a 'model reader', in Eco's (1994) sense.

Perhaps the most obvious source of understanding of plot relations is the excitement of the depicted events, from which comes the necessity to turn the page. But that is not all there is to say about the resource of the text for this learning. How is the sense of event and, perhaps more importantly, the significance of event, given by the patterning of the resources of language and image?

Consider those images in which Max looks directly at the viewer/reader, in contrast with those in which his gaze is directed 'within' the represented world. There are three such images. The first occurs just after the bedroom begins to become a forest, and just before Max begins to take advantage of it. He looks directly at the viewer, with a smile which seems to invite complicity. As readers we appear to be instructed that something slightly different is about to happen as we turn the page. Perhaps it will seem akin to one of those moments when somebody makes momentary eye contact, in a classroom or at a party, from which it is evident that more will follow. That is to say, at this point the text 'asks' us to begin to adopt a slightly different relationship with Max through the form of the image.

How does the image 'ask' something new of the reader? In a recent analysis of the semiotic resources of visual images, Kress and van Leeuwen (1990) describe direct gaze from the depicted figure to the viewer as the means through which demands, in comparison with offers, are made. Following their lead we might say that prior to this point the text has offered information, but in this image it makes a first demand on a reader to adopt a particular orientation of expectation to the sequent events. We might predict that what follows will therefore have some particular significance for the narrative development, as indeed it does as Max begins to act in the transformed world of his room.

The next moment of 'demand' comes soon after. It is the image in which Max sets out in his private boat to begin his voyage to the Wild Things. Max's gaze here is very clear, very direct – in some contrast with the furtiveness of the earlier image. The combination of the gaze, the disposition of the arms, the smile and the frontal angle of Max's body all seem to suggest a request which is something like 'come and play this game with me'.

There is one last image in which a demand is made. The wild rumpus has begun at Max's command and, of course, the following three images assume the full volume of the page. In the first of these Max dances in parallel with the wild things, but below them; in the second, he swings in the tops of the trees, equal with them; and in the third, he is on top of them, riding triumphantly, mace in hand. It is in the second that the new demand is made, just prior to his ascendancy to a position of total domination.

Direct gaze from the depicted character to the reader is, of course, just one of the many meaning resources which contribute to a sense of the plot. Going back through the images we can see many other ways in which subtle variation cues readers to adopt a variable role relationship with Max, or with the other participants. Consider just one further example of the significance of variation, the vertical angle at which the characters are depicted. As viewers we are positioned at eye level in the first image, at a slightly higher angle in the second, and at a much higher angle again through the images of Max in his bedroom, but then the angle drops back to eye level as he sails off through night and day, and then to a much lower angle as he encounters the first Wild Thing (cf. Nodelman 1988: 183).

Again, what is the significance of this variation? In Western European visual semiotic resources, angle of view is the primary means through which a relation of power between viewer and represented image is construed. (Consider, for example, the variable construal of a politician's power through press photographs shot at various vertical angles.) In this text the images instruct us to adopt variable power relations with Max as part of the plot development – first, we are more or less his equal; then, in his moment of abandonment we become 'superior' in power – or, perhaps more accurately, Max is relatively diminished in power; and then, as the plot develops, our power diminishes relative to the participants in the ensuing monstrous clash.

The significance of variation in the patterning of meanings might equally be pursued with regard to language. For example, we might ask how, linguistically, readers *initially* are given a sense that this night – the night of Max's transgression, journey and restoration – is a night with singular qualities.

Grammatically, the text has an unusual beginning which 'foregrounds' the particularity of the night. This comes about because of the choice the author has made for the initial element of the first clause of the text. Halliday (1994) describes how English gives readers a choice as to which constituent is placed in first position in a clause. As a consequence there is a meaning significance attaching to the initial element, which gives information about the textual organisation of the message by indicating the speaker/writer's 'point of departure'. Speakers may begin a clause with the grammatical Subject, as the writer of the publisher's introduction did in the Puffin edition:

Max's wonderful adventure began the night he put on his wolf suit.

Alternatively, a speaker might begin with an atypical choice or marked choice as Sendak did when he brought to the foreground not Max, nor his adventure, but instead

The night Max wore his wolf suit and made mischief of one kind and another his mother called him 'WILD THING!'

Notice, too, that grammatically a good deal of information about the particular night is built up immediately around the noun 'night' itself. Technically this is achieved through embedded clauses in the noun group, which are constituted by all the words in italics after 'night'. The physical distribution of the language on the page also supports this marking of the moment in time since the noun group is extended over the first two pages. Grammar and orthography together draw attention to the particularity of the moment.

To return, then, from the detail of the particular text to the general argument. The point to which Meek and others draw attention is this: many literary texts written for children enable readers to take up ways of meaning relevant to literary readings of text through the patterning of semiotic resources in both language and visual image. On this account children do not become 'literary' readers by first developing a bank of skills in 'decoding' and 'comprehension', and then apply these skills to literary (and other) texts. They learn how to act as literary readers partly because the resources of the texts they care about make it possible for them to act as literary readers.

The sense of 'act' is important. It draws attention to the fact that literacy is constructed in action, in and through the reading of texts and through engaging in the forms of interpretation which these texts make possible. The selection of verb here in fact owes much to Vygotsky's insight into the resources which mediate meaning in interaction and over time become part of a child's ways of meaning (Vygotsky 1986).

Literary texts are thus a necessary requirement for the development of literary readers. They are not, though, a sufficient condition. In Meek's formulation there are two conditions, the second being the necessity of 'sharing our readings with others'. The benefits of sharing readings have been so widely discussed in the children's literature field they may appear to require no further analysis, but this is not so.

Since for children the two main sites for this sharing are families and schools, relations between ways of sharing readings in these sites are crucial for development. Since sharing is always by definition with socially situated others, whose locations in socio-cultural practices vary, there is an important potential for different forms of interpretive practice to develop in and around literary text. Therefore, how readings are shared in classrooms, and how these classroom ways of saying relate to ways of meaning that children have developed in their families, have a deep significance for literacy pedagogy and are the focus of the next section. In the following discussion I will initially consider changes to early school literacy pedagogy which are based on observations of family reading practices, then raise some questions about the effects of the notion of a close partnership between home and school in literacy education.

Story Reading and Early Literacy Pedagogy

From case studies of precocious readers (for example, Clark 1976; Durkin 1966), and correlational studies of early development of schooled literacy (for example Wells *et al.* 1981; Wells 1985; 1987), there have been consistent findings of strong associations between joint book reading in families and early success in school literacy. The findings have been widely used in Australia, Britain, Canada, New Zealand and the USA to fashion literacy education in the early years of schooling. In Australia, joint book reading has become one of the orthodoxies of the 'whole language' approach.

In classroom joint book reading, teachers have been encouraged to simulate family interaction by reading 'big book' versions of children's literature with whole classes of young learners (Holdaway 1979). Interaction during school joint book reading usually takes the form of an initial reading of a text and discussion of story features based on children's individual responses to it, then further readings in which children progressively take more responsibility for reading the written language aloud.

However, the foregrounding of continuity in reading practices between home and school, tending to universalise the practice of joint book reading in the home, comes at a high price for some young learners. In contrast with the universalising tendency of much of the pedagogical literature, a significant body of evidence points to the relativity of literacy practices in different social locations, including ways in which caregivers read to their children and hence the orientations which children develop to different 'ways with words' (Heath 1983). Since only some of these practices are selected into school discourse, even those children who are read to extensively at home may experience significant discontinuity between home and school literacy practices.

In fact, even in the early correlational studies of early reading achievement, important differences in family story-reading practices were evident. This was so in Wells's Bristol study (1985, 1987), and in a range of small-scale studies, for example Tizard and Hughes (1984) and Teale (1986). Researchers such as Wells have been clear that certain characteristics of linguistic interaction during the reading of text are related to school literacy development. He comments:

> it is not the reading of stories on its own that leads children towards the reflective, disembedded thinking that is so necessary for success in school, but the total interaction in which the story is embedded. At first they need a competent adult to mediate, as reader and writer, between themselves and the text; but even when they can perform the decoding and encoding for themselves, they continue to need help in interpreting the stories they hear and read and in shaping those that they create for themselves. The manner in which the adult – first parent and later teacher – fulfils this latter role is almost as important as the story itself.
>
> Wells 1985: 253

Despite the strength of these assertions, repeated frequently in both research reports and pedagogic handbooks, only rarely has linguistic interaction during joint book reading been a topic of intensive analysis. Among such detailed studies, Heath's ethnographic comparison of literacy events in three communities in the south-east of the USA is the most widely known. With respect to joint book reading specifically, Heath found crucial variation in interaction between caregivers and children in the white fundamentalist Christian community of 'Roadville' and the 'maintown' middle-class social location of 'Gateway'. (The practice was found to be virtually non-existent in the third community, 'Trackton'.) The Gateway variant was the only one which approximated school practices. Heath argues that the variants signify different historico-cultural literacy traditions in these communities.

Additional to Heath's study of 'inter-cultural' variation, intra-cultural variation by social class locations was considered by Williams (1995). Many hours of interaction between mothers and 4–year-old children, and between teachers and kindergarten classes in the first two months of schooling, were audiorecorded. Semantic features of each clause of this interaction were analysed to describe typical semantic patterning during talk about books. Findings from the study confirm the sensitivity of literacy practices to social location and, additionally, indicate that it is aspects of the practices of only one social class group which are projected into school pedagogy.

The sensitivity of joint book reading practices to social location represents a radical challenge to the image of naturalness in interaction around children's literature which strongly typifies teaching handbooks. In these environments children become, in Bernstein's phrase, the 'imaginary subjects' of instruction (Bernstein 1990) and the account of the complexity of what they have to learn for success in school literacy is significantly reduced.

One of the most important current challenges for early literacy educators is to find ways of talking about books which can be made genuinely inclusive of children, or at least genuinely clear to them. Another is to avoid impressions that literacy differences are simply educational differences in another guise, and therefore successfully 'treated' by parent education strategies. Both challenges will have to be addressed through greater knowledge about both the subtlety and effects of meaning variations in relation to different socio-cultural locations.

Talking About Literary Texts and their Meanings in Classrooms

The metaphor of *personal response* to story currently dominates thought about the function of children's literature in education. Under this metaphor children are involved in a wide range of activities which amount either to forms of retelling the constructs of the text, for example by mapping the plot, or by recreating elements of a scene (draw a picture of Terabithia), or to acting imaginatively within the constructs of the text (write to Gilly Hopkins to encourage her in her new life with her grandmother). What is specifically encouraged is an individual response which effectively takes the fictive world as given.

At its best this work can be interesting for children, particularly by creating opportunities to explore the internal coherence of a fictive world. But, in so far as these approaches to 'using' children's literature dominate classroom work, they actually create significant problems for many children. ('Using' literature is by far the most common verb representing these processes in literacy pedagogy.) Activities of the imagination are refracted through the metaphor of personal response as though they were universal features of childhood rather than specific forms of interpretive activity which are learned through specific social practices. Consequently, because textual meaning and modes of interpretation are taken as given under this metaphor, the longer-term significances of classroom work based on it remain opaque for many learners. They may appear to participate willingly, and certainly to enjoy themselves, but their understandings of *why* they are engaging in such work are likely to be another matter.

A rather different approach is taken by teachers who include explorations of the nature of literary text itself in classroom work, even with emergent readers. In this approach teachers position children as apprentice collaborators in the investigation of meanings and how they are made, rather than as reactors to given meanings. Such teachers find in the textual play of books like Browne's *Bear Hunt* and *Piggybook*, Burningham's *Granpa* and Scieszka's and Smith's *The Stinky Cheese Man and other Fairly Stupid Tales* resources which enable them to encourage children to investigate literary meaning-making as textual practice.

Experienced readers sometimes fear that such explorations of how meanings are made will destroy embryonic reading pleasure through disturbing the 'magic of narrative', no doubt with memories of their own experiences of interminable and arbitrary classroom readings of texts still vivid. However, children do appear to be able to learn to read variably. Much in the way that Barthes describes in his introductory discussions in *S/Z* (1974) children can learn to read, on the one hand, as though for the moment a character were a real psychological entity and there were such places as midnight gardens and, on the other hand, as though there was nothing but the patterning of language which was the source of their pleasure. It is the integration of these two forms of pleasure which makes pedagogies which include investigation of how meanings are made so distinct: different ways of reading, each with its own satisfactions. What is importantly changed is the level of abstraction at which children learn to think about the nature of literature, and language.

In such approaches the search is always for the patterning of meaning, and never for the isolated textual instance of a felicitously used adjective or some other 'good word'. It is, after all, the patterning of relations which gives a literary text the kind of distinctive significance which Culler (1977) accords it. Although classroom readings begin by taking the figures of a text as given, it is usually not very long before children can be helped to notice features such as intertextual play and the repetitions and parallel structures of wordings which are the very basis of how literary texts mean.

One interesting example of such work is given by Aidan Chambers (Chambers 1985, 1993). Chambers's provocative question, first raised in *Booktalk* (1985) was this: are children critics, where the work of critics is understood in the terms Auden proposed in *The Dyer's Hand and Other Essays* (1948)? His evidence suggests that they may be. Chambers and his teacher collaborators describe children's participation in three types of 'sharing': sharing enthusiasms, sharing puzzles and sharing connections. The third is subtitled 'discovering patterns', and includes a framework of discussion through which sharing of ideas might take place, including the highly significant question 'Were there any patterns – any connections – that you noticed?' As with any proposal for a general framework, there is a danger that such a methodology might come to restrict what might be talked about with a particular text. Chambers himself warns repeatedly against this (for example, 1993: 87). But it is a danger which is a problem for any specific pedagogical proposal, and therefore not a criticism of the approach itself. Pedagogical proposals which avoid the specific transmit their own invitations to rigidity.

In investigating the patterning of text it eventually becomes necessary to say something about what it is that is patterned. This requirement leads directly to a need for metasemiotic tools: a language to talk about language, or about other meaning systems. Here we come full circle to the beginnings of this discussion, to ask a question which it has only been possible to raise within reading pedagogy during the last few years. The question is this: as people with an interest in various facets of children's literature learn more about the nature of textuality by using a range of metasemiotic tools (Doonan 1993), is it possible that children might also learn to participate in such explorations through accessible metasemiotic tools?

To exemplify, and in a sense to offer a test case, I will describe a specific, exploratory instance of work of this kind as the final movement of this chapter. The work was with a class of 11-year-olds and forms part of a research project concerned with children's development of knowledge about language being conducted at the University of Sydney. The teacher, Ruth French, is part of the small research group. The general purpose of this work is to explore children's understandings of the significance of variation in language. So far as literary text is concerned, the children were encouraged to investigate effects of variation in the patterning of certain kinds of meaning within a specific text. It is important, though, in order to place the literary work in the more general context to begin by describing aspects of the work on language variation.

The children knew well, from sharing between various members of the class, that languages themselves vary. The majority had a language other than English as their mother tongue, including Tamil, Mandarin, German and Italian, and their knowledge was an important resource for the rest of the class. For example, Giridhar taught the class something of the Tamil alphabet, Cathy showed them how difficult it is to write Mandarin, Eric talked about differences between his (Austrian) German and the German spoken in Germany itself. Since all of the children were learning to speak Italian they could make their own comparisons with English. They also knew that English varies in different contexts of use, and that this variation comes about partly because of the role language plays in making meaning.

The specific metasemiotic tools they were learning to use derived from a functional grammar of English (Halliday 1994), which describes English from the perspective of language as a resource for meaning rather than as a set of prescribed grammatical rules. Observations about grammatical patterning, and the significance of variation in patterning, were a prominent aspect of this work. The children knew, for example, that typically texts which give people instructions about how to do something are linguistically organised in a way different from texts which argue for a particular point of view: they are different genres, in Bakhtin's (1986) sense. Their knowledge of semiotic design generally, and linguistic variation more specifically, were then important bases for further insight into how literary texts mean.

A literary text which particularly attracted the children's attention was Anthony Browne's *Piggybook*. They laughed loudly as Ruth read it to them, exclaiming as they noticed the transformation of the setting through the occurrence of the pigs in wallpaper, light switches and lampshades. Their conversations about the book extended over several lessons. They began with the details of the represented figures, but soon extended their discussion to notice the patterning of colours, especially the colour selections and relative saturation. They also began to make some tentative observations about the different perspectives from which the images were drawn.

Their enthusiasm was so great that Ruth extended their observations to features of the language. They focused initially on Mr Piggott and the two sons, noticing that these figures *do* a lot of physical action, but their actions do not extend to anything else. So they learned some new descriptive terms of a functional grammar to further their observations. They learned, for example, that in a clause such as 'he went off to his very important job' Mr Piggott is the grammatical actor in the process 'went'. In contrast, in a clause such as 'Mrs Piggott washed all the breakfast things', Mrs Piggott is the grammatical actor and the process 'washed' extends to the goal 'all the breakfast things'. They found many similar examples in the first movements of the text and discovered that the males were never involved in physical processes which extended to anything else. In contrast, Mrs Piggott was almost always involved in physical processes which had some aspect of housework as goal, not only washing the dishes but also making the beds, vacuuming the carpets and so on. They played extensively with this new idea, discovering that a character can be made to seem very different by the types of physical process in which they are made to participate and the goals to which the processes extend. 'Janet made a new dress', or 'Janet made a mess' or 'Janet built a tree house'. All of this, they knew from their play, was a matter of a writer's choice, however unconsciously, in effecting specific meanings.

Finally, they went back to *Piggybook* to look at the last movement. They had, of course, already realised that the family relations were different by this time. That had been clear from their understanding of the sense of the characters and plot on the first reading. Their teacher's further question suggested that a different type of understanding might be possible. She asked: how does variation in the language itself make the family relations different now from the beginning of this book? After much further discussion and practical mapping of grammatical differences this is what the children themselves recorded about their discovery.

What we learnt about the grammatical patterns in *Piggybook*

Beginning

All the goals Mrs Piggott did were to do with housework.

Only Mrs Piggott had goals. This shows she is the only one doing something *to* something else.

Mr Piggott and the boys only did things for themselves; they did not do work in the home. This is shown by the fact that they didn't have any goals. They were the only characters that talked. They told Mrs Piggott to hurry up.

Resolution

At the end, everyone did an action to something – to benefit the whole family, not just themselves. Everyone had goals at the end.

Now the goals for Mrs Piggott included more than housework.

She mended the car.

Just one moment in one class with one text and one particular teacher. But perhaps there is a suggestion here that children might be able to participate, with enthusiasm, in the search for linguistic patterning and its significances.

Margaret Meek observes that 'Children read stories they like over and over again; that's when they pay attention to the words – after they've discovered what happens' (1988: 36). What we have yet to find more about is the means through which children can be assisted to attend to 'words'. Heath's work, and that of others who have followed her lead, suggests there is nothing natural about these processes. Indeed Vygotsky's meticulous analysis of the ontogenesis of voluntary attention shows just how deeply social these apparently natural processes of attention are (Vygotsky 1981). It seems that offering children some access to semiotic tools which enable them to describe visual and verbal patterning in literary text may have some potential to develop a different reading pedagogy, remaking it to include the possibility of children delighting intelligently and critically in the nature of a text's composition without excluding their enjoyment of the constructed story.

References

Auden, W. H. (1948) *The Dyer's Hand and Other Essays*, London: Faber.

Bakhtin, M. (1986) *Speech Genres and Other Late Essays*, trans. C. Emerson and M. Holquist, Austin: University of Texas Press.

Barthes, R. (1974) *S/Z*, trans. R. Miller, New York: Hill and Wang.

Bernstein, B. (1990) *Class, Codes and Control*, Vol. 4, London: Routledge and Kegan Paul.

Browne, A. (1986) *Piggybook*, London: MacRae.

Chambers, A. (1985) *Booktalk: Occasional Writing on Literature and Children*, London: Bodley Head.

—— (1993) *Tell Me: Children, Reading and Talk*, South Woodchester: Thimble Press.

Clark, M. M. (1976) *Young Fluent Readers: What Can They Teach Us?*, London: Heinemann Educational.

Culler, J. (1977) *Structuralist Poetics: Structuralism, Linguistics and the Study of Literature*, London: Routledge and Kegan Paul.

Doonan, J. (1993) *Looking at Pictures in Picture Books*, South Woodchester: Thimble Press.

Durkin, D. (1966) *Children who Read Early: Two Longitudinal Studies*, New York: Teachers College Press.

Eco, U. (1994) *Six Walks in the Fictional Woods*, Cambridge, MA: Harvard University Press.

Halliday, M. A. K. (1994) *An Introduction to Functional Grammar*, 2nd edn, London: Edward Arnold.

Heath, S. B. (1983) *Ways with Words: Language, Life and Work in Communities and Classrooms*, Cambridge: Cambridge University Press.

Holdaway, D. (1979) *The Foundations of Literacy*, Sydney: Ashton Scholastic.

Kress G. and van Leeuwen, T. (1990) *Reading Images*, Victoria: Deakin University Press.

Meek, M. (1988) *How Texts Teach What Readers Learn*, South Woodchester: Thimble Press.

Nodelman, P. (1988) *Words About Pictures: The Narrative Art of Children's Picture Books*, Athens, GA: University of Georgia Press.

Sendak, M. (1970) *Where the Wild Things Are*, Harmondsworth: Penguin.

Teale, W. H. (1986) 'Home background and young children's literacy development', in Teale, W. H. and Sulzby, E. (eds) *Emergent Literacy: Writing and Reading*, Norwood, NJ: Ablex.

Tizard, B. and Hughes, M. (1984) *Young Children Learning: Talking and Thinking at Home and at School*, London: Fontana.

Vygotsky, L. S. (1981) 'The genesis of higher mental functions', in Wertsch, J. V. (ed.) *The Concept of Activity in Soviet Psychology*, New York: M. E. Sharpe.

—— (1986) *Thought and Language*, ed. and trans. A. Kozulin, Cambridge, MA: MIT Press.

Wells, C. G. (1985) 'Pre-school literacy-related activities and success in school', in Olson, D. R. Torrance, N., and Hidyard, A. (eds) *Literacy, Language and Learning: The Nature and Consequences of Reading and Writing*, Cambridge: Cambridge University Press.

—— (1987) *The Meaning Makers: Children Learning Language and Using Language to Learn*, London: Hodder and Stoughton.

——, Bridges, A., French, P., MacLure, M., Sinha, C., Walkerdine, V. and Woll, B. (1981) *Learning Through Interaction: The Study of Language Development*, Cambridge: Cambridge University Press.

Williams, G. (1995) *Joint Book Reading and Literacy Pedagogy: A Socio-Semantic Examination*, Ph.D. dissertation, School of English and Linguistics, Sydney: Macquarie University.

14 Can Stories Heal?

Hugh Crago

Editor's introduction

The question of how texts influence their audience has always been of particular interest for those in the field of children's books. The books have always had a strong element of the didactic, and they have generally been assumed to have directly beneficial effects on their readers. Hugh Crago's discussion of the question of whether, or how, books can be used as a mode of psychotherapy relates to reader-response theory, psychology, and literacy.

P. H.

Bibliotherapy is one of an enormous range of methods for helping human beings in distress. The word itself suggests a specific therapeutic modality (as in 'art therapy' 'occupational therapy' or 'dance therapy' – all of which were developed specifically to meet the needs of patients perceived to be wholly or partly beyond the reach of mainstream psychotherapeutic methods). In fact, bibliotherapy has not remotely established its claim to such status, and may never do so, but it still has a direct, though peripheral, relationship to the whole field of *psychotherapy*.

However, because the printed text (*biblio-*) is the medium through which the helping/healing is considered to occur (whereas, the concept should really cover non-printed 'texts' such as oral story-telling and the viewing of visual narratives like films and picture books), bibliotherapy must also be considered in relation to the study of literature as received by its audience, a field now categorised as reception theory (Tabbert 1979) and reader response. With these bibliotherapy once again enjoys a presently tenuous but potentially significant connection.

Indeed, we may as well say clearly at the outset that both the theory and the practice of bibliotherapy have suffered from a failure fully to explore (or even in many cases to recognise) these connections. Few advocates of bibliotherapy have had much knowledge of reader-response theory – much of which postdates the pioneering work in bibliotherapy. Even fewer have had much personal acquaintance with the wider fields of psychology and psychotherapy. For their part, most psychologists have simply avoided dealing with a subject as complex and difficult to quantify as the potential effects of narrative on human lives. Much of what purports to be received wisdom on the subject of bibliotherapy is thus of dubious value, and perhaps it is not surprising that bibliotherapy has not been taken seriously by many people.

In so far as bibliotherapy has been seen as particularly relevant to children and adolescents, its proponents have been influenced by misleading assumptions about the nature of childhood, in particular, the Rousseau-derived belief that children are especially susceptible to suggestion through print in comparison with adults, and ignorance of the real similarities and differences between child readers and adult readers (outlined briefly in Crago 1979) In fact, as we shall see, there is little difference between children and adults at the level of reading where lasting 'influence' is most likely to occur.

What Psychotherapy Is

Psychotherapy comprises a body of knowledge about what goes wrong with human beings, along with a set of practices designed to improve happiness and competence in the face of life's inevitable stresses. Lay people commonly assume that such work is the province of psychologists, but the academic discipline of psychology has no compelling claim on the practice of psychotherapy, and many 'scientific' psychologists eschew psychotherapy except in extremely restricted forms. Psychiatry, because of its association with mental illness, is the other profession most often associated with psychotherapy, but once again, psychiatrists need not necessarily practice it.

Psychotherapy, which Freud called 'the talking cure', is best understood as something which may be practised by nurses, social workers, family therapists, doctors, marriage counsellors and occupational therapists, as well as by psychiatrists and psychologists. In non-Western cultures, shamans and other traditional healers operate out of a totally different conceptual framework from that employed by European psychotherapists, but at a fundamental level satisfy the same needs in their troubled clientele – needs for reassurance, meaning and healing confrontation. This makes it clear that there is no universally 'true' system of psychotherapeutic theory, and that no single professional guild in our own, or any other, culture, 'owns' psychotherapeutic practice.

The Co-Evolution of Story and Consciousness

In pre-literate cultures, narrative has always functioned in multiple ways, preserving accumulated knowledge, articulating meaning, offering cathartic release and pleasure, and promoting 'healing' in the broad sense of reassurance as to each listener's place in the scheme of things. A single myth or ceremony may embody all of these functions simultaneously. We can reasonably assume that the prehistoric antecedents of our own culture were similar. The earliest written versions of oral narratives that we possess appear to have operated in much the same way as prime time television does today: offering their audiences culturally central messages that confirmed listeners in their existing understandings of what was right and wrong, acceptable and unacceptable, heroic and ignoble.

In the European Middle Ages, where story-telling occurred – whether in church, or around the hearth at night – it would probably have been experienced in the same shared way, and with the same multiple dimensions, as myth and bardic epic. One reason why it has been possible for scholars in our own century to 'discover' the therapeutic potential of traditional folk tales (for example, Bettelheim 1976) is precisely because it has always been there. Those tales formed part of a collective, oral culture which spoke to a collective psyche, not a collection of individual psyches, and which inevitably embodied messages of broad relevance to the community in general.

The coming of print to Western Europe, followed a few centuries later by the spread of mass literacy, formed part of a process of gradual individualisation of consciousness. Jaynes (1976) and Wilber (1986) have independently constructed speculative overviews of the evolution of consciousness which differ in details, but agree on a shift from a collective consciousness in which individuals were embedded in a 'group mind' (brilliantly simulated in William Golding's *The Inheritors* (1955)) to the form of consciousness we know today, where people experience themselves as 'separate', and in which the 'private space inside the head' is experienced as under the control of the individual, and inaccessible to other individuals except under certain conditions. John Fowles's extraordinary novel *A Maggot* (1985) presents one of the best descriptions of this shift from pre-modern to modern consciousness.

There are some grounds for believing that the concept of 'private thoughts' was actually assisted by the development of diary-writing among the Protestant middle class in the seventeenth century (Stone 1976). Private writing enhanced the individual's awareness of his or her own uniqueness, just as the private documentation of the development of one's own children, which seems to have commenced during the nineteenth century (Steedman 1982), enhanced parental consciousness of those children's individuality. Simultaneously, an increasing life span, and a better standard of living (including the possibility of a 'room of one's own') for a larger proportion of the population in the centuries following the industrial revolution supported the movement to value the lives of individual human beings other than the famous and powerful.

The Romantic movement, coinciding as it did with the first phase of industrialisation, was a powerful cultural stimulus to the emergence of the individual sensibility, setting the tone for almost two centuries in which the individual mind, personality and emotions would become the central subject for poets, novelists, dramatists and (ultimately) film makers. As human beings increasingly experienced themselves as separate and even isolated ('I am a rock, I am an island', sang Paul Simon in the 1960s, explicitly contradicting Donne's seventeenth-century 'No Manne is an Islande'), it became doubly important for literature to offer validation for that individuality, by opening windows into the private worlds of other individuals, and by increasingly portraying a whole range of highly specialised subjects, which would of necessity appeal only to particular audiences who could identify with them. 'Bardic' literature had by contrast offered only matter that appealed to the common denominator, and had spoken only to the values which all its listeners possessed in common. Thus highly individualised fictions support and extend the development of highly individualised consciousness.

The emergence of individual psychotherapy as practised by Freud, and as elaborated vastly throughout this century, can also be seen as part of the development of an individualised consciousness, setting up a relationship similar to that of the confessional, but extending its scope to deal with the entire realm of emotional, existential and behavioural distress, now conceived in more secular than spiritual terms. Psychotherapy at its inception and still predominantly today deals explicitly with the inner world of the individual. It is commonly assumed that a highly individualised relationship must be established between client and therapist in order for any intervention strategy to work. The client or patient must first feel understood, valued and empowered before he or she is likely to accept challenge to existing habits of thought and feeling.

The encounter between a modern reader and a printed text is similar in many ways to the therapeutic encounter we have just examined. What happens between reader and printed text is a mystery – unless the reader chooses to tell us about it, and even then, there will be much that has occurred in the reading process that will have been below the level of consciousness. Once again, it is a question of a very 'private' transaction, in which an exquisite degree of 'matching' is required between the external agent (book) and the individual if any self-insight or change on the reader's part is to be elicited. The whole notion of bibliotherapy rests on the possibility of such matching.

The growing popularity of psychotherapy has in turn influenced narrative, which has become increasingly confessional (dealing explicitly with aspects of inner life hitherto considered entirely private), and increasingly concerned with abnormal mental and emotional states. This has been true equally in adult and in young people's fiction, where 'problem novels' for adolescents have been a burgeoning area in publishing over the past twenty years. The existence of such novels, dealing with highly individualised problems (such as anorexia nervosa, see Pantanizopoulos 1989), appears to be the most recent fictional manifestation of the individualisation of consciousness.

Bibliotherapy: a Twentieth-century Notion

In its broadest historical context, the concept of 'bibliotherapy' forms part of the ancient *dulcis et utile* debate, in which some scholars advocated a role for literature as 'useful' or 'instructive' in some moral sense, while others maintained that stories and books existed primarily or even purely to give pleasure. Since Greek and Roman times, one side or the other has prevailed for periods of a century or more, but the weight of evidence has always suggested that people continued to listen and read regardless of what the 'experts' thought. Within the field of children's literature, the debate has focused in particular on the ambiguous category of fairy tales, originally oral narratives which, having been appropriated by 'child culture' from the nineteenth century, have been at varying times attacked as dangerous, defended as 'pure escapism', and re-conceptualised as 'morally instructive' or psychologically growthful.

In fact, there are few examples of successful and popular literature which do not offer both delight and 'instruction' in some form or other. The debate seems rather to reflect a continuing moral uneasiness, in which the intensity with which humans have always immersed themselves in 'story' has prompted us to seek justification for an involvement so seemingly unrelated to the hard business of daily life.

Simsova (1968), Hatt (1976) and Nell (1988) all draw attention to the extraordinary work of Nicholas Rubakin in the USSR in the 1920s, work which anticipates by nearly half a century the claim of reader-response theory that readers experience texts in their own images (Holland 1975). Rubakin also argued for something akin to Piagetian 'schemas' as facilitating comprehension, and recognised the possibility of 'scientifically' matching types of readers with types of books (the typology of reader personalities being broadly based on Jung's system). Such an enterprise of social engineering was likely enough to appeal to a revolutionary government, but Rubakin's ideas were never fully operationalised even in the USSR, and in the West (like his fellow Russians Vladimir Propp and Kornei Chukovsky) Rubakin achieved no recognition until many years after the first appearance of his work.

Rubakin's pioneering efforts were not strictly directed towards 'therapy'. The idea of bibliotherapy as such seems to have originated in Germany and the USA in the early years of the century, but in Britain the term 'reading therapy' has been preferred until relatively recently. Jean M. Clarke (in Clarke and Postle 1988) summarises the development of this practice in Britain from the initial stage in which the provision of libraries for patients in mental hospitals was vaguely seen as 'a good thing' and reading as vaguely 'curative' without any apparent grasp of the dynamics involved (or the manifest potential difficulties). Much later in the century, librarians working in hospitals were joined by a handful of social workers who had independently concluded that reading might be a source of insight and cure.

In the idealistic and therapeutically oriented culture of the USA, the idea of bibliotherapy has enjoyed a somewhat wider constituency (Pardeck 1984). Fader and McNeil's *Hooked On Books* (1969) directed attention to a single client group (alienated and anti-print teenagers) and their enthusiastic anecdotal evidence of triumphant success in transforming teenagers into bookaholics inspired a generation of teachers. The idea that reading was in itself a 'wonder drug' with the power to 'transform lives' was not new, but it led to a number of attempts to use books to alleviate individual and social ills; thus Manning and Casbergue (1988) outline 'Bibliotherapy for children in step families'. In Pittsburg, Elizabeth Segal and Joan Friedberg set up a modestly-conceived but eventually nationally influential programme to bring quality picture books into the homes of the city's poor, in order to encourage early literacy and to promote cultural enrichment (Segal 1989). More strictly 'therapeutic' was Butler's work in New Zealand. *Cushla and Her Books* (Butler 1979) argues that picture books were instrumental in the rehabilitation of a multiple handicapped child.

The basic idea of bibliotherapy, as established by (predominantly) librarians runs approximately as follows. A child or adult has a problem. A skilled librarian, teacher or (Clarke would prefer) 'reading therapist', suggests a story which in some way bears on that problem. If the intervention is successful, the reader recognises that the book has something personally significant to say to him/her, perhaps becomes conscious of the dimensions of his/her own problem, and sometimes perceives potential solutions to it. The reader then returns the book to the professional, perhaps wishing to discuss it (and through it, his or her own problems), perhaps asking for more books 'like that one', which the professional then sensitively provides on the basis of feedback as to the reader's reception of the first.

The practical obstacles to the widespread employment of such a process, as opposed to the broader applications of 'reading as enrichment' mentioned above, are considerable. With the possible exception of staff in small private mental institutions or private boarding schools, few librarians are likely ever to know their constituents well enough, or have time enough, to play such a role, which requires both intimate knowledge of the individual and wide knowledge of literature. Moreover, bibliotherapy is open to ethical objections if it is foisted upon mental patients or older children without their having requested it, and (more pragmatically) will in such cases almost certainly be resisted openly or covertly. Worse still, existing bibliotherapeutic theory seems inadequately informed as to how narratives actually interact with human lives.

How Stories Affect Individuals

Pre-literate children in our own and other cultures spontaneously compose songs, chants, monologues and other forms of 'phatic' expression, often to the accompaniment of motor play, and apparently in rough imitation of adult talk, song and story. Children who grow up with television emulate its manner and matter in their compositions (Sutton–Smith *et al.* 1981); those brought up on oral stories are influenced by that mode, and print-soaked children imitate the mode of print (Crago and Crago 1983). There are, however, distinctive structural principles in children's compositions which mark them off from adult models, and which suggest some innate paradigm that modifies direct imitation.

Later in life, such spontaneous story-making 'goes underground', taking the form of the 'inner newsreel' discussed by Becker (1972) and Klinger (1971). Adults do not normally chant aloud as they make beds, tee off on the golf course or type at their computer station, but their minds do run an endless stream of loosely arranged images, thoughts and inner dialogues – a waking version of dreaming.

All of this evidence suggests that story-telling, or at least, arranging the raw material of experience into some sort of pattern, is a process almost as fundamental to human life as breathing. In these ur-narratives, we are both 'creators' and 'audiences', both 'participants' and 'spectators': the roles are not substantially distinguished.

'Absorbed' or 'ludic reading', as investigated by Victor Nell (1988) is virtually a trance state, where readers willingly become oblivious to the world around them. Normal consciousness is put on hold and the print seems to guide the 'inner newsreel's' production of highly personalised images. Thus the reader 'merges' with the characters and events of the work. Nell, one of the few mainstream psychologists to offer anything useful on the affective dimension of reading, points out that it is useless to distinguish fiction from non-fiction or popular fiction from 'good literature' where ludic reading is in question. However, it is unlikely that ludic reading would normally occur unless in response to narrative material. It is as if there is something intrinsically consciousness-altering about the narrative form itself. Ludic readers are skilled in seeking out texts which will offer them the experience they desire, and can often successfully select on the basis of only small samples of writing (a process akin to that by which we 'instinctively' assess strangers after a few minutes' acquaintance).

If deep absorption in narrative has nothing to do with literary quality, then adult ludic readers are probably functionally identical with child readers/listeners, for whom aesthetic sophistication has little to do with enjoyment. Schlager (1977) found that children's preferences among award-winning children's books had more to do with 'matching' between the themes of the books and the developmentally appropriate themes of middle childhood than with literary sophistication or level of textual difficulty.

Together, these findings suggest that the optimal conditions for 'bibliotherapy' would be when a reader (child or adult) already capable of ludic reading (many readers do not read in this deeply absorbed manner) encounters a text (fiction or non-fiction, pot-boiler or classic) which matches his or her personal criteria for 'a good read', and where the themes are in some way appropriate to his or her developmental stage and inner world.

But whereas the bibliotherapists have proposed a fairly crude model in which the reading therapist seeks for a literal correspondence between the content of the text and the reader's own 'problem' or life situation, it is far more likely that the 'merging' of reader and text will occur when the correspondence is partly or wholly metaphorical rather than literal.

Human addiction to 'story' is an aspect of our symbol-making nature: our very language is strongly metaphorical and our dreaming almost always uses the language of symbol and analogy. When we read a story that is obviously very similar in its characters and events to our own life experience, we may read it with enjoyment and appreciation, consciously appreciating the parallels; but if our life experience is painful, then we may reject such a story altogether.

Thus when offered a short text (Wild's *Beast* (1993)) featuring a protagonist with obsessive-compulsive symptoms, three early adolescent boys with similar symptoms read only a few pages, or failed to read the novel at all, although their reading skills were more than adequate for the task, because, as they said, the protagonists were too much like themselves. Daniels (1992), on the other hand, describes an orphaned Vietnamese adolescent living in Britain who was deeply affected by a novel about a porpoise who becomes separated from its mother and is cruelly treated by its human captors.

The emergence of ur-narrative so early in human life strongly suggests that story is indeed a 'natural' mode of self-expression and self-healing. But for a print text to 'plug into' the inner newsreel and temporarily replace it as an ongoing source of images, feelings and self-talk, exquisitely fine unconscious matching must occur, so that the reader 'recognises' something of high personal significance, while simultaneously failing to pin down its precise meaning. I maintain (Crago 1993) that such matching is akin to 'falling in love'. In both cases, an instinctive, largely unconscious recognition of similarity occurs, while consciously, the individuals concerned are aware only of a powerful emotional 'pull' and a sense of 'rightness' or 'fitness' in being with the other person (or text). Texts that are self-selected on such a basis are likely to be read and re-read with total absorption.

In this 'systemic' model of reader–text interaction, readers 'influence' books, rather than the other way around (Holland 1975) But when preferred texts are read again and again, or are brooded over in memory, they become, in turn, potent shaping influences over the reader's future self concept and life path. Key texts then become 'potentiating devices', eliciting from individuals the full development of what is already latent within them, but which might never flower otherwise. Needless to say, such potentiation can occur both for good and for ill. *Der Ring des Niebelungen* and *Also Sprache Zarathustra* may have 'potentiated' Hitler's grandiose and paranoid fantasies; Wagner and Nietzsche are not therefore responsible for the Holocaust or the Second World War.

Here the theory of literary response begins to converge with recent developments within the field of psychotherapy where, quite independently of the bibliotherapy movement, the 1980s brought a new consciousness of the power of 'therapeutic story-telling' as an intervention device. Probably originating in Jay Haley's (1973) lively account of the therapeutic 'wizardry' of Milton Erickson, the concept of therapeutic story-telling has been picked up and popularised. Cameron-Bandler (1978), Gordon (1978), and Mills and Crowley (1986) all emphasise the power of metaphor to 'slip past' the defences of the conscious mind.

Such practitioners have little acquaintance with literary history – otherwise they would surely have recognised that their 'therapeutic metaphor' amounts to little more than a re-tooling of the time-honoured genres of allegory and fable. However, what is new is their highly individualised focus. Stories, they maintain, must be constructed specifically to suit the emotional dynamics of individuals. Also worth noting is their insistence that 'the unconscious does not recognise negatives' ('whatever you do, please don't smoke' becomes 'smoke!'); thus stories attempting to be 'curative' through the language of symbol and metaphor must be positive in intent and in the specific propositions they employ.

Not to be confused with 'therapeutic metaphor' is the development of so-called 'narrative therapy' (Epston and White 1989). A variant of strategic psychotherapy, but employing Foucauldian notions about power, language and meaning, 'narrative therapy' invites clients to become aware of how they have been participants in the construction of a 'dominant story' of their own life (for example, 'my life is a total failure') and instead to consider alternative ways in which they might have constructed their stories. This encourages the noticing and valuing of instances when the person subverted or resisted the 'dominant story' – and the construction (for example) of an alternative self-narrative of success and heroic resistance.

Whither Bibliotherapy?

The sobering truth about bibliotherapy is that such a form of healing is more likely to occur through the reader's own unconscious selection of texts that will 'speak' to her or him than through the planned recommendations of a professional mediator. This is not to say that bibliotherapy in its existing form cannot offer modest contributions. First, the reading of narratives that literally or symbolically parallel one's own condition can provide a language in which a child or adult may begin to talk about what has previously been inchoate. Thus the intense interest shown by many adolescent girls in accounts of anorexia, drug addiction and sexual abuse even when they themselves do not have such problems, suggests that these stories provide a way of articulating their own sense of alienation, aggression or low self esteem.

Second, the reading of books can provide the comfort of knowing that one is not alone, and thus function as a 'safer', more private version of a psychotherapy or self-help group. Third, reading can provide vicarious insight into one's problems, and even a measure of integration of previously disowned feelings. In the sense that it is entirely private, reading is thus far safer than seeking an interview with a therapist or counsellor; but on the other hand, it is far easier to put a book down than to walk out of a therapist's office at the mention of an uncomfortable truth. Fourth, reading can, at a metaphorical level, and sometimes even at a literal one, provide suggestions, akin to hypnotic suggestions, for ways of resolving the reader's problems – suggestions which may bypass conscious resistance on the sufferer's part.

On the other hand, reading by itself, like any other form of 'therapeutic' activity, from painting to gardening or sport, is not likely to embody the element of caring confrontation that seems fundamental to much successful psychotherapy. If the theory of emotional 'matching' is correct, then readers will nearly always reject a text that contains too painful a self-confrontation; and they will be drawn again and again to those narratives which will encourage them to construct their lives much as before, albeit, perhaps, in a more vivid, enriched way.

This leaves a heavy onus on the bibliotherapist to provide what the text itself cannot, and while a sensitive librarian may do as well as a professional therapist with a relatively 'easy' client, it is likely that clients (child or adult) with more deeply-rooted dysfunctions will prove far beyond even a well trained teacher or librarian's ability to help.

If bibliotherapy is to fulfil its promise, its practitioners must learn to diagnose their clients' patterns of preferred reading through careful observation and questioning over time. Personally significant texts, which are read again and again, are the most efficient indicators of those patterns. The professional could then recommend further texts which embody the same patterns, or seek to engage the client in discussion of one of his or her existing 'special books'. If bibliotherapy is understood as a way of affirming and extending an individual personality rather than as a way of 'curing' or 'changing' a person, then its chances of being useful will be far greater. In her Earthsea quartet, Ursula le Guin's Mages can call up a magical wind to fill their sails if required; but they cannot magically compel an existing wind to blow in the opposite direction.

References

Becker, E. (1972) *The Birth and Death of Meaning*, 2nd edn, Harmondsworth: Penguin.
Bettelheim, B. (1976) *The Uses of Enchantment: The Meaning and Importance of Fairy Tales*, New York: Knopf.
Butler, D. (1979) *Cushla and Her Books*, London: Hodder and Stoughton.
Cameron-Bandler, L. (1978) *They Lived Happily Ever After: A Book About Achieving Happy Endings in Coupling*, Cupertino, CA: Meta Publications.
Clarke, J. and Postle, E. (eds) (1988) *Reading Therapy*, London: Clive Bingley.
Crago, H. (1979) 'Cultural categories and the criticism of children's literature', *Signal* 30: 140–150.

—— (1993) 'Why readers read what writers write', *Children's Literature in Education* 24, 4: 277–290

Crago, M. and Crago, H. (1983) *Prelude to Literacy: A Preschool Child's Encounter with Picture and Story*, Carbondale, IL: Southern Illinois University Press.

Daniels, J. (1992): 'Stories we tell ourselves: stories we tell others', in Styles, M., Bearne, E. and Watson, V. (eds) *Exploring Children's Literature*, London: Cassell.

Epston, D. and White, M. (1989) *Literate Means to Therapeutic Ends*, Adelaide: Dulwich Centre Publications.

Fader, D. and McNeil, E. (1969) *Hooked on Books*, London: Pergamon.

Gordon, T. (1978) *Therapeutic Metaphors: Helping Others Through the Looking Glass*, Cupertino, CA: Meta Publications.

Haley, J. (1973) *Uncommon Therapy: The Psychiatric Techniques of Milton H. Erickson, MD*, New York: Norton.

Hatt, F. (1976) *The Reading Process: A Framework for Analysis and Description*, London: Bingley.

Holland, N. (1975) *Five Readers Reading*, New Haven: Yale University Press.

Jaynes, J. (1976) *The Origin of Consciousness in the Breakdown of the Bicameral Mind*, Boston: Houghton Mifflin.

Klinger, E. (1971) *The Structure and Function of Fantasy*, New York: Wiley-Interscience.

Manning, D. and Casbergue, R. (1988) 'Bibliotherapy for children in stepfamilies', *Clearing House* 62, 3: 124–127.

Mills, J. and Crowley, R. in collaboration with Ryan, M. (1986) *Therapeutic Metaphors for Children and the Child Within*, New York: Brunner-Mazel.

Nell, V. (1988) *Lost in a Book: The Psychology of Reading for Pleasure*, New Haven: Yale University Press.

Pantanizopoulos, J. (1989) 'I'll be happy when I'm thin enough': the treatment of anorexia nervosa in adolescent fiction', *ALAN* 17, 1: 9–10.

Pardeck, J. and Pardeck, J. (1984) *Young People With Problems: A Guide to Bibliotherapy*, New York: Greenwood Press.

Segel, E. (1989) 'Collaborations: putting children's literature to work for children at risk', in Gannon, S., Thompson, S. and Thompson, R. (eds), *When Rivers Meet: Selected Papers from the 1989 International Conference of the Children's Literature Association*, West Lafayette, IN: Children's Literature Association.

Schlager, N. (1977) 'Predicting children's choices in literature: a developmental approach', *Children's Literature in Education* 9, 3: 136–142.

Simsova, S. (ed.) (1968) *Nicholas Rubakin and Bibliopsychology*, Hamden, CT: Archon/ London: Bingley.

Steedman, C. (1982) *The Tidy House: Little Girls Writing*, London, Virago.

Stone, L. (1977) *The Family, Sex and Marriage in England, 1500–1800*, London: Weidenfeld and Nicholson.

Sutton-Smith, B. *et al.* (1981) *The Folkstories of Children*, Philadelphia: University of Pennsylvania Press.

Tabbert, R. 'The impact of children's books: cases and concepts', *Children's Literature in Education* 10, 2: 92–102.

Wilber, K. (1986) *Up From Eden: A Transpersonal View of Human Evolution*, Boston: Shambhala.

Further Reading

Appleyard, J. (1990) *Becoming a Reader: The Experience of Fiction from Childhood to Adulthood*, Cambridge: Cambridge University Press.

Crago, H. (1985) 'The place of story in affective development: implications for educators and clinicians', in Curry, N. (ed.) *The Feeling Child*, New York: Haworth.

—— (1985) 'Prior Expectations of "Great Expectations": how one child learned to read a classic', *College English*, 58, 6: 676–692.

Holland, N. (1975) *Five Readers Reading*. New Haven: Yale University Press.

Kottler, J., Sexton, T. and Whitstone, S. (1994) *The Heart of Healing: Relationships in Therapy*, San Francisco: Jossey-Bass.

Lesnik-Oberstein, K. (1994), *Children's Literature: Criticism and the Fictional Child*, Oxford: Clarendon Press.

General Bibliography

This list does not include items which are in the chapter bibliographies.

Criticism, Theory and General Approaches

Broadbent, N. *et al.* (1994) *Children's Literature Research: A Coming of Age?*, Southampton: LSU.

Butts, D. (ed.) *Stories and Society: Children's Literature in its Social Context*, London: Macmillan.

Egoff, S. *et al.* (eds) (1996) *Only Connect. Readings on Children's Literature*, 3rd edn, Toronto, Ont: Oxford University Press.

Fox, G. (ed.) (1995) *Celebrating Children's Literature in Education*, London: Hodder and Stoughton.

Hendrickson, L. (1987) *Children's Literature: A Guide to the Criticism*, Boston, MA: G. K. Hall.

Hollindale, P. (1997), *Signs of Childness in Children's Books*, South Woodchester: Thimble Press.

Hourihan, M. (1997) *Deconstructing the Hero. Literary Theory and Children's Literature*, London: Routledge.

International Youth Library (ed.) (1991) *Children's Literature Research: International Resources and Exchange*, Munich: K. G. Saur.

Nikolajeva, M. (1996) *Children's Literature Comes of Age. Toward a New Aesthetic*, New York: Garland.

Reetz, M. (1994) *Professional Periodicals in Children's Literature: A Guide*, Munich: Internationale Jugendbibliothek.

Styles, M., Bearne, E., and Watson, V. (eds) (1994) *The Prose and the Passion: Children and their Reading*, London: Cassell.

History and Bibliography

Alderson, B. (1986) *Sing a Song for Sixpence: the English Illustrative Tradition and Randolph Caldecott*, Cambridge: Cambridge University Press in association with the British Library.

Avery, G. (1975) *Childhood's Pattern: a Study of the Heroes and Heroines of Children's Fiction 1770-1950*, London: Hodder and Stoughton.

Barr, J. (1986) *Illustrated Children's Books*, London: British Library.

Bottigheimer, R. B. (1996) *The Bible for Children from the Age of Gutenburg to the Present*, New Haven, CT: Yale University Press.

Carpenter, H. (1985) *Secret Gardens: A Study of the Golden Age of Children's Literature*, London: George Allen and Unwin.

Demers, P. (1993) *Heaven Upon Earth. The Form of Moral and Religious Children's Literature to 1850*, Knoxville,TN: University of Tennessee Press.

Fever, W. (1977) *When We Were Very Young*, London: Thames and Hudson.

Foster, S. and Simons, J. (1995), *What Katy Read. Feminist Re-Readings of 'Classic' Stories for Girls*, London: Macmillan.

Green, M. (1980) *Dreams of Adventure, Deeds of Empire*, London: Routledge and Kegan Paul.

Griswold, J. (1992) *Audacious Kids: Coming of Age in America's Classic Children's Books*, New York: Oxford University Press.

Hilton, M., Styles, N., and Watson, V. (eds) (1997) *Opening the Nursery Door. Reading, Writing and Childhood, 1600-1900*, London: Routledge.

Opie, I. and Opie P. (1951/1980) *The Oxford Dictionary of Nursery Rhymes*, Oxford: Oxford University Press.

—— (1955) *The Oxford Nursery Rhyme Book*, Oxford: Oxford University Press.

—— (1959) *The Language and Lore of Schoolchildren*, Oxford: Oxford University Press.

—— (1969) *Children's Games in Street and Playground*, Oxford: Clarendon Press.

—— (1974) *The Classic Fairy Tales*, Oxford: Oxford University Press.

Opie, I. (1985) *The Singing Game*, Oxford: Oxford University Press.

Pickering, S. F. (1981) *John Locke and Children's Books in Eighteenth Century England*, Knoxville, TN: University of Tennessee Press.

—— (1993) *Moral Instruction and Fiction for Children, 1749–1820*, Athens, GA: University of Georgia Press.

Reynolds, K. (1994) *Children's Literature in the 1890s and the 1990s*, Plymouth: Northcote House.

Richards, J. (ed.) (1989) *Imperialism and Juvenile Literature*, Manchester: Manchester University Press.

Salway, L. (ed.) (1976) *A Peculiar Gift: Nineteenth Century Writings on Books for Children*, Harmondsworth: Penguin.

Slade, P. (1954) *Child Drama*, London: University of London Press.

Summerfield, G. (1984) *Fantasy and Reason: Children's Literature in the Eighteenth Century*, London: Methuen.

Trease, G. (1964) *Tales Out of School: A Survey of Children's Fiction*, 2nd edn, London: Heinemann.

Warner, M. (1994) *From the Beast to the Blonde: On Fairytales and their Tellers*, London: Chatto and Windus.

Types and Genres

Auchmuty, R. (1992) *A World of Girls*, London: The Women's Press.

Bader, B. (1976) *American Picturebooks from Noah's Ark to The Beast Within*, New York: Macmillan.

Bennett, J. (1979) *Learning to Read with Picture Books*, South Woodchester: The Thimble Press.

Blount, M. (1974) *Animal Land: the Creatures of Children's Fiction*, London: Hutchinson.

Bolton, G. (1979) *Towards a Theory of Drama in Education*, Burt Mill, Harlow: Longman.

Cadogan, M., and Craig, P. (1976) *You're a Brick, Angela!: A New Look at Girls' Fiction from 1839–1975*, London: Gollancz.

Chambers, A. (1982) *Plays for Young People to Read and Perform*, South Woodchester: Thimble Press.

Cook, E. (1976) *The Ordinary and the Fabulous*, 2nd edn, Cambridge: Cambridge University Press.

Dusinberre, J. (1987) *Alice to the Lighthouse*, New York: St Martin's Press.

Fisher, J. (1994) *An Index of Historical Fiction for Children and Young People*, Aldershot: Scolar Press.

Fisher, M. (1975) *Who's Who in Children's Books*, London: Weidenfeld and Nicolson.

—— (1976) *The Bright Face of Danger*, London: Hodder and Stoughton.

Gifford, D. (1971) *Discovering Comics* (rev. 1991), Prices Risborough: Shire.

Haymonds, A. (1996) 'Pony Stories', in Hunt, P. (ed.) *International Companion Encyclopedia of Children's Literature*, London: Routledge.

Kuznets, L. R. (1994) *When Toys Come Alive: Narratives of Animation, Metamorphosis and Development*, New Haven, CT: Yale University Press.

Lewis, D. (1990) 'The constructedness of texts: picture books and the metafictive', *Signal* 62: 131–146.

Lurie, A. (1990) *Don't Tell the Grown-Ups: Subversive Children's Literature*, London: Bloomsbury.

Lynn, R. N. (1989) *Fantasy Literature for Children and Young Adults: An Annotated Bibliography*, 3rd edn, New York: R. R. Bower.

Mellon, N. (1992) *Storytelling and the Art of Imagination*, Rockport, MA: Element.

Morse, B. (1992) *Poetry Books For Children, A Signal Bookguide*, South Woodchester: Thimble Press.

Quigley, I. (1982) *The Heirs of Tom Brown: The English School Story*, London: Chatto and Windus.

Richards, J. (1988) *Happiest Days: The Public Schools in English Fiction*, Manchester: Manchester University Press.

Steele, M. (1989) *Traditional Tales: A Signal Bookguide*, South Woodchester: Thimble Press.

Sullivan, C. W. III (1989) *Welsh Celtic Myth in Modern Fantasy*, Westport, CT: Greenwood Press.

—— (ed.) (1993) *Science Fiction for Young Readers*, Westport, CT: Greenwood Press.

Tucker, N. and Reynolds, K. (eds) (1997) *Enid Blyton: A Celebration and Reappraisal*, London: National Centre for Research in Children's Literature.

Turner, E. S. (1975) *Boys Will Be Boys*, 3rd edn, London: Michael Joseph.

Watson, V. and Styles, M. (ed.) (1996) *Talking Pictures. Pictorial Texts and Young Readers*, London: Hodder and Stoughton.

Contexts

Barker, K. (1986) *In the Realms of Gold: The Story of the Carnegie Medal*, London: MacRae.

Buckingham, D. (1993) *Children Talking Television: The Making of Television Literacy*. London: Falmer Press.

Burress, L. (1989) *Battle of the Books: Literary Censorship in the Public Schools*, Metuchen, NJ: Scarecrow Press.

Darling, R. L. (1968) *The Rise of Children's Book Reviewing in America, 1865–1881*, New York: R. R. Bowker.

Fox, C. (1993) *At the Very Edge of the Forest: The Influence of Literature on Storytelling by Children*, London: Cassell.

Goldthwaite, J. (1996) *The Natural History of Make-Believe*, New York: Oxford University Press.

Heeks, P. (1982) *Ways of Knowing*, South Woodchester: Thimble Press.

Jones, D. B. (ed.) (1988) *Children's Literature Awards and Winners*, Detroit, VA: Neal-Schuman.

MacLeod, A. (1983) 'Censorship and children's literature', *Library Quarterly* 53, 1: 26–38.

Meek, M., Warlow, A. and Barton G. (eds) (1977) *The Cool Web: The Pattern of Children's Reading*, London: The Bodley Head.

Oittinen R. (1993) *I Am Me – I am Other: On the Dialogics of translating for Children* [Acta Universitatis Tamperensis ser A vol 386], Tampere: University of Tampere.

Pinsent, P. (ed.) (1997) *Children's Literature and the Politics of Equality*, London: David Fulton.

Postman, N. (1983) *The Disappearance of Childhood*, London: W. H. Allen.

White, M. (1992) 'Children's books from other languages: a study of successful translations', *Journal of Youth Services in Libraries*, 5, 3: 261–275.

Whitehead, W. (1988) *Different Faces: Growing Up with Books in a Multicultural Society*, London: Pluto Press.

Applications

Bennett, J. (1991) *Learning to Read with Picture Books*, South Woodchester: Thimble Press.

Butler, D. (1980) *Babies Need Books*, Sevenoaks: Hodder and Stoughton.

Mathias, B. and Spiers, D. (1982) *A Handbook on Death and Bereavement: Helping Children to Understand*, Wokingham: National Library for the Handicapped Child.

Styles, M., Bearne, E., and Watson, V. (eds) (1996) *Voices Off: Texts, Contexts, and Readers*, London: Cassell.

Thomson, J. (1987) *Understanding Teenagers Reading*, London: Croom Helm; Melbourne: Methuen.

White, D. N. (1954) *Books Before Five*, Wellington: New Zealand Council for Educational Research.

Wolf, S. A. and Brice Heath, S. (1992) *The Braid of Literature: Children's Worlds of Reading*, Cambridge, MA: Harvard University Press.

International

Coughlan, V., and Keenan, C. (eds) (1996) *The Big Guide to Irish Children's Books*, Dublin: Irish Children's Book Trust.

Danish Literature Centre (1992) *Roots in Denmark, Danish Children's Literature Today*, København: Danish Literature Centre.

Egoff, S., and Saltman, J. (1990) *The New Republic of Childhood. A Critical Guide to Canadian Children's Literature in English*, Toronto, Ont: Oxford University Press.

Griswold, J. (1992) *Audacious Kids: Coming of Age in America's Classic Children's Books*, New York: Oxford University Press.

Khorana, M. (1991) *The Indian Sub-Continent in Literature for Children and Young Adults*, New York: Greenwood Press.

Lees, S. and MacIntyre, P. (1993) *The Oxford Companion to Australian Children's Literature*, Melbourne: Oxford University Press.

MacLeod, A. S. (1975) *A Moral Tale: Children's Fiction and American Culture 1820–1860*, Hamden, CT: Archon Books

Scott, D. H. (1980) *Chinese Popular Literature and the Child*, Chicago, IL: American Library Association.

Segun, M. D. (1992) 'Children's literature in Africa: problems and prospects', in C. Ikonne *et al.* (eds), *Children and Literature in Africa*, Ibadan: Heinemann Educational.

Glossary

This Glossary contains technical terms which are not adequately explained in the text, and which are not (usually) readily available in standard dictionaries. An excellent source of definitions in this field is Katie Wales's *A Dictionary of Stylistics* (London: Longman 1989); more generally, I have referred to the *Shorter Oxford English Dictionary* (SOED).

branching   A way of describing the complexity of sentences. In 'left-branching' sentences, the complex information comes before the verb or main noun ('Although it was hot outside, the cat sat on the mat'); in 'right-branching' sentences, it comes after the main word ('The cat sat on the mat, although it was hot outside'). Right-branching sentences are generally thought to be easier to understand.

cohesion   Cohesion refers to the ways in which sentences are linked together – by meaning, sound, words, or grammar.

deconstruction   A theory and practice of reading (rather than a 'method' of criticism) which looks on texts as possessing infinite complex meanings rather than as being reducible to simple, 'static' meanings or interpretations. It looks, for example, at the 'blindnesses' or 'silences' of texts – the things that they do not say (or which they suppress). Deconstructive readings can, of course, be deconstructed themselves (infinitely).

dialectic   Logical argument.

dialogical   'Double-voiced' language which responds to and is sensitive to the language and society around it (used by Mikhail Bakhtin); compare **monological** – 'single-voiced' language which operates in isolation, dominated, perhaps, by the aims of the writer.

diegetic   In narrative, 'telling' rather than 'showing': a report of an action.

discourse   Broadly, communication; a communicative act, or series of acts.

efferent   Moving outwards.

epistemological   Dealing with knowledge and the theory of knowledge.

focalisation   Sometimes taken to be the same as 'point of view' – the 'angle', viewpoint, or perspective from which or through which the story is told. The 'focaliser' may be the narrator (in a first-person narrative) or the person through whose eyes we see things (in first- or third-person narrative), usually the central character of a story.

formalism   An early form of structuralism, which looked for recurrent patterns in texts.

'free' and 'bound' forms of speech   Speech and thought can be presented in texts either 'directly', using inverted commas ('Hello!') or 'indirectly', where the speech or thought is 'reported' (How careless of them!) If there is no 'tag' (he said, she thought) the phase is 'free'; if a tag is used ('Hello!', she said; How careless of them, she thought), the phrase is 'bound'. There is some disagreement among linguists as to the use of the terms, but broadly 'free' forms allow (or force) readers to use their imaginations; 'bound' forms allow authors more (potential) control.

gender   Now widely taken to mean characteristics given to individuals through 'nurture', rather than the physical sex characteristics given by 'nature'.

gestalt psychology   Believes that perceptions, reactions, etc., are gestalts: integrated perceptual structures conceived as functionally more than their parts (SOED).

hermeneutics   Dealing with theories of interpretation.

historiography   The writing of history.

isomorphic   Linking the same forms.

Leavisite   Strictly, following the critical ideas of F. R. Leavis (1895–1978), an immensely influential Cambridge academic who was instrumental in shifting the emphasis of literary studies from history to the text. Leavis was broadly anti-theory, using close readings to produce judgements purporting to derive from the text, but actually lodged in a right-wing, if idiosyncratic, ideology. 'Leavisite' is now often used as a synonym for conservative and authoritarian (or alternatively, sensible) readings.

lexical set   Words which are linked together by occurring within similar grammatical or cultural contexts (such as supposed gender characteristics), or forming 'natural groups' (like the months of the year); genres and individual authors will recurrently use similar lexical sets.

literary stylistics   The application of 'objective', non-judgmental analytical techniques to the language of texts designed for 'non-functional' reading.

metafiction   Self-conscious fiction, which draws attention to its fictiveness.

metalepsis   A term coined by Gerard Genette to mean the intrusion of the 'voice' of an author, narrator, or character into a narrative, to give a great impression of realism.

metonym   An attribute standing for an object ('the stage' = the theatre).

monological   see **dialogical**.

polyphonic   'Having many voices' – texts which are not dominated by a single narrative or authorial authority (associated with Bakhtin).

postmodernism   The idea that towards the end of the twentieth century there has been a fragmentation of the certainties of culture, society and individualism in 'advanced' capitalist societies.

poststructuralism   In reaction to the intended universality of structuralism, a criticism which questions all readings of texts (including its own) and emphasises instability and ambiguity.

pragmatics   The study of language in context, in the sense of what it does, rather than what it is; intention and affect are important, rather than form.

psychological phenomenology   Deducing what goes on in an author's mind from the text.

register   Language used in a certain context or situation: there is, for example, language thought appropriate to, and therefore more likely to occur in, a church sermon, or on a football field, or in literary genres.

semiotics   The study of sign-systems.

structuralism   Criticism which examines the patterns, codes, forms, convention and structures of texts and larger cultural systems; generally descriptive rather than interpretative.

systemic analysis   The analysis of language according to the system developed by Halliday, which sees language as a network involving choices which are influenced by context.

ur-narrative   Primitive, original, theoretical or underlying narrative.

Weltanshauung   A particular philosophy or view of life; the world-view of an individual or group (SOED).

Index